910.4 WHE
Access all areas : selected
writings 1990-2011
Wheeler, Sara.

RU MAR 2015
VE AUG 2016

Amit Lennon

SARA WHEELER

Access All Areas

Sara Wheeler is the author of six books of biography
and travel, including *Travels in a Thin Country: A
Journey Through Chile*, *Terra Incognita: Travels in
Antarctica*, and *The Magnetic North: Notes from the
Arctic Circle*. She lives in London.

FU MAR 2015
VE AUG 2016

ALSO BY SARA WHEELER

Evia: Travels on an Undiscovered Greek Island

Travels in a Thin Country: A Journey Through Chile

Terra Incognita: Travels in Antarctica

Cherry: A Life of Apsley Cherry-Garrard

Too Close to the Sun: The Audacious Life and Times of Denys Finch Hatton

The Magnetic North: Notes from the Arctic Circle

ACCESS ALL AREAS

ACCESS ALL AREAS

Selected Writings 1990–2011

SARA WHEELER

North Point Press
A division of Farrar, Straus and Giroux | New York

North Point Press
A division of Farrar, Straus and Giroux
18 West 18th Street, New York 10011

Copyright © 2011, 2013 by Sara Wheeler
All rights reserved
Printed in the United States of America

Originally published, in slightly different form, in 2011 by Jonathan Cape,
Great Britain
Published in the United States by North Point Press
First American edition, 2013

Library of Congress Cataloging-in-Publication Data
Wheeler, Sara.
    Access all areas : selected writings 1990–2011 / Sara Wheeler.
        p.   cm.
    ISBN 978-0-86547-877-0 (alk. paper)
    1. Wheeler, Sara—Travel.   2. Travelers' writings, British.
    3. Biography as a literary form.   I. Title.

G246.W54 A3 2013
910.4—dc23
                                                            2012021399

Designed by Abby Kagan

www.fsgbooks.com
www.twitter.com/fsgbooks • www.facebook.com/fsgbooks

1 3 5 7 9 10 8 6 4 2

FOR EZRA PAYNE

Happy travels

Language is like a cracked kettle on which we beat out tunes for bears to dance to, when what we long to do is make music that will move the stars to pity.

—FLAUBERT, *Madame Bovary*

At the sight of this filth and disorder, my spirits rose.

—PAUL THEROUX, *Ghost Train to the Eastern Star*

Contents

PART V: WHAT DO I DO NOW?

Introduction

I became a foreigner. For myself that is what a writer is—a man living on the other side of a frontier.　　　—V. S. PRITCHETT

The happiest moment of my life presented itself one cool February afternoon in the Transantarctic Mountains, many years ago. I was hiking up a valley. Fearful of losing my bearings, I stopped to fish a USGS map from my pack and spread it on the ice. Tracing my route by topographical landmarks (including an especially pointy mountain glaciologists had baptized the Doesn'tmatterhorn), my finger came to a straight line drawn with a ruler and marked "Limit of Compilation." Beyond that, the sheet was blank. I had reached the end of the map.

I went to the Antarctic and put my tent up and down for half a year because I found the continent a potent symbol of terra incognita. More of that later. But here's the point. The polar wind was uplift for the prose. There are many and varied landscapes in this book, and the pieces they inspired mark my progress as a writer, for better or worse. Rereading them revived the pleasures of crossing unimportant African borders using a kidney donor card as ID; of sharing a bathroom with a harp seal; of mixing a cocktail of six parts vodka and one part something else (they didn't revive any memories of that, because I can't recall what happened next). Throughout my writing life, travel has lent a vehicle in which to explore the inner terrain of fears and desires we stumble through every day. Writing about travel allowed flexibility and freedom within a rigid frame of train journeys, weather, and a knackered tent. The creative process is an escape from personality (T. S. Eliot said that), and so is the open road. And a journey goes in fits and starts, like life.

My chief endeavor, in my work, has been books: travel books, biographies, and a lumpy mix of the two. I wrote these essays, reviews, and squibs along the way, for love and for money. Having made the selection, I arranged the material in categories. The first section consists of travel pieces. The second is a sequence of essays on my role models: writers I admire who took inspiration from foreign lands in one way or another. In the third section I have assembled pieces about a particular person in a foreign land: I called it "Putting a Figure on the Landscape," and its subjects range from a contemporary Chinese artist to Henry Stanley. The fourth, short section is an indulgence consisting of skits I wrote when confined to barracks in London. The fifth and final section gathers up articles that appeared after my life changed irrevocably and I—well, you will see what I did when you get there.

The appendix contains my sole foray into fiction, an exercise never to be repeated, though, as the reader will see, it threw up some interesting issues. Finally, an obituary I wrote of myself for an anthology that, for reasons too complicated to divulge, failed to materialize. I reproduce it here for the first time, in case the reader is curious about the person who slept on Captain Scott's bunk, was a rubbish stripper, and peered into the lavatory with Ronald Reagan (though not all at the same time).

I chose not to take the chronological approach, as it seemed to me that the arrangement I have described imposed a more coherent logic on what is a wide range of subject matter. I hope that recurring patterns of thought and theme draw together material written twenty years apart. Roots and rootlessness; domesticity and the open road; the murky unknowability of our own motives (let alone anyone else's); the funk of hopeless, lovable humanity in a world gone wrong: these are the topics that slither through this collection like the cobra the skin of which I smuggled back from Libya and nailed on the kitchen wall. Those, and the struggle with despair, the need to make order, our relationship with landscape, and the unbreakable bond between past and present.

The pieces cover a twenty-one-year span. When I wrote the first, nobody I knew had an Internet connection. That year John Major went to Downing Street, Nelson Mandela walked free, and Iraq invaded Kuwait, while the Cure headlined at Glastonbury and Gazza wept at the World Cup. Two decades on—but you know what's happening now.

Some of the pieces in *Access All Areas* are conventional essays—new introductions to classic works of travel literature, for example—others you could call incidental journalism. This latter might be an enemy of promise, but it gets me out of the house, often to places I would not otherwise go. Dropping in to a village in Kerala for six days might not yield any profound experience, but it offers suggestions and opens up possibilities. This collection, by its existence, examines the difference between the magazine assignment, for which the writer must travel fast and purposefully, and the book, for which the journey evolves its own inner logic. Although, as I have said, I am in my bones a writer of books, I got a lot out of these short pieces. Let's face it, writing is hell, so an essay or feature curtails the agony. Producing a book, over the long haul, has a hostage-like feel. That said, I love the deep research a book demands. Every day is a success when you research, every one a failure when you write.

I often hear it said that tourism has murdered travel writing. I don't think so. Mass travel has liberated the form. No amount of package tours will stop the ordinary quietly going on everywhere on earth. When I lived in Chile in the early 1990s, I found my weekly trawl around the supermarket gripping beyond belief: watching women decide between this jar of *dulce de leche* or that one, weighing out their *chirimoyas*, loading up with boxes of washing powder. In Greece a decade earlier I often joined girl-friends at their weekly weigh-in at the local pharmacy (domestic scales had to wait for more prosperous times). Don't you some-times find daily life almost unbearably poetic? Minute curiosity is a requirement of the travel writer—and of the biographer, nov-elist, and poet. The significance of the trivial is what makes a book human. Out there on the road, I have often found that the most aimless and boring interludes yield, in the long run, the most fertile material.

In short, the notion that all the journeys have been made is just another variation of the theme that the past exists in Tech-nicolor while the present has faded to gray—that everything then was good and everything now is bad. A theme, in other words, as old as literature. I add the point that there are no package tours to the Democratic Republic of the Congo, still the heart of dark-ness, or to the parts of Saudi Arabia where women live in a per-petual ethical midnight.

An element of memoir clings to these pages, perhaps inevita-bly. The attentive reader will deduce that I grew up, with metric money but without computers, in that literally gloomy interlude in British history when the lights went out. Embedded in the St. George district of Bristol for as long as records revealed, my family fell neatly into two groups: the paternal tribe supported Bristol City, the maternals the Rovers, the Reds' mortal rivals. Every Saturday, during the season, I accompanied my father to the terraces at Ashton Gate. When the first team was playing away, we watched the Robins' Reserves.

At the age of eighteen, the family home having ceased to exist in the wreckage of my parents' marriage, and the Robins about to plunge three divisions in consecutive seasons, I moved to Paris to work as a shopgirl in a fashion emporium in the Forum des Halles. This was the beginning. I found it inspiring to be a stranger in a foreign land. I had an acceptance letter from an Oxford college in my pocket and found, via an advertisement in the window of a tobacconist's (oh, those long-gone days), a maid's room in an apartment share in the sixteenth arrondissement. At work, Madame Regnier, the manageress and a former Dior model, insisted on Pink Floyd's *The Wall* at all times on the store's new quadraphonic surround-sound system. The customers never complained, but it almost killed me. Frenchwomen categorically refused to wear leg warmers, but they bought our glitter jump-suits and tube tops by the thousand. After a year of little but fun and poor behavior, I converted my francs into dollars and took a Greyhound bus around the United States.

More of all that later too. When I was deciding what to include in this collection and what to discard, I sought pieces illustrative of their time, as well as of my own interests. Besides covering a geographical spread—pole to pole, via Poland—the stories ricochet between luxury (an oceangoing liner) and fantastic discomfort (a poorly constructed igloo), and between the frosty crunch of the Russian Arctic and the sweltering swamps of Malawi's Kasungu, a place so hot that toads explode. I also aimed for a variety of lengths and formats, in the interest of pace and rhythm: like different distances at an athletics meet.

It has been said, all too often, that I was "brave" to stride forth across pack and tundra, alone with a bar of Kendal Mint Cake. This is absurd. Brave people risk their lives to protect others or to protect democracy; brave people battle to live a compromised life in the teeth of horrific marginalization, and to live it well. Besides, I seek refuge in the protection of solitude: I prefer being there alone to being here with you, as the reader will quickly see. I like the sense of being homeless. It's a good starting point for a writer. The trick is to find sustenance in what Nathaniel Hawthorne called "the written communications of a solitary mind with itself." Booze has a similar effect and is easier to find than the sober self-communication Hawthorne had in mind. But those days too have gone, alas.

So we can disregard talk of bravery. I will admit only to a sliver of courage in always returning to sit still behind my desk, facing every morning the tyranny of the blank page. Every journey yielded energy, joy, and, above all, hope. There was always a dash of human dignity to lift a story out of absurdity and farce, however ugly the background. The world everywhere and simultaneously is a beautiful and horrible place.

Whatever the subject here, whether frivolous (belly dancing) or grave (HIV orphans in East Africa), I have striven to be true to life and faithful to the world's multiplicity. And although overarching themes are discernible in these pages, I reserve the right to be inconsistent in my opinions. I learned from a gang of atmospheric chemists on the top of the Greenland ice sheet that nothing in nature is isotropic—meaning, looking the same from each side.

My publishers have brought out this collection to mark my fiftieth birthday. Fifty, perhaps, is the time of life when most of the places you visit you will never go back to and nearly all the books on your shelves you will never read again. It marks the stage another writer recently called "the retreat from Moscow." At the beginning, I was afraid they wouldn't take me seriously. Now I am afraid they'll take me seriously. I see in many of the earlier pieces here a fumbling search for certainties. But as one gets older, one realizes there are no questions, only stories. And who can deny that the willingness to experiment vanishes? I find myself reading almost no contemporary fiction. I have not reached the point identified by Kingsley Amis when he said he only wanted to read novels that begin "A shot rang out." But it might not be far off.

Schopenhauer said the first forty years are text, the rest commentary. So I thought I had better nail this collection down. As I put it together, I had a vague sense of getting out of the woods before the trees arrive.

So here I am at fifty. I never thought it would be *luxe, calme,* and *volupté.*

But I never dreamed it would be like this, either.

2011

ACCESS ALL AREAS

I | FINDING THE STORY

The End of the Bolster: Romance in Poland

In 1981, I purchased a round-trip ticket to Warsaw on LOT airlines. I was twenty, with a year of university behind me. Why Poland? I can't remember, except that the country had been in the papers a lot that year. I had been waitressing throughout the holidays and accrued the absurdly small sum required to buy, in addition to the plane ticket, a monthlong Polish rail pass.

It was already dark when I arrived in Warsaw, but I had the address of a government accommodation office and managed to get there on a tram. There was throughout the Soviet bloc at that time a scheme under which visitors could stay in people's homes. It was cheap, and I thought it would be a good way of getting to know Poles.

The office had a full-length glass frontage, behind which a poorly stuffed eagle molted kapok. A heavy revolving door scraped through its revolution like an orchestra tuning up. Two gorgons swathed in black behind a Formica desk looked up, briefly. I could see that they found the interruption to their knitting an irritation.

A double room, it quickly emerged, was all that was available. I said I'd take it. It was against the rules, snapped Gorgon One, revealing a row of gold teeth, for a single person to take a double room. She returned to her knitting with a triumphant clack of needles. I said I was prepared to pay double rates. "Also illegal," chipped in Gorgon Two, eager not to miss out on the opportunity to ruin someone's day. In addition, they alleged there was not one hotel room available in the entire city.

I deployed a range of tactics, including tears. No dice. It was dark, and I was in a strange city without a word of Polish.

At that moment the revolving door spluttered to tuneless life once more. All three of us looked up. The crones muttered darkly, no doubt about the damnable inconvenience of a second customer. A tall, blond man with marble-blue eyes and a rucksack sauntered athletically into the room.

"We'll take the double room," I said to the crones.

One looked at the other. So it was all true.

The blond man put down his rucksack and held out his hand to shake mine. A Band-Aid covered his right thumbnail. I knew from the first syllable that he was Australian. It turned out that he had already been on the road in the Eastern bloc for a month, so when I explained the non-accommodation situation, he found it perfectly normal that we should share a room.

We stayed in a high-rise in the industrial suburbs, guests of a saturnine family who had been instructed not to speak to us. (In those days, Poland was still a boiling sea of suspicion, and people who rented out rooms were vetted. So much for meeting Poles.) Once we had settled into our chilly billet, my new friend took up the cylindrical bolster that lay at the head of the double bed and placed it down the middle. "No need to worry," he said. "This is my half," and he pointed to the left side of the bed, "and that's yours."

The Security Service had been busy that year, doing what it most liked to do—shutting up everyone else, brutally if possible. Millions of Poles naturally reacted with anger, and in March Solidarity activists had coordinated an extraordinary general strike unique in the Eastern bloc. Tension had subsided somewhat, but the economy was a car crash. Even though every food shop was empty, a queue snaked outside, the people waiting for some tiny rationed bit of something to be doled out from behind the counter. A Solidarity poster on the telegraph poles showed a black skull with a crossed knife and fork under it.

As for Teddy, following in the footsteps of so many of his compatriots, he had taken six months out to have a look at the world. His mother was a Pole who had arrived in Western Australia as a twenty-four-year-old refugee. She had married Teddy's father, a wood turner from Perth, and they had worked hard and made good. Teddy, who was twenty-three, was the youngest of seven. He turned out to be a fine companion, with a relaxed antipodean attitude to everything that the Polish system tossed in our path. We decided to travel together. But before leaving Warsaw, we paid twenty pence for opera tickets in Teatr Wielki, installing ourselves in the magnificently restored Moniuszko Auditorium to listen to a fine coloratura soprano sliding up and down Amina's arias in *La sonnambula*. Afterward we sat in bars kippered with smoke, downing tiny glasses of vodka. We left the capital to wander through the mildewed rooms of baroque castles and tore our jeans climbing to hermitages teetering on Gothic outcrops. We visited Teddy's mother's birthplace, where I took his photograph, and traveled to the Tatra Mountains, where we swam in Lake Morskie Oko, climbed Mount Kościele, and ate spicy wild boar sausages.

One day, at the end of our second week together, we took an overnight train to Wrocław. Early in the morning Teddy procured a cup of acorn coffee from a vendor through the train window and brought it to me, waking me by stroking my arm. When I opened my eyes, I felt a rush of emotion. Despite all Poland's exotic unfamiliarity, I learned then that the most foreign country is within.

We visited Chopin's birthplace, a modest manor in Żelazowa Wola, a hamlet nestled in the Mazovian heartland. A group of musicians from the Warsaw Conservatory were giving Chopin piano recitals in the grounds; as we approached, they were belting out mazurkas, but when we took our seats, a young man began to play the C-sharp minor Scherzo. The fierce opening octaves uncoiled over forest, glades, and the willowed hills behind the fast-flowing Utrata: a perfect setting for the music of an ardent patriot. But Chopin finished the piece at George Sand's summer house in Nohant, on the northern rim of the Massif Central. He was twenty-nine, consumptive, and guilty at his self-imposed exile in Louis Philippe's France. Folded into the devotion, a betrayal. But one forgot all that, and one even forgot Poland as the genius of the music took hold. The small amphitheater of chairs gave onto a clearing infused with the butterscotch light of late summer, and the intense final harmonies of the incomparable Scherzo—a climax of desire and longing—drifted away over the silver beeches. We sat there in the checkered shadow of the trees, Teddy rested his fingers on the nape of my neck, and that was the end of the bolster.

1998

POSTSCRIPT

The story rolled on for some years, the highlight, at least in retrospect, an extended camping tour up the west coast of Australia. One saw Teddy as he was made to be seen: wading into the ocean to spear supper. We both loved the open road. Every two or three days a gas station emerged from the red dust of the distance. Each had a bar and a shop. We stood at one bar on our way to the Ningaloo Reef, and I asked Teddy about the gutter at our feet, running along the wooden partition.

"Blokes used to piss in it," he said. "So they didn't waste time going to the toilet round the back."

Writers have compared a love affair to the mapping of an unexplored land; it seems a good analogy. If it is seen through to its logical conclusion, the lover does less well than the cartographer. That, too, has a truthful ring.

As a writer, I have learned to see the past as a friend. What else is there? The present is never around for long enough. I chose this next piece as it illustrates—rather clunkily, it now seems—the way landscape can work as a mirror to history. In these lines I can also see, dimly, the notion that I was working to keep the shadows at bay; what we all do, all the time. The grope for redemption, or at the very least respite, recurs throughout these pages, in different disguises.

Tierra del Fuego

Tierra del Fuego is an archipelago that drips off the tail of South America. Separated from the Chilean and Argentinean mainland by the waters of the Strait of Magellan, the largest island is itself divided between the two republics by a vertical line drawn with a ruler. This is the bottom of the world, a region where the curve on the globe turns steeply inward.

Before I turned thirty, some years ago, I found myself down there, marooned at Puerto Williams on Isla Navarino, the southernmost permanent settlement in the world. I was at the end of a six-month journey through Chile. I was writing my second book, and I had learned Spanish on the way down the thin country. It would have been easier if I had not spent the previous two years learning Italian at night school in London. But I ended up with a strong Chilean accent, still noted with disdain by Madrileños today. It had been a great time. My heart was fresh. So were my legs, as I had just recovered from a bout of scabies picked up in a boardinghouse in Puerto Natales. I had got to Tierra del Fuego. It was Land's End: the place where the whole world stopped. What could be more beguiling?

A white man first sighted land there in 1520. He was the Portuguese-born navigator Ferdinand Magellan, standing on the deck of *Victoria*, and he named what he saw Smoke Land, after the spires rising from the natives' fires. When he got home, his patron, Charles I of Spain, announced that he wished the place to be called instead Fireland, on the basis that there was no smoke without fire. Nobody knew that Fireland was an archipelago. It was Francis Drake who discovered that, when he pushed past the icebergs in the flagship *Pelican*, not yet renamed *Golden Hinde*, fifty-eight years later. Drake had already lost three of his six ships and barely weathered the horse latitudes, that subtropical region in which the old sailboats were so frequently becalmed, their captains ordering the crew to throw the horses overboard to conserve drinking water.

Navarino is Chilean now, and Williams its only village. The settlement was named after John Williams, a sea captain from my hometown of Bristol whom the young Chilean government dispatched in a twenty-seven-ton armed schooner in 1843 to claim the Strait of Magellan for Chile. Williams is a harsh and frigid place, squeezed in between three oceans: the Atlantic shoulders in from the east, the Pacific from the west, and the Southern Ocean from below. The westerlies in particular come freighted with rain and snow. Even in summer, the temperature averages just 52°F without windchill—and it is windy all the time in Tierra del Fuego.

It was a place where nothing ever happened. The low houses with their corrugated-iron roofs were separated by dirt tracks carved with puddles, and when you walked away from them, they slunk back into the purple mist. My billet was a guesthouse, though whether any other guest had ever appeared there was a matter for conjecture. One day, to pass the time, I hitched a ride in a lorry that was to deliver wood to a police station at the western tip of the island. The driver had called at the guesthouse on his way out to deliver some sausages. We clunked through miles of deciduous southern beech forest, the silvery trunks swaddled in pale primrose lichen and twisted into alphabet configurations by the prevailing southwesterlies. A band of white mineral deposits circled every pool, and their metallic whiff percolated the unheated cab.

The station consisted of a hut in a clearing that sloped down to the water's edge and a small jetty. It was an odd place for a police station, but Navarino lies directly below Argentinean territory, separated from it by a twelve-mile strait. As the two countries existed in a permanently tensile state, the Chileans kept a keen eye out lest a marauding naval force were to surge over to claim the bounty of Navarino for Argentina. Three unarmed policemen served the station, and it was difficult to see what they would do under those circumstances, but nobody worried too much about the detail down there.

The memory of the Falklands conflict was fresh, and any enemy of the Argies was a friend to Chile. At the end of the afternoon, as I was about to leave with the lorry, which had by now disgorged its firewood, the head policeman asked me if I'd care to stay for a while. My diary for that day notes, "Magritte clouds, beaver wigwams in the sphagnum bogs. No toothbrush. Must stay. What will I read?"

My carabineros took me mushroom picking and taught me which ones were for eating. We fried them in butter with a bright orange spherical fungus we snapped off the beech trees. Every evening, the head carabinero got out his photograph album, and we leafed through it in the flickering candlelight: here was José at Viña, at a party, on the beach. He was living off his memories in the back end of Tierra del Fuego.

In the early morning, when the cleaver peaks of the Darwin Cordillera turned baby pink, we took the horses to patrol the bays of the Beagle Channel to the southwest. The horses stamped the tussock grass, steam dissolving off their coats into the chilly morning air, and lumpy steamer ducks careered over the rocks, redundant wings flapping. We strolled about, and the policemen showed me where grass had grown over mounds of shells and ash left by Yahgan Indians, who used to paddle their beech-bark canoes from bay to bay, diving for shellfish and hunting seal. The name is Westernized; they called themselves Yamana, which means "people." They were nomadic and moved around the part of Tierra del Fuego that stretches from the Brecknock Peninsula to Cape Horn, though their territory shrank as they were hunted by white men, and they ended up confined to the canals around Isla Navarino. They spoke five mutually intelligible dialects, which together constituted a distinct linguistic group, and enjoyed one-word verbs meaning things like "to come unexpectedly across a hard substance while eating something soft" (like a pearl in an oyster). But they had no words for numerals beyond three: after you got to three, you said "many."

The Yahgan were killed off by imported Western diseases and by European settlers who sliced off their ears in order to collect the reward offered for each dead Indian. The last pure Yahgan died in 1982.

When we rustled the gorse bushes, fat upland geese took off against the Hockney-blue sky, unfolding white-striped wings. To the south, mountains trickled down into the ocean, last visible remains of the longest range on earth—one that runs forty-three hundred miles from the Caribbean to Cape Horn, where it goes underwater, and who knows what happens to it then. In the peaty light of early evening we rode toward the mountains called the Navarino Teeth in the heart of the island, a gleaming, uneven row of lower canines. Polar winds hurried across the ocean at that hour, and winter gusted in from the south.

On my last night we went at sunset on a final trip: my cara-bineros wanted me to see a beaver. There were many clearings of leafless and chiseled trunks enfolded within the luxuriance of the forest, but although we saw their wigwams and their swimming pools as we sloshed through the mud, we did not see any beavers. I heard the policemen expressing disappointment among themselves. The clouds hung low like white canopies, illuminated from underneath. The mountains turned shades of indigo, and the mirrored water darkened, cracked by trails of ducklings. On the highest peak of Hoste Island, a slender column of rock jutted upward just before the perpendicular walls of the summit.

"That," said José, "is what we call the monk entering the monastery."

When I woke on the last day, a three-foot-long stuffed beaver glared up from the end of my bed, baring horrid little yellow teeth.

This was fifteen years ago. When I think of it, costive at a desk behind the rain-splattered windows of home, staring into the sulfurous halos of London streetlights, I see the ghostly outlines of beech-bark canoes paddling eagerly from Wulaia to Douglas Bay. And I look back not just at a landscape I loved deeply. Shipwrecked now in another life, here where the curve on the globe is barely perceptible, I can just make out too the hopes and dreams of a young woman I once knew, down there in Tierra del Fuego.

2005

POSTSCRIPT

Since that visit, the Chilean government has sold tracts of the dense southern beech forest at the eastern edge of Navarino to Japanese paper manufacturers, and a plankton known as *marea roja* (red tide) has poisoned the shellfish that nourished generations of Yamana. And so it goes.

In the first years of the millennium I spent a lot of time in East Africa researching *Too Close to the Sun*, a biography of Denys Finch Hatton, the white hunter and lover of Karen Blixen immortalized by Robert Redford in the film of Blixen's *Out of Africa*. The coast cast a spell I could never break. Centuries before the railway opened up the interior, Arab merchants capitalized on an alternation in the monsoon winds to found harbor towns from Somalia to Mozambique. Lamu, Zanzibar, Kilwa, Mombasa, Pemba—ports that retain the easeful elements of the Orient, where you can still drink coffee served from brass jars by vendors tending tiny charcoal braziers behind the plain ashlar beauty of the Arab mansions. Once, in the Quirimbas Islands of northern Mozambique, I traveled south by dhow in a soft night breeze. What, I found myself thinking, was so strikingly unusual about the long black band of shoreline spooling out ahead? The wake of the dhow stimulated light-emitting plankton that glowed in the warm waters of the Mozambique Channel. Then, as I listened to the low Kimwani murmuring of the boatmen, I realized what it was. There was no artificial light anywhere—not a single pinhead of sodium breaking up the solid darkness of the East African coast.

When the Portuguese arrived in what is now Mozambique in the fifteenth century, they set up their provincial capital in the Muslim trading port of Ibo in the Quirimbas and from it grew fat on slaves and ivory. Ibo today is a study in sultry dilapidation. Far from home, where I like to be, I loitered among whitewashed mosques with walls three feet thick and blowsy almond trees heavy with swollen pods. In the Fort of São João Baptista, below cannons still trained on ghostly pirate ships, silversmiths sat hunched over their burners late into the night.

I had just recovered from a fever, possibly malarial, and had spent delirious nights in a strange bed. In the Quirimbas, I felt elated to be well, taking an attenuated delight in a quietly swelter-ing landscape of mangrove channels and fish eagles, of outrigger canoes filled with still-gilling barracuda, and of the lateen wings of dhows rising from the water like fins. On the uninhabited Rolas (pronounced "Rolash"), half a dozen families camped out, waiting for their catch to dry on racks—anglers with the tubular eyes of the bottom dweller, octopus, snapper, parrot fish—and under a makeshift shelter boys were smoking kebabs of spiny sea cucumber. The women's faces were painted white with a *mucira* beauty mask made from the pounded root of a bushy plant (Anita Roddick used it some years ago for a Body Shop product). Before long I was installed under a coconut palm turning my face up to Manessa, a dowager in a nightie printed with the words "Starry Dreams." Once applied, the mask is finished off with a particular pointillist pattern, in my case involving rivulets of "tears" signi-fying that my boyfriend was sleeping with another woman. When I got through to him on the phone a week later, he denied it.

Over on the mainland of Cabo Delgado, outside a broken-down customs house the national flag flapped in the wind. It is the only flag in the world to bear a firearm—the silhouette of an AK-47. This exemplifies the paradox of northern Mozambique: one senses a chained phoenix beating its wings in the ashes of civil war. Inland, the wreckage of capital projects marked out the terrain like the trading towns of precolonial days: manufactur-ing plants that failed because there were no engineers to main-tain them; agricultural projects sited in the wrong place on account of well-intentioned consultancy schemes out of touch with African reality—every conceivable half-built liberal dream a robust re-minder of the African politician's cash-siphoning skill.

Imagine the hope that filled my heart after *The Telegraph* sent me off to meet Peter Ryan. I was eighteen when Margaret Thatcher became prime minister. It took me a long time to understand how comprehensively she had murdered my socialist dreams. I wanted a world in which politicians built societies on truth for the good of the people. I thought there was a moral center. The joke was on me. But I was desperate to find a grain of hope, and I found it in Malawi.

Malawi: Dead in the Long Run

Catherine Mbalaka stands in the shallows of Lake Malawi squinting at the horizon as the fine mist they call a *chiperoni* drifts off the surface of the water and rises toward the western escarpment. We are looking out for her two dugouts, fetching back bulging nets. A wizened forty-one, with cropped hair and kinetic energy, the smiling Mbalaka is chuckling. After decades of hungry misery, her small fishing business is doing well. She started with a dugout and two homemade nets. After a year, she could afford another dugout; now she plans to buy a motorized boat so her fishermen can work in deeper waters. She did it with the help of managed borrowing from a dynamic young British-based charity that directly helps the poorest of the poor. The MicroLoan Foundation gives them a hand up, not a handout.

In November I toured Malawi to meet a wide range of women engaged in the fight out of near destitution through the small-loan system. A few had secured access to clean drinking water for the first time in their lives. Some were able to send their children to secondary school (only primary education is free). Many had made the transition from mud hut to brick house. So it is possible. "My life," Mbalaka told me once the latest haul of *chambo* were flailing on the sand, "has been transformed."

The small miracle taking place in Malawi is the result of the vision of one man: an affable fifty-four-year-old Devon-born businessman called Peter Ryan. Tall and angular, with raven hair, strong features, and a ringing laugh, Ryan looks like the archetypal Englishman abroad. He wears sandals and socks, and as soon as our plane touched down on African soil, he changed into a blinding Malawi-made print shirt he had stowed in his hand luggage. "Giving money away is a bad idea," Ryan explained to me as we set off from the capital, Lilongwe. "We lend very small amounts—from £15 to £180—and provide borrowers with training, a carefully managed financial plan, and ongoing support. They set up in a variety of fields, from sewing to market trading, and end up with a steady income from a sustainable business."

Malawi, the landlocked former tea protectorate of Nyasaland, is a worm-shaped country that wiggles between Zambia, Tanzania, and Mozambique. Its eponymous lake runs for 310 miles down the eastern flank, though in reality it is more of an inland sea (when you swim, every day it's a shock to rediscover that the water isn't salty). Beyond the lake westward, bush and saddle-back mountains yield to uncultivated plains and the characteristic bouldery hills of the Rift Valley.

Malawi is the ninth-poorest country in the world. According to World Bank figures, 90 percent of the twelve million Malawians live on an average of seventy cents a day. Unlike many of its neighbors, the country has virtually no minerals; delayed and erratic rains, a changing climate, and rampant deforestation mean crops regularly fail; there is no visible industry, no economic infrastructure, and next to no tourism; and there are no public universities or teeming game reserves. After leaving Lilongwe airport, we were in empty scrub after five minutes; there was none of the ribbon development that spools through the suburbs of other East African cities. Hour after hour we barely passed another vehicle, just uninterrupted rivulets of trudging people.

I sat in on a MicroLoan borrowers' meeting in Sasani in central Malawi and watched a loan officer coaching twelve women in the newly formed Sitigonja group (the name means "we will not give up" in Chichewa). To foster collective responsibility and a support network, the charity lends to small groups, not individuals. The loan is divided out equally, and each member is responsible for her own repayment. "It's basically joint and several liability," said Martha Nkhoma, a regional manager who also looks after credit operations for the whole program. At the meeting we sat on rush mats in the shadow of a spreading *gmelina* tree, conversation punctuated by the timeless Malawi thud of maize kernels being pounded in a mortar. Three women were suckling babies. Sasani has no sanitation or running water. The nearest clinic is a four-hour walk. Everyone has malaria at least once a year. When I asked the twelve women under the tree how many look after AIDS orphans as well as their own children, eight hands shot up.

After the meeting I talked to the group's chairwoman, twenty-four-year-old Loveness Banda. We loitered in her MLF-funded tea shop, a windowless brick room in which Banda dispenses tea, rice, and buns under a handwritten sign announcing, NGONGOLE MAWA—EATING ON CREDIT TOMORROW (meaning pay up). She had dolled up the decor by stringing up lines of colorful sweet wrappers twisted into butterflies. Infants wandered in and out; Banda had her first when she was fifteen. Slight and muscular, she looked me in the eye and talked steadily in alliterative and highly inflected Chichewa. "One day a week is a buying day," she explained when I asked about her routine. "It's a four-hour walk each way to catch a minibus to the town market, where I pick up supplies." After only three months in business she already had a stall selling okra and red beans as well as the tea shop, and plans for future loans tumbled out of her. She exuded entrepreneurial flair: in another life, she might have been a CEO. "All I had before discovering MLF through a friend," she said as we parted with the elaborate triple-grip Malawi handshake, "was a strip of cassava plants."

Loans are arranged in four-month cycles; once one cycle of repayments is made, the money is recycled into another loan, and the group borrows a higher sum, thus enabling businesses to grow. Borrowers are charged 24 percent interest on the first cycle and 20 percent thereafter. And it works: MLF enjoys a repayment rate of over 96 percent, a figure that would excite our own banks. I asked Ryan why he only lends to women. "I've asked our loan directors if we should start including men," he said, "and they are adamant that we shouldn't because we know that families benefit far more when women receive the cash."

Banda was completing her first loan cycle. At the other end of the MLF path out of poverty I found thirty-year-old Christina Mzula, currently repaying her ninth loan from a stall in the old town of Nkhotakota. "Incremental small amounts of capital," she told me, "have allowed me to expand from a tiny range of products to this"—and she gestured toward three walls of shelves crammed with hundreds of items, from batteries to chloroquine tablets, eggs (sold individually), and skin-lightening cream. While we were talking, a procession of children arrived clutching a handful of kwacha to purchase one of the small plastic bags of gleaming groundnut oil hanging from the roof like goldfish at an amusement park. (Two tablespoons of oil for five kwacha, or three cents.) "I am about to purchase a fridge," Mzula told me, "so I can sell cold drinks." She works at the stall from six in the morning till nine at night, six days a week; her husband, a salt trader, buys the goods wholesale when he is in Lilongwe.

Make-work schemes and cottage industries are not new to the charity sector. In *Bleak House*, Dickens satirizes Mrs. Jellyby's fellow philanthropist Mr. Quale, who plans to teach the denizens of Borrioboola to make piano legs. But the majority of these schemes have no business underpinning to make them sustainable. "You have to manage it tightly," says Ryan. "It doesn't just come." Now based in Chiswick in west London, Ryan is married with two grown-up children, and on non-MicroLoan days he works as a consultant in the consumer field. Crucially, he has in-depth experience of fledgling small businesses. A surfeit of compassion and a deficit of hardheaded business skills arrest the development of many small charities. It was the application of rigorous business methods and good practice that most impressed me as I toured MicroLoan offices and projects in Malawi.

Ryan is driven by the conviction that it is possible to enable even the poorest of the poor. He started the foundation in 1998 in a classic spare-bedroom start-up, initially to support a program lending to low-income individuals in the Philippines. Seeking an environment for a new project, he went to Malawi in 2001. "It was a conversion on the road to Lilongwe," said Ryan. "Malawi was the ideal place to introduce the self-sustaining charitable model I had in mind." He recruited one employee, the redoubtable Kenson Chiphaka, and the foundation made its first loan to a group of women selling sugar and tomatoes. It got 100 percent of the money back. The charity currently employs thirty-two local staff (with Chiphaka as country director) based in six regional offices; Ryan plans to roll out four more offices next year. Patrons include Sir Bob Geldof, and the U.K. operation is run only by a recently recruited CEO, a fund-raiser, and a squadron of volunteers. Ryan himself draws no salary. And nobody ever, ever flies business class.

Ryan is one of the growing band of apostles of microcredit, arguably the most significant trend in the aid sector in a generation. Sometimes known as microfinance, microcredit was pioneered by Muhammad Yunus, the charismatic Bangladeshi who earlier this year won the Nobel Peace Prize. "As a professor of economics in the seventies," explains the genial, round-faced Yunus, "I used to get excited teaching my students how economic theories provided answers to economic problems of all types." But in 1974, when famine ate up Bangladesh, Yunus began to have doubts. "What good were all these elegant theories," he wondered, "when people died of starvation on pavements?" Finding that no formal institution was available to cater to the credit needs of the poorest—he refers to "the prison walls of collateral"—in 1976 Yunus conducted an experiment, lending $27 worth of taka in a carefully monitored scheme to forty-two women to make bamboo stools. Repayments—including interest—were small (daily at first), rather than the lump sums demanded by banks; but they were made. Contrary to conventional financial wisdom, the poor turned out to be reliable borrowers. The philosophy of aid was turned on its head.

Yunus converted his program into a bank he called Grameen. To date the institution has lent $5.3 billion to six million families from Ecuador to Eritrea (there were lots of fights with the World Bank along the way). Some time ago I visited the lush villages in the Chittagong Hills close to the border between Bangladesh and Myanmar. I was amazed to find small Grameen bank branches tucked away in the remotest spots, catering to, and managing, the needs of illiterate women with no other access to credit. In his autobiography, *Banker to the Poor*, Yunus rails against the corruption and bureaucracy of international aid. "If foreign aid does reach Bangladesh at all," he thunders, "it usually goes to build roads, bridges, and so forth which are supposed to help the poor in the long run. But in the long run you are dead. And nothing trickles down to the poor."

Opponents of microfinance argue that it remains a palliative measure that does nothing to bring about the systemic reforms essential to the reduction of poverty. But how many millions of pounds and dollars have been poured into the black hole of aid to no effect? I traveled through the Nkhotakota reserve in northern Malawi on a seventeen-mile "road" recently built at vast expense with donor finance. It was so poorly constructed that the first rains washed it clean away. The fleets of shiny white four-wheel drives emblazoned with the logos of multinational NGOs have overtaken the declining elephant population. But they rarely benefit the poorest in a sustainable way. The writer Paul Theroux spent two years teaching in Malawi in the 1960s (he encountered his first dictator there, he recounts in *Dark Star Safari*, and got his first dose of the clap). When he returned in 2001, he was bewildered at the deterioration: his school had all but collapsed, and the only businesses that remained in Soche Hill were coffin makers. Large-scale international charity, Theroux concluded, was failing.

In the 1960s, of course, there was no HIV/AIDS. An estimated one in five Malawians carries the virus; recent random testing revealed the figure to be as high as 30 percent. Average life expectancy has dropped to thirty-six, and those left alive cope with four hundred thousand AIDS orphans, a figure that is rising. I was shocked at the low level of AIDS education and awareness. At a meeting of the Vinjenje HIV/AIDS Coping Group, I watched a sick woman breast-feeding her three-month-old twins—a known means of transmitting the virus. But nobody had told her not to breast-feed. "The only information we have," one woman in the group told me, "comes from the radio." I asked those who had a radio to raise their hands. Fewer than half those present did so. Frequently, husbands abandon ailing wives and find someone else to infect. I saw at least a hundred preschool orphans in that small district alone. None were adequately nourished. Many had no family. The unlucky ones are abandoned, and God knows what happens then. Mr. Kurtz himself couldn't have foreseen the horror.

Despite their proliferating numbers, women living with HIV/AIDS are still stigmatized, and MicroLoan tries to reach as many as possible. I visited Jennifer Chemdala in the village of Malasa, a pleasant hilly jumble of huts, houses, and small boys chomping mangoes. Chemdala greeted me among pots of canna lilies outside the smart wooden front door of the house she built from the profits of her secondhand-clothes business. Her husband, lying under a mango tree nearby, was very ill. Chemdala herself had tested positive. "When my husband got poorly," she told me, "MLF helped me scale back my borrowings so I did not default on loans while taking care of him." Tall and dignified, with the ready smile of most Malawians, she has four children and four orphans and hopes to stay alive until all eight can fend for themselves.

When borrowers complete their cycle of loans, the foundation prepares them for the next phase: becoming a bank borrower. On my last day in Malawi, I attended the opening of the new MicroLoan regional office in Kasungu, eighty miles northwest of the capital. There I met Thandiwe Gama, a grocer who had paid back her final £180 loan (the highest available) and was learning about what to expect when she enters the intimidating environment of a bank branch. Britain's high commissioner to Malawi, Richard Wildash, a keen supporter of MicroLoan, drove up from Lilongwe to cut the ceremonial ribbon, greeted by a troupe of dancers ululating choruses of welcome. The imperial past was so close in this backwater that the people of Kasungu bowed to the high commissioner when they left his presence. It was a glimpse of what my countrymen had done there in Nyasaland before me, and I didn't like it. "The empowerment of women in Malawi is something we very much want to support," Wildash told me. He acknowledges that while the anticorruption drive still has some distance to travel in the public sector, MicroLoan can offer almost total transparency. As Chiphaka told me as we sipped celebratory Fanta at the conclusion of the ceremonials, "None of our money is siphoned off. It goes directly from us to the borrower."

Most women I met exuded optimism, strength, and, frankly, a joyful spirit. Many were widows ("MicroLoan is our husband now," one said). But some were too weighed down to be cheerful. I spoke to Alima John outside her home off the old Nkhotakota market. The porch was crowded with children and goats, and as we talked, the sun set with its tropical haste, and paraffin lanterns began to glimmer through glassless windows. John's was a handsome, large face, her mouth naturally turned up in a smile—ironically, under the circumstances. She is an established MLF borrower. Besides selling vegetables, she rents a sewing machine for her eldest son to generate extra income. But as her business began to take off, six orphans joined her own brood of four—first her sister's three, then her brother's. "I could manage with seven," she told me, "because my brother shared the load, but then he died too . . ."

Microcredit has gained so much ground over the past decade that even corporate big hitters are clambering onto the bandwagon, arguing that microfinance should rely on investors, not donors. The UN designated 2005 the International Year of Microcredit, in the same year Citigroup, the largest banking outfit in the world, established a microfinance division, and many young Silicon Valley entrepreneurs are investing in the field. Some argue that the whole future of microfinance lies in the for-profit sector, not its charitable equivalent. Ryan disagrees. He considered taking MLF down the bank route and rejected it, arguing, plausibly enough, that banks are beholden to investors seeking a return—even the new breed of "ethical investors."

By the end of this year the charity will have made ten thousand loans. Ryan plans a further seven thousand next year. His long-term vision includes MicroLoan branches in other sub-Saharan countries as well as the expansion of an embryonic fair-trade venture exporting products from Malawi to the U.K. "We're close to being self-sustaining already," he said as we boarded the plane home, the loud print shirt already replaced by a Pringle sweater. "This is the crucial stage for MicroLoan. We are on a long journey." Bon voyage.

2006

Colorado: Bringing Lynx Home

High in the San Juan Mountains, on the southernmost spur of the Rockies, an elongated tawny cat with amber eyes and chocolate ear tufts lifts a paw like a small tennis racket and softly crunches the deep snow of a spruce forest threaded with stands of silver-trunked aspen. She looks around, wide-eyed, and starts at the beat of a red-tailed hawk's wing. Then she begins to trot, rotates her stumpy, black-tipped tail, and disappears into the forest.

It's been a long journey for a small cat. Twenty-five days previously, minding her own business thousands of miles away up in the Yukon, the two-year-old lynx was looking for a snowshoe hare for breakfast. Sniffing her prey underneath a mature spruce, she crept right into a metal trap. It was a bad move, but it wasn't catastrophic: unlike most traps, this one had been designed to capture the animal unharmed. When the trapper arrived an hour later, he was able to extricate the lynx and maneuver her into a small, portable cage without blood being drawn. As he did it, through his thick gloves he could feel that she was pregnant.

The trapper will be paid $1,000 for this female, a sum that reflects the extra effort required to capture a cat alive. His job ended at Whitehorse airport, where the lynx joined five other cats being examined by vets before boarding a plane to Denver, Colorado. From Denver, the pregnant lynx was loaded into another truck for a six-hour drive to a small camp in a remote corner of the San Luis Valley. There, sharing a large pen with another female, she was fattened on rabbits. Though her food was caught for her, she was not allowed to acclimatize to humans.

This bizarre feline journey was organized, monitored, and

financed by the state of Colorado's Division of Wildlife, and in particular by the biologist Dave Kenvin. Three weeks after the Yukon lynx arrived at the camp, Kenvin reckoned that she had reached prime condition. She was examined by more vets and fitted with a radio-tracking, mortality-sensing collar. The next morning, Kenvin inveigled her (she hissed and snarled throughout) into a custom-made perforated aluminum cage that he and a colleague hefted into the back of his oversized Ford pickup. The five other Yukon cats followed in three more vehicles.

Kenvin's patch, where he has spent thirty-five years observing wildlife, covers eight thousand square miles of the San Luis Valley and southwestern Colorado. A bearded, genial individual who hunts his own meat and displays a healthy disregard for bureaucrats, Kenvin led his small convoy up to about ten thousand feet in the San Juan Mountains. When the eight team members jumped down from the cabs, they quickly layered up with down jackets, fleece balaclavas, and gloves, as it was ten degrees colder up there, even though the sky was cloudless. For the last half mile of the trek, the cages were hauled off the trucks, loaded onto sledges, and towed by snowmobiles to a slope on the edge of a brush thicket overlooking white-brown tracts of Colorado wilderness. One by one, the front walls of the cages were lifted out. The lynx were free.

The six cats vanished into the heart of the San Juans, hunting for hares just as they did in Canada. It cost the Division of Wildlife $1,000 on top of the trapper's fee to capture, transport, and release each one, and in 1999 it brought forty-two down from the Yukon and Alaska. You have to want an animal badly to do that. But there aren't many lynx left in Colorado. There at the southern edge of their range, numbers of these secretive, forest-dwelling cats have declined to the point of extirpation as logging, oil, agricultural, and recreational industries have encroached upon their habitat: the last lynx seen in Colorado was trapped in 1973. So the Wildlife people have set about the difficult job of reintro-duction. Until now, only one state in America—New York—has tried to reintroduce lynx. That program, in the Adirondacks, was judged a failure (though in fact funding was cut, so it couldn't be properly followed up, and the biggest mortality was from roadkill).

The wide open spaces of Colorado traditionally belong to the men who farm them, ten-gallon-hatters with big herds and big swaggers. Ranchers perceive the whole bring-back-the-lynx busi-ness as a threat to their livelihood—which means a threat to the traditional use of public lands for grazing cows and sheep. A lynx is three feet long and only weighs about twenty-two pounds, but in the words of Todd Malmsbury, spokesman for the Colo-rado Division of Wildlife, "This is bigger than the lynx. It's about who controls the West. Traditional interests, which means fami-lies who've been farming the land for generations, or people who've moved in from the coast, bringing with them a strong environmental ethic?"

The polarization of Old West and New West has a lot to do with the shifting demographics of Colorado, a state that has swol-len from a population of 3.2 million in 1990 to 4 million now, making it the nation's third-fastest-growing state. Most of the immigrants are wealthy folk from California, and land prices have soared not just in the fashionable enclaves of Vail, Aspen, and Steamboat Springs but also around Pagosa Springs and other less well-known areas. The influx has created resentment. Many Coloradans told me the story of out-of-staters who move to the wilderness in search of the good life, then ring the Division of Wildlife in a panic saying, "Help! There's a bear in my garage!" "This is a wilderness," says the man at the DOW. "There are sup-posed to be bears."

Freeman Lester runs 250 beef cattle off Highway 160, a long, lonely road linking moribund mining towns. He owns nine hun-dred acres and buys permits to graze ten thousand more. He is also president of the Colorado Cattlemen's Association. The yard of his ranch is strewn with agricultural equipment in varying states of decay, a belching tar barrel, log pens, yapping animals, and an astonishingly small cabin he built himself thirty-two years ago. "Never got round to finishing it!" he said, extending a hand like a root vegetable. The buckle of his low-slung Wranglers shouts "FREEMAN!" and the skin on his face is like the bark of one of his ponderosa pines.

Like farmers everywhere, Lester enjoys moaning. Agricultural depression, GATT, NAFTA, loss of market share, inheritance tax, global famine—while he ranged widely over these and other topics, the one that caused him to lean forward over the rough wood table, take off his cap, and smooth his hairless head is the baby-sized furry lynx.

"Lynx are no threat to our livestock," he admitted straightaway. "But we have a long list of concerns about the Endangered Species Act."

The lynx was designated an endangered species in Colorado in 1976, but this state-level status protects only the animal, not its environment. In January 2000 the U.S. Fish and Wildlife Service will decide whether to list the lynx as a threatened or endangered species, and ranchers are afraid that federally designated status would extend its protection. "The act shut down the whole logging industry in the northwest quarter of the U.S. in the case of the Mexican spotted owl," said Lester, pinching tobacco from a battered tin. "It closed towns and put thousands out of work. We're frightened of it. Real frightened. The western slope of Colorado basically runs on forest permits, which means that ranchers buy licenses to graze on public land. We're worried that ESA listing of the lynx could result in grazing restrictions."

Ranchers are not the only group opposed to the reintroduction of the big-pawed cats. When the first lynx were released back into Colorado in the spring of 1999, four died of starvation right away. Animal rights activists quite literally stood shoulder to shoulder in the malls of Denver and Boulder with hyper-conservative ranchers, screaming for lynx to go home.

Dave Kenvin acknowledges that carnivore reintroduction is a difficult game. When the most endangered mammal in North America, the black-footed ferret, was decimated by distemper, the federal government brought the remaining population into captivity. When the ferrets were first reintroduced to the wild, they suffered a 90 percent mortality rate as they had forgotten that they were supposed to look up for hawks. In addition, sometimes the animals' instinct foils human intervention. "When we moved some black bears recently," said Kenvin, "they beat us home."

So far, ground and aerial tracking indicates that the lynx aren't heading back north, though thirteen of the forty-two that came south in 1999 have died. Reintroduction can work: biologists like Kenvin are fond of citing successful programs that they have pioneered. In 1990–1991 a Colorado team brought in moose for hunting, and river otters were reintroduced in a program that was ultimately successful despite an initial 40 percent mortality rate. In addition, the Division of Wildlife has transported pronghorn antelope and bighorn sheep into areas where they had disappeared. "The lynx are a long-term project," says Kenvin. "I'm cautiously optimistic."

It was an idea that grew from the bottom up. Having looked hard for remnant populations of lynx for some years, Kenvin sat down with a bunch of other biologists and decided that although there might be a few in the forest, if there were to be a viable population, they were going to have to introduce more. They knew their scheme involved risk. Progress usually does. "We may have changed Colorado so much in the last fifty years that lynx might not be able to survive here anymore," says Kenvin. "We learn as we go."

The program is coming to the end of its second year and has two more years to run. It looks likely that fifty more lynx will be released in April and May 2000. About one-fifth of the $250,000 annual budget comes from license fees paid by hunters and fishers (the Division of Wildlife collects about $60 million a year in license fees) and the rest from grants. The foundation of the media mogul and multiple-ranch owner Ted Turner has pledged $70,000 in the next budget cycle, beginning in July. The major developer Vail Associates Inc. gave $200,000 from its environmental fund. In 1997, this company earned net revenues of $291 million from public lands in Colorado, and the U.S. Forest Service approved its latest expansion into 885 acres of prime lynx habitat (not to mention elk calving grounds). A request for an injunction to halt the expansion failed in a federal court. So Vail Associates is simultaneously paying to reintroduce an animal and cutting off its best chance of a home.

Wildlife regulation in the United States involves a symbiotic and often uneasy relationship between federal and state agencies. Forty-two percent of Colorado is public land, and the U.S. Forest Service is its biggest agent. Brad Morrison is a Forest Service officer covering the lynx reintroduction territory. Besides handing out cattle-grazing permits, his job involves writing an environmental impact assessment report for anything that might happen on federally owned land—the sinking of an oil well, for example. While Morrison speaks in favor of the Endangered Species Act, he stresses—crucially—the importance of interpretation. The act also brings him problems of his own. "I'm often not deciding between man and animals," he says, "but animal and animal."

American environmentalists believe that large carnivores are essential for the protection of biodiversity and that in order to save the Colorado wilderness the wolf and grizzly have to come back.

Mention the word "wolf" to a Colorado rancher and the temperature rises. Wolves, sheep and cattle predators that used to exist in every American state, are now only found in Minnesota and Montana. An opinion poll recently revealed that 70 percent of Coloradans would like to see them back, and an environmental group is working on their reintroduction from Casper, Wyoming, south through Colorado to northern New Mexico under the program called the Southern Rockies Ecosystem Project. If it goes through, it will be wildly controversial. While the gray wolf reintroduction program worked in Yellowstone, ranchers have fought it all the way and are still suing. Half the Mexican red wolves reintroduced to Arizona in 1998 were shot.

The fear that reintroduced lynx will set a precedent for reintroduced wolves has moved the cats to the eye of the storm. The pages of *High Country News* are vibrating with conflicts between backcountry recreationists, ranchers, and environmentalists: one letter described the lynx program as "the worst case of animal cruelty any of us have ever witnessed." And this being America, everyone involved is suing everyone else. Conservation organizations and private individuals sued the Fish and Wildlife Service for dillydallying over the listing of the lynx. A coalition of farmers and hunters challenged the lynx reintroduction on the grounds that it violated national environmental laws. Their case was thrown out of court.

Wildcats, ranching, the hegemony of humans: these issues stir up a lot of hate in the West. In October 1998 ecoterrorists in Vail caused $12 million of damage in an arson attack on the nation's biggest ski resort, claiming they did it "on behalf of the lynx." The Colorado Division of Wildlife is under persistent attack from traditionalists. "People want to be able to do anything they want, anytime they want, and live like they used to," said Todd Malmsbury. "But everyone has a right to a voice in what's happening in Colorado, and that's why this whole battle's coming down. It's about the regulation of the Wild West, and it's going to run for a long time."

The Lynx Recovery Team, meanwhile, is monitoring its newly

released cats closely. Each animal's collar emits a unique radio frequency that is tracked by single-engine Cessnas equipped with antennas and radio telemetry. The planes take off from a badly cracked strip of tarmac outside the former silver-mining town of Creede on the Rio Grande, and above early-morning herds of a thousand elk they scrape the top of the fir forests searching for the *cheep cheep* that identifies each lynx. Once a cat has been located, ground trackers like Minnesota-born Jenny put on their snowshoes and take up the trail. When she finds the remains of a kill, her joyful voice crackles over the radio.

"Go, kitty, go . . ."

1999

POSTSCRIPT

In September 2010 wildlife officials in Colorado announced that the lynx birthrate was outpacing mortality and that the reintroduction scheme had surpassed best expectations. (The year after this piece appeared, the U.S. Fish and Wildlife Service did indeed declare the lynx an endangered species.) As I write, descendants of the kitty I had seen cautiously emerging from her cage on that cold morning in the San Juan Mountains are happily hunting snowshoe hares up and down the Rockies. But after much Sturm und Drang, the National Park Service decided against taking the next step and bringing wolves back to Colorado. Elsewhere, reintroduced wolves have done so well that Washington took the beast off the endangered species list and in 2009 Montana and Idaho even reintroduced wolf hunts. Then, in another twist, in late October 2010 the government relisted the wolf in response to a lawsuit from an environmental organization—a telling symptom of the competing interests involved in matters lupine.

Species reintroduction remains deeply divisive. Everyone still disagrees about who controls the West, the East, and all points in between. The issue has begun to attract more attention in the U.K., and attempts to reintroduce the Eurasian beaver are currently under way on the west coast of Scotland. In 2010, the Cairngorms National Park published a report identifying twenty-three potential species for reintroduction, including lynx and wolf. But, as in Colorado, the idea ignites anger and passion in equal measure. Last year wildlife campaigners labeled a plan backed by the British equivalent of the Audubon Society to reintroduce the white-tailed sea eagle to Suffolk a "PR stunt" and a potential environmental "disaster." The project had already been batted from county to county as interested parties successfully campaigned to get it shifted off their patch. But if scientists from Natural England get the permission they require, twenty young birds will be released annually over a six-year period.

Meanwhile, the most vivid memory I have of that assignment for *The Telegraph* was a tracking flight over the Rockies. We had taken off from Creede in a three-seater—it was more of a two-seater really, but the pilot and the copilot wedged me behind them. The updrafts and downdrafts of the gorges, and our acrobatic swoops when we heard the bleep of a lynx collar, made it a very rough flight indeed. Fighting hard to keep my breakfast down, I had to listen to the other two over the headset discussing what we would choose from the Mexican restaurant just over the border in Arizona where we were headed for lunch.

Kerala: Killing Elephants, and How to Avoid It

Viscous blood colored the tender shoots, the stain on the soil like a map. A thin banana farmer stood on a bank of the fast-flowing Kalindi, under the spires of the Western Ghats. "I didn't want to kill it," Chami explained in the lurching staccato of Malayalam. "But what can I do?" He raised an efflorescence of eyebrows, bony fingers wringing a torn lungi. "Three times this elephant destroyed my crop." He had tapped a power cable to electrocute the elephant as it returned for a fourth session.

Currently out on bail, Chami faces a mandatory minimum of three years in jail if he's found guilty.

In the heart of a teak forest less than a mile from Chami's wrecked little plot, Mark Shand bent over a chart spread on the bonnet of a shiny jeep. A passionate English buccaneer of the central-casting variety, even if the pecs are a bit saggy these days (whose aren't?), Shand, brother of Camilla, Duchess of Cornwall, was planning the next stage of his campaign to preserve a vital elephant migration route. Like Chami—both men are fifty-eight—Shand has a long history with elephants.

"The Asian elephant is at an all-time low," he boomed, swinging one arm as if it might be a trunk. "I predict extinction if we don't do something to secure its shrinking habitat. Can we really allow this magnificent beast to vanish on our watch?" This is not a story of good against evil. It is more complex than that. It is about poor people and an endangered species, each fighting for survival in a shrinking environment.

India's twenty-nine thousand elephants now compete for space with 1.2 billion people. First agriculture depleted the forests, then a shifting zeitgeist compelled Congress to ban both hunting and the capture of wild elephants: a devastating double whammy that resulted in more animals and less space. Elephants deprived of traditional feeding grounds took to crop invasion; hungry farmers retaliated. Currently, elephants kill between two hundred and three hundred Indians a year. Up in the West Garo Hills of Meghalaya, I once saw rioting villagers brandishing flaming torches on the streets after elephants trampled four children to death.

Shand connected in the late 1980s. On a whim, he bought an emaciated captive elephant, christened her Tara, and rode her 750 miles from Konarak on the Bay of Bengal to the Sonepur Mela, the ancient elephant trading fair on the Ganges at Patna. The bestselling *Travels on My Elephant* that emerged from the trip recounts an unlikely love story. "My mouth went dry," Shand wrote of the moment he first saw Tara. "I knew then that I had to have her." A film is scheduled to start shooting next year.

An ex-playboy of the Imran Khan set (Shand's former lover Marie Helvin wrote in her autobiography that he was in possession of "the most beautiful body I'd ever seen"), Shand has a public school tribalism that suits a hierarchical society in which each caste has its place. For his next book, *Queen of the Elephants*, set in the shadow of the Himalaya, Shand qualified as a mahout, or elephant handler, spouting the special language evolved from Sanskrit and nimbly mounting his charge via the trunk. In *Travels* he had noted that "the Indian elephant was simply running out of living space." By *Queen* four years later, he was witnessing open warfare. "It was the first time," he wrote, "I had seen these majestic and beautiful animals reduced to the level of common and rather cumbersome thieves. Stripped first of their forests and now of their dignity, they ran like frightened rabbits in the headlights."

Horrified at what he had observed, Shand returned home to London and founded the charity Elephant Family. "Actually, it wasn't me who founded it," he says. "It was Tara." Hokey anthropomorphism might be cloying, but you can't blame Shand for using every fund-raising weapon in his arsenal. "Look," he tells me conspiratorially on the first leg of our Indian field trip. "Elephant Family is the only U.K. charity solely dedicated to the Asian elephant. There are only fifty thousand of them, compared with half a million African ones. Yet bigger, uglier African elephants grab all the attention."

After several false starts, Shand realized that the erosion of migration routes lay at the heart of the problem. Elephants eat so much that they have to keep moving: they are big, social nomads. Herds have followed the same routes for centuries. If their passage is blocked, they seek food elsewhere—among crops. Preservation of the corridors between habitats has become crucial for both sides in the battle for land in India.

The slender southwestern state of Kerala on the Malabar Coast is defined by the Western Ghats, the mountain range that for centuries protected Kerala from mainland invaders. (On the other side, the Ghats form an edge of the Deccan Plateau.) At the good end of many human development indices—infant mortality, life expectancy, reduction of rural poverty—the state also boasts the highest literacy rate in India (91 percent). Shand and I were headed for the Wayanad highlands in the far northeast of Kerala, a landscape of rosewood groves, shimmering rice paddies, and misty peaks. Although the region is now a patchwork of rubber and tea plantations, swaths of deciduous secondary forest remain intact, and as a result Wayanad hosts the largest single elephant population in Asia.

In the heart of Wayanad, the fields around Thirunelli are known for cardamom, cashews, and multitudinous banana species (Malayalam has as many words for banana as Guam for coconut and the Hidatsa language for cuts of buffalo). The land is pocketed with modest farms and roadside stalls peddling coconut jaggery to pilgrims on their way to the Vishnu temple on the Thirunelli escarpment. This is the world conjured by R. K. Narayan, India's greatest English-language novelist. Often, while I was traveling through those remote settlements, I glimpsed a character from Narayan's Malgudi: a woman harvesting jackfruit or a youth shinning up a hundred-foot trunk to harvest betel nuts with a kukri knife bandaged to a bamboo pole. But Thirunelli, with its dense bamboo groves, is a hot spot of elephant-human conflict, especially around the crucial migration corridor linking the Nilgiri Hills to the south with the much smaller Brahmagiri Hills to the north.

After a lively five-hour drive from the coast along a slope so vertiginous that I several times had to restart my heart, we arrived at Thirunelli. There Shand and I met up with Vivek Menon, founder of the Wildlife Trust of India. The two men met long ago on a conservation project in India, and Menon's WTI now implements the Elephant Family program in the country. Menon had flown down from Delhi to join WTI field officers working on a long-term project to protect a migration corridor. As we drove into the jungle, rays filtered through bamboo hatchings, dappling stands of turmeric. A troop of langur monkeys swung between yellow laburnum blooms, and a mongoose darted behind a termite mound. "The migration route through here," Menon explained, "is one of the most imperiled in the country." A tall, mustachioed figure with rocket fuel in his veins, Menon is the son of the engineer who designed the fabled Ambassador car, long a fixture of urban India. ("As a child I rode in one of the prototypes," Menon recalled as we bumped through the jungle. "I said to Dad, 'Everything in this car makes a noise except the horn.'") Having trained as an ornithologist, Menon junior worked his way up the hierarchy of the Indian World Wildlife Fund before leaving to found WTI from his spare bedroom. Eleven years later, the organization employs 150 staff and has more conservation projects on the go than any other NGO in India. But foreign funding accounts for 80 percent of revenues, and, as Menon admitted, "It's still a hard sell. When people think of India, they don't think of wildlife. They think of swami and the Himalaya. Africa is wildlife."

"The elephant has a totally different cultural role here," Menon went on after a long, yapping exchange with the driver about directions, "which is partly why we've never gone down the culling route like South Africa. In India you don't sell your mother, your wife, or your elephant." Reserves—the short-term conservation solution for large, endangered mammals—have a mixed record, and anyway compete for priority: newly discovered coal deposits in Chhattisgarh are currently threatening a planned sanctuary to check rising human-elephant conflict in that region. Population growth, industrial development, poverty, political incompetence, corruption—everything is stacked against the

Asian elephant. Small wonder that hardly a day goes by without a gory story appearing in the papers somewhere in India reporting on hungry, marauding tuskers killing people in their desperate search for food. Small wonder too that farmers like Chami take the law into their hands.

The author of half a dozen influential books on the politics of conservation, Menon focused in the 1990s on poaching, going undercover in Japan and China for two years to expose illegal ivory trading. "Legislation," he said, lifting his binoculars, "has reduced poaching. So now we are concentrating on conflict killing and trying to reduce it by creating safe space for both elephants and people."

Menon suddenly asked the driver to stop and to cut the engine. He had spotted pugmarks. "Young male," he whispered. The silence of the forest was broken only by the sound of an elephant trunk cracking bamboo. Then we heard the low, grieving trumpeting of a ship leaving port, and a magnificent tusker crashed through the rosewood, ears slowly flapping. That close, its horny bulk blocked the sun. "Mock charge," muttered Menon calmly. We watched. A blue-winged Malabar parakeet streaked across the glade in an iridescent flash. After a few minutes, the elephant backed into a patch of wild lilies, executed a slow three-point turn, and vanished back into the forest.

Elephant Family works in partnership with WTI to secure the forty-two-mile Thirunelli-Kudrakote corridor, a vital funnel route for elephants and just over a half mile wide at its narrowest point. "The preservation of an elephant corridor is complex in scope, size, and scale," explained Menon. "First you have to get the state to declare the land an official corridor, then establish a field office and put men in to get to know the communities, find out what they want. Third, you have to relocate some of the people actually living within the corridor to create a contiguous migrating environment."

Relocating is notoriously difficult, painstaking, and expensive, but it is possible. We visited one of the first successful Malayalee relocations: a thriving community of families who four years ago, with WTI assistance, shifted from Thirulakunnu, bang in the middle of the elephants' route. On the front porch of a tiled bungalow, a carpet of coffee beans lay drying under a satellite dish. Inside, Kali-awa, the wrinkled chatelaine, pointed out amenities, her tough hands closely patterned with henna. "I like it much better here," she said, "though I miss the moving water [the river]. Our new house is nearer the market where we sell our crops. And we got three bullock loads more coffee this year." She eyed four unmarried daughters sashaying in the yard for the *Telegraph* photographer.

At the relocated Valiya Emmadi community five miles away, a sequence of more compact bungalows sloped between neat rows of amaryllis. Coffee bushes and pepper vines extended up the hill behind. As we sipped tiny glasses of sugary ginger tea, I asked Menon why such a small settlement had two wells. "Tribal and non-tribal," he said. "They won't share a well." Malayali talk proudly of their state's religious pluralism, omitting to mention the plight of its economically disenfranchised tribal peoples. After Bihar and Orissa, Kerala has a larger tribal population than any other state (1.1 percent of almost thirty-two million). "It's hard to break down taboos," said Menon as we moved off. "A recent dung-fueled biogas project failed as the two groups refused to share the other's animal dung."

Two years ago Congress passed an act to protect tribal communities by granting each adult a hectare of land. (Some environmentalists said the legislation represented "the end of the elephant.") But, as Shand explained, tribal peoples gained little, as, to garner more votes, Congress has altered the terms of the act to make it apply to all forest dwellers. "Misuse of this law is a disaster," fulminated Shand. "Only five percent of those who apply for protection are tribals; the rest are forest dwellers and chancers."

On the way back to camp I asked Menon how he managed to focus on animals when Oriya mothers were feeding their babies roasted mud so they didn't cry out with hunger as they died. His face twisted in the late-afternoon light. "With grave difficulty," he replied. Later, he told me he found solace in the Hindu concept of acceptance.

The success of WTI relocations has made an impact in the Indian media. But sustained funding is crucial. "A relocation is a five-year project, minimum, and you can't stop halfway through where people are involved," said Shand. As his most ambitious fund-raiser to date, he is about to stage Britain's largest-ever public art exhibition. In May, 250 five-foot-tall fiberglass elephants will stand on plinths across London, only to vanish mysteriously overnight later in the summer in a cunning representation of extinction. Each animal will be decorated by an artist or celebrity—Jack Vettriano, Diane von Furstenberg, and Sacha Jafri have signed up—and later auctioned. The project was inspired by a similar event in Rotterdam in 2007. The Dutch organizers Marc and Mike Spits, father-and-son marketeers guilty of launching the Smurfs and Hello Kitty, subsequently auctioned the models to the tune of almost three-quarters of a million pounds. "The success of Elephant Parade [Holland]," said Mike, "proves that people are insistent on keeping the elephant around in this world."

Meanwhile, Chami, the thin banana farmer who electrocuted an elephant he found tearing up his livelihood, is still awaiting trial. (Ever tried to bury a dead elephant under the patio?) He is the only breadwinner in a family of nine.

On the long drive back to camp, Menon, Shand, and I discussed the prospects for Chami's wife and children if, as seems likely, he gets put in prison. Was it really possible to protect the likes of this hapless farmer and to allow the wild Asian elephant to thrive unmolested? At that moment, I had my doubts. But, as Shand said, can we let this majestic animal go extinct on our watch? In the last westering rays of sun, a matriarch and her calf were chewing bamboo. On the other side of the road, a few hundred yards off, a man led a bullock through a freshly harvested paddy field. We stopped. An air of unearthly calm overlay the scene. The elephant raised her head, the profile of the trunk sharp against the setting sun. Ancient and wise, she looked, it seemed to me, with longing to the distant hills.

No: not on our watch.

2010

Albania

L ate in the afternoon a Vlach shepherd and his mule coerced a string of goats to pastures high in the Lunxherise mountains. Below, a man hooked the blade of a scythe around his neck and walked from his hut, wordlessly leaving his wife, who was churning butter with a paddle in a wooden pail. I looked far out over the yellows and greens of the Albanian mountains, and I thought, *Where else in Europe is it still like this?*

Albania is a country waking up after a long, dark night. After almost fifty years of its own particular brand of communism, its people subsist on the lowest per capita income in Europe (a professor I met at the School of Medicine earns $130 a month). The country was effectively sealed off from the rest of the world by the megalomaniac dictator Enver Hoxha (pronounced "Hodga"). Hoxha was barking mad and a murderer to boot. He banned beards and made people call him Sole Force. He squabbled with all his erstwhile allies—the Soviets, the Chinese, the Yugoslavs—and he had thousands of his people sent to labor camps in the chrome mines for crimes such as listening to the

BBC World Service on the wireless. His Sigurimi—secret police—buried priests alive. ("The only religion of Albania," Hoxha declared, "is Albanian.") Young Albanians were shot for playing a Rolling Stones tape. Thousands died. Albania might be 112 miles from Italy, but as far as the rest of the world was concerned, it could have been the Antarctic.

In the heart of the capital, Tirana, the vacant plinth that once supported a fifty-five-foot bronze statue of Sole Force stands redundant in Skanderbeg Square. Beyond the Stalinist monster buildings radiating off Skanderbeg, and beyond the rows of handsome yellow house-offices thrown up by the Italians during the occupation, half a million Tiranians live in concrete apartment buildings built during the communist era, graffitied now and leprous with corrosion.

I found the city full of cafés and the cafés full of men. The click of billiard balls came flying through open doors. Finding out how much you weigh was a popular pastime, and on the sidewalks men squatted next to pairs of scales, charging a few leks for use. And everywhere the whiff of open drains, exhaust fumes, and piles of decaying refuse.

Sheep grazed in the scrubby central park, but the rest of Tirana was a perpetual snarl of traffic. Yet when the communist regime fell in 1992, there were fifty cars in the capital, and it was illegal for an ordinary citizen to have a motor vehicle. Now the country enjoys the highest Mercedes ownership in the world, almost entirely due to cars stolen from Germany by Albanian gangs and the Italian Mafia and sold in the port of Durres, twenty miles west of Tirana. In many, the red-and-white pennant of Bayern Munich still dangles proudly from the rearview mirror.

Tucked in between Greece in the south, Montenegro in the north, Kosovo and Macedonia in the east, and a large slice of the Adriatic in the west, Albania's land surface is about that of Maryland. To get around, I hired a car and a driver. I paid $100 a day for my man, which included all gas and his food and lodging. You can get a driver for less, but I wanted someone with a driver's license. You pay extra for that.

I cannot say that it was an easy trip. The fact that nobody speaks English is exacerbated by out-of-date guidebooks and the erroneous nature of much of the information extracted from helpful passersby. Maps became legally available to foreigners only recently, telephones often don't work, and there are many power cuts. Confusingly, people usually quote prices in old leks, which means ten times the actual cost. While I experienced only friendliness from Albanians (the dynamite incident was an accident), it was impossible not to be aware of a general lawlessness. Shortly before my arrival, someone stole the prime minister's car.

Communicating with my driver, Qazim, in pidgin Italian (though the truth was that he was reluctant to speak at all), I set off for the south over the semiarid Krabbe mountains and down to Elbasan along the Shkumbini valley, the latter wrecked by a Chinese-built steel mill, now mostly defunct, like all Albanian heavy industry. The small part of it in operation was exuding acrid orange clouds. In Elbasan the apartment buildings were flowering with satellite dishes. Out to the east, the road followed the Shkumbini to the shores of Lake Ohrid and Lin, a fishing village overlooking Macedonia. Three women were guiding donkeys freighted with corn along the viny Lin lanes, carding wool as they went. On the lakeside road from Lin to Pogradec we ate red-speckled trout at a fish restaurant on stilts. Even the sphinx-like Qazim was impressed. During Hoxha's rule it was illegal for ordinary people to catch this delicious fish (to ensure the conservation of supplies for party bosses), and if you got found trying in an attempt to feed your starving family, you were sent to the camps for fifteen years.

Hoxha was convinced that Albania ran a grave risk of being invaded by Western forces jealous of the country's success, and so he ordered the construction of hundreds of thousands of reinforced-concrete domes with machine-gun slits. These bunkers are a sinister feature of every Albanian landscape and a potent symbol of paranoia that will still be there in five hundred years.

In Korça, a town at the foot of the Morava mountains, a couple of solid Ottoman *hans* hid modestly among the concrete sprawl—caravansary posts where traders rested, prayed, and stocked up for the next leg. The Turks occupied Albania for half a millennium, and their hand is everywhere—in the architecture, language, food, and the fact that 70 percent of Albanians are Muslim. Yet I had no sense of being in a Muslim country. Women wore miniskirts in the cities and bikinis on the beaches, and I did not hear a single call to prayer.

We crossed a scrubby plain outside Korça to visit the old Christian village of Boboshtica, where a dozen families were living off one cow each and an old woman in a lean-to stirred a vat of blackberry raki over an open fire. It took ten minutes to get from Korça to Boboshtica, but it was like going back a thousand years.

At another village, Barç, a Muslim one in the mountains on the other side of Korça, we were told that the only doctor had immigrated to Canada the previous month (who could blame her?). I spoke in Greek to two young men in jeans who had returned home for the summer from their jobs laboring on Athenian building sites. "It's like Pakistan here," one of them said, sweeping a hand round the mud streets. Yet at six o'clock, the hour of the evening stroll throughout southern Europe, a couple of young women emerged from their shack in high heels and lipstick to pick their way among the cow pies.

All over Albania, I met people with apparently irreconcilable feelings about their country: an attenuated awareness of national inferiority and an engorged sense of patriotic pride. They were embarrassed at being hoodwinked by the communists for so many years, but how were they to know?

We pressed on south through the Gramoz mountains, a wolfy hinterland and established robbery zone. The dun shades of the flatlands rippled upward, gradations of color shifting through purples and opalescent ambers up to the last glassy mountain ridge. The air was heavy with wild thyme. Armed police stopped us three times on the crumbling switchbacks, though they were less interested in protecting us than in rifling through Qazim's papers until they found something for which they could extort a fine. At Erseka there were two donkeys at the taxi stand.

Shortly we entered ancient pine forest and in two hours passed only a group of men in equally ancient suit jackets gathered at a pyre to make charcoal. At an altitude of about four thousand feet we stopped for lunch at a village called Leskovik. This place, sheltering under a bare, tawny shoulder of the Nemërçka range, was isolated even by the standards of the Albanian mountains. Horses and carts outnumbered cars in Leskovik by some margin, and haystacks the shape of fat obelisks nestled up to the ubiquitous concrete. All Albanian haystacks wore tiny waterproof capes crowned with a tire hat.

A large tractor-servicing factory just outside the village had been burned out. The Albanian landscape was a living oxymoron: the advent of democracy triggered a construction spree, and there were building sites everywhere, each unfinished structure displaying a ghoulish dummy to ward off the evil eye. Yet everywhere too were the decaying skeletons of communist collectivization.

If Albania had a tourist industry, Gjirokastra would be on the poster. A granite medieval and Ottoman fortress presides over everything else from a small hill, the slopes below crowded with nineteenth-century merchants' houses with pale gray slate roofs, the whole lot sitting like crumbs in a bowl of limestone mountains. It was a spectacular spot all right, but I did not feel safe in Gjirokastra, and even the inscrutable Qazim militated for an early departure. The narrow streets up at the castle walls seemed particularly tense, as the Greek consulate was up there and a three-hundred-strong visa-seeking crowd was eddying volubly around its walls.

Turning toward the coast, we drove on to the palm trees of Saranda, where Corfu looms so near across the strait you wonder why, in the dark days, they didn't all swim for it (it can't be more than a mile or two at the narrowest point). Then you learn that they did. Before they got far, armed security boats fished them out in order to dispatch them—yes, to the camps.

South of Saranda the unpaved road ran parallel with the sea through miles of olive groves and petered out at Butrint, probably the best of Albania's many archaeological sites. According to book 3 of the *Aeneid*, Trojan exiles founded Butrint in the twelfth century B.C. The Romans were there, the settlement's strategic position on the east-to-west trade routes kept it going all through the Byzantine period, and by the fourteenth century it was part of the Venetian Empire. When we got to it, Butrint was empty. Qazim procured a bag of figs, and we ate them in the shade of a eucalyptus, right below the Bronze Age acropolis.

We proceeded up the coast known as the Albanian Riviera on a perilous corniche. Above miles of untrodden beaches (notwithstanding a few hundred bunkers, but to these I was now inured), the road eventually dipped down to Himara. There I holed up in a hotel hard on the sandy beach. The cafés on the front were permanently crowded with old men taking turns at an open-air billiard table and shouting orders to wives laboring back from the fields. A taverna was so close to the sea that I swam between ordering and eating.

Right at the top of Dhérmi, a depopulated hill town to the north of Himara, I visited the tiny thirteenth-century church of Shen Maria, where Byzantine saints and reptilian devils paraded across sixteenth-century frescoes. It was quiet, and rods of buttery light beaming through the high windows cast checkered shadows on the flagged floor.

The proprietor of the small hotel at Dhérmi had promised fresh fish for supper. And indeed it was fresh. He dynamited it out of the water thirty feet out in the small cove right in front of the hotel. I was swimming in the cove at the time. A flake of spent dynamite landed on my head.

North of Dhérmi the road leaped from zero to three thousand feet in minutes. The large flocks of black goats on the mountainside were the only healthy-looking animals in Albania. A handful of holiday cabins tottered in a state of imminent dereliction, looted to death in 1997 during the riots that followed the collapse of government-endorsed Ponzi schemes. Virtually nothing escaped this period of plunder—industrial sites, factories, schools, museums (people ran around brandishing hundred-year-old swords), state arsenals, hospitals, and even jails, from which all the prisoners escaped.

On the way back to Tirana, in the palmy main street of Vlora, a police van stopped in front of our car, and half a dozen policemen piled out wearing black balaclava hoods with eye slits. Blood feuds are so prolific in Albania that if a policeman shoots a criminal, he is likely to be murdered in turn by the criminal's avenging family. So policemen sometimes patrol in disguise. Blood feuds are especially prolific in the highlands to the north of Tirana, the territory of the Gheg tribe, where clan loyalty is more powerful than toothless national law. And remember, this is 112 miles from Italy. As so often in this lawless land, what should have struck terror in my heart instead rang a note of bathos: as the sinister masks had no mouth holes, the policemen were obliged to wear them half rolled up to allow the obligatory cigarette to dangle from their lips.

How long will it take before the package tourists debouch into Albania and turn it into another southern European resort? The government has begun work on Corridor 8, a planned highway from Durres down the Riviera. Whether Albanians will ever have enough money to complete the project is debatable. Inward investment remains poor, inhibited by frequently changing laws, along with several hundred other inhibiting factors, including endemic corruption and the instability of the Balkans in general. I think it will be a long time before Club Med ousts the donkeys grazing among the Albanian bunkers.

1999

The Sea Islands of Georgia

On the door to the ladies' bathroom, a sign said, NO FIRE-ARMS. Beyond a live oak trailing Spanish moss, sunshine glanced off the lighthouse pebble glass. Apart from that, there was nothing but salt marsh—miles of spartina grass quietly whirring in the still spring Georgia air.

When the soldier-statesman James Oglethorpe pitched up on St. Simons Island in 1733, he found little but oyster shells, discarded in the millions across the Yamacraw seasonal hunting grounds. It was tough country to settle. But Oglethorpe's patron George II was desperate to establish a buffer zone between his prosperous South Carolina colony to the north and the hostile Spanish garrisons in Florida on the other side. With a royal charter in his pocket, Oglethorpe founded a colony on St. Simons Island and named it after the king. The land grants he allocated kick-started the plantation system. The men tried various crops—indigo was too smelly, as it had to be cured with urine—but it was the salt-and-moisture-loving Sea Island cotton that enabled the Georgia Colony to put down roots. (Sea Island remains the most expensive cotton fiber, but it grows in Egypt now.) A succession of treaties dispatched the indigenous peoples: at a congress in Augusta in May 1773, the season of the Green Corn

Moon, twenty-three hundred square miles of Creek and Chero-kee lands around the Savannah River were ceded to His Majesty. St. Simons prospered until the Civil War. Without slaves, its cotton withered, and the population of Georgia shifted inland— leaving St. Simons to sink back to its miasma of refracted light and oyster middens.

Known today as the Sea Islands, the stringy Georgian archipel-ago is mostly under public ownership. Oglethorpe would recog-nize the landscape, its salty tang, and the iridescence of light particular to tropical tidewater marshes. The islands present a different Georgia from the plateaus of the Piedmont, the north-ern mountains, or the Atlanta metropolitan region, and a differ-ent Atlantic America from the barrier islands of the Carolinas. The coarse yellow marsh grass is bleak from a distance, but close-up it flickers with migratory birds and shellfish nurseries. St. Simons is a spread-out place of low-country seafood boils, boardwalks, and summer houses where ruby-throated humming-birds feed on sweet bay magnolia. Cumberland Island, on the other hand, has no permanent population and no public transport links. Seventeen miles long and covering twenty-three thousand acres, the Cumberland wilderness is ringed by honey-colored beaches where egrets gorge on the fat-filled eggs of horseshoe crabs and wild horses with potbellies have adapted to a salty diet. Behind the beach, ranks of dunes literally roll toward the main-land. The Sea Islands are piles of sand and sediment without a rocky spine: the root system of the sea oats holds the loose sand together and stabilizes the dunes.

Toward the end of the nineteenth century, the industrialist Thomas Carnegie, brother of Andrew, came to Cumberland in search of a rural winter idyll far from the Pittsburgh smog. It was a country retreat of the Gilded Age variety: Thomas and his wife, Lucy, employed two hundred staff at their Queen Anne mansion. The couple loved the island so much that they gave each of their nine offspring $10,000 with which to build a home among the crabs and egrets. These houses, some seasonally occupied, still dot the jungly interior. Green balls of mistletoe hang in the hickory trees, swags of muscadine vine loop from the cedars, and northern gannets bomb the ocean. No wonder JFK Jr. and Carolyn Bessette got married there, in a plain chapel in the forest that still stands (if you can find it).

If St. Simons is a benign seaside resort and Cumberland a southern Garden of Eden, Jekyll Island between the two is pure fin de siècle glamour. Bored with the overcrowded north, in 1886 a band of Vanderbilts, Astors, and Pulitzers turned up on the Georgia coast to found the Jekyll Island Club, built to look like a monster lighthouse. The tycoons went skeet shooting, guzzled martinis, and competed for the biggest yachts. (J. P. Morgan's was so huge it couldn't dock.) The club remains a hotel—a little hokey, and less elite, but a glimpse of a long-gone world.

When Oglethorpe founded Georgia, he identified an alluvial plain eighteen miles inland as his capital. He called it Savannah. It was close to the border with South Carolina, on a broad and placid river of the same name. The capital has moved many times over, but Savannah remains the jumping-off point for the Sea Islands. It's hard not to love the city's courtly allure, especially early in the morning, before traffic breaks the spell, when a misty sheen darkens the bricks of the cotton exchange on Factors Row and slicks the cobbled ramps to the wharves (the cobbles came from England in sailing ships, as ballast). Behind the river, the grilled gateways and half-concealed gardens of the planters' town houses recall the Georgian England of the founding fathers. In the Owens-Thomas residence on the northeast corner of Oglethorpe Square, the Bath-born architect William Jay showed himself to be incapable of placing a feature on one side of the house without adding its mirror image on the other side. Jay even incorporated a bridge into the second floor, and the building enjoyed indoor plumbing before the White House. In the belowground slave quarters, West African Gullahs painted the ceiling haint blue to ward off evil spirits.

In *Gone with the Wind*, Margaret Mitchell calls Savannah "that gently mannered city by the sea." Since she had her bestseller, decades of economic decline and its associated problems have sharpened Savannah's edges: the modern city is more Tennessee Williams than Scarlett O'Hara. But so much the better. Despite some dire urban renewal projects in the 1950s and the dead hand of "historic preservation," Savannah still has a heartbeat. The restaurants serve sushi with grits, and the biggest art school in America, the Savannah College of Art and Design, has colonized the mottled cotton warehouses on the west side. As for *Gone with the Wind*: for a more realistic depiction of slavery in Georgia, read the English actress Fanny Kemble's brilliant *Journal of a Residence on a Georgian Plantation*, set on St. Simons Island in 1838 and 1839. Tara, it seems, was the plantation to be on.

2011

Tips About Icebergs: The Polar Regions

I mentioned earlier that my second book described a three-thousand-mile journey down Chile and that it ended at Cape Horn. That last part is not quite true. When I was in Chile, I noticed a triangular segment hanging—redundantly, it seemed—at the bottom of every map. On the television weather forecasts, in bus terminals, on badges sewn to Boy Scouts' arms—there it was, a pendulous slice of cake. This proved to be Antártida Chilena, a segment of the Antarctic continent claimed by Chile. Nobody recognizes the claim—no claimants to Antarctic territory are recognized under international law—but that wasn't going to put Chileans off the scent. They were citizens of a young country sensitive about borders and territory and, hell, Argentina was a claimant. So they made it illegal to publish a map without the cake slice, dispatched a platoon of soldiers to the Antarctic, established a post office on the ice, and made some poor woman have her baby there, all to show how desperately Chilean it was.

This was rotten news for me. It had been hard enough to get to Robinson Crusoe Island, to Isla Mocha, to the top of the Andes, to Cape Horn (I had weaseled my way onto a supply ship delivering a coffin to a cruise ship); now I had to get to Antarctica as well, if my portrait of Chile were to have credibility. I knew nothing of the polar regions. To cut a multivolume story short, after a series of meetings with a Chilean admiral that at one point looked set to continue until one of us died, I secured a seat on a military plane to King George Island and landed at the Chilean base. There I climbed a mountain with a glaciologist, and as he tap-tapped specimens into a jar, I looked out across the bergs in the bay at an ice desert bigger than Europe. There I saw my next book. It was a good moment.

A freelance life requires constant juggling, one eye always on the bank statement. I was not yet published in the United States, or in translation, so a single publisher's advance had to go a long way. I made a little money from book reviewing, and when the bills piled up, I took on larger, pseudonymous writing projects. Once a television network commissioned a novel based on two episodes of a police procedural series. I moved the clunky eighties computer and the humpbacked eighties TV and, watching frame by frame, built a novel. At the end, I had thirty thousand words. The contract required ninety thousand. During this period, Alan Ross provided encouragement. He was the revered editor of *The London Magazine*, known among aspiring litterateurs for his rejection postcards. Before taking me on, Ross had dispatched a number of these to my flat in Mornington Crescent.

One depicted the public lavatories in Westbourne Grove, apparently of interest to connoisseurs of civic architecture. Someone had sent the card to Ross, and he had recycled it by sticking a blank label over the message. On the label he had written, "Not quite." After I came back from the Antarctic, I spun off magazine features to scrape up some extra cash. Here are three pieces about living in the far south, followed by two much later pieces about my experiences in the far north. They represent a kind of work in progress, as they were staging posts on the way to the book—my third—that became *Terra Incognita*.

THE IGLOO PAPERS

It was one damned thing after another in the igloo. You struggle out of the bag to solve one problem, and a battalion of others queue up for recognition.

There was a perfectly good high-altitude tent in my kit. But I was in a remote field camp on the West Antarctic Ice Sheet, and I spent two days building the igloo, helped by the team of bearded seismic geologists with whom I was camping, the weather having temporarily buggered up their chances of setting off bombs. As part of a long-term project to map the mountain range immured within a mile of ice beneath our tents, seismologists make holes in the ice—sounds easy, doesn't it?—pack them with nitroglycerine, stand well back, and light the fuse. A series of REF TEK computers laid on the ice measure the waves that bounce back from the earth's crust hiding somewhere below. It is a long job, with whiteouts imposing extended periods of inactivity.

When camping in the Antarctic, you take so many items into the sleeping bag to prevent freezing that there is barely room to get in yourself. You always need your water bottle in with you, and in crowd the baby wipes (the polar substitute for washing), camera, batteries for the tape recorder, underwear defrosted for the next day, and any odd scientific equipment that happens to be lying around. It is like sleeping in a cutlery drawer, in a deep freeze. In the igloo, the rake of the wall resulted in a shower of fine ice crystals down the back of the pajamas whenever one raised one's head from the *semifreddo* pair of wind pants doubling up as a pillow. One's nostrils hardened in the night. The toothpaste froze.

Having said all that, when I crawled out each day and blinked up at the blue lid of sky and the ice-crystal sun dogs shimmering alongside the high sun, and when I walked up my ice steps to the fluttering Union Jack the Beards made for me and crunched onto the welcome mat carved in the snow, and when I looked out over the plateau and scanned the 360-degree horizon and I saw the curvature of the earth, as if I were in space, and the sun a white stain on the blue, at that moment each day, I thanked God out loud for bringing me to the most heartbreakingly beautiful place on earth, and I forgot about the igloo. No five-star hotel could have provided an experience that even came close.

The liquid waste facility at the seismic camp consisted of a pee flag. It was in full view: otherwise in a blizzard you would die weeing. (A poor end to your obituary.) Not all camps involve quite such communally oriented urination. Once, when I was camping on sea ice with a small group of benthic geologists, the scientists drilled a hole ten feet down to the ocean and placed a wooden drop lav over it, topped with a warm polystyrene seat. With a windbreak set up behind, this luxurious khazi offered a world-class view over a glacier. Perfection. Until one morning a member of the team came skidding across the ice with his wind pants around his ankles. "Mike!" I cried. "Whatever's the matter?" "I was sitting on the john," he gabbled, "and a seal came up through the hole." Imagine: all that hot fishy breath.

My best-ever camp was on the ice just off Ross Island. With the munificent assistance of the U.S. Antarctic Program and the companionship of Lucia deLeiris, an accomplished Rhode Island artist, I set up a camp that later appeared on that season's sea-ice maps as "The Ant Art Chicks." As it was still only September, the scientists hadn't yet arrived. Lucia and I were the only people out camping in an area larger than the United States. It was the continent's brief cusp between darkness and light, and we had twenty minutes more light each day until October 22, when the sun failed to set and we lost all our diurnal clues.

Home consisted of two huts on ski-runners that we towed out from McMurdo, the American base camp, using a tracked vehicle. We positioned the huts in the lee of Mount Erebus, an active volcano, and opposite the Transantarctic Mountains. We called the camp Sea View as, when the weather was bad, sea was all we had to look at. It might have been frozen, but it was sea. The ambient temperature hovered around minus 40, and with wind-chill it plunged to minus 175°F. The huts were heated by drip-oil diesel stoves, though by morning a drift had always crept in past the blanket we hung over the doorjamb. When we threw a mug of boiling water in the air outside, it froze before it landed. Temperature inversion created mirages that shimmered around the horizon. When a whiteout blew in, Lucia had to paint me.*

We had drilled bamboo poles into the ice outside Sea View and strung out an aerial for our high-frequency radio, and once a day, at an appointed time, we checked in with McMurdo to tell them we were still alive. In the minus 20s we found it appallingly difficult to fix the antenna wire after a blizzard blew it down. It was impossible with gloves; without gloves, one's fingers turned to frozen chipolatas in under a minute. But we had to keep our radio schedule. If we didn't, the search-and-rescue team would launch a chopper. The risk involved in deploying a helicopter in the Antarctic in September conditions—well, it was easier to countenance losing a few digits.

For recreation, we crawled around the configuration of ice

*See www.luciadeleiris.com for pictures of Sea View camp.

caves beneath the Erebus Glacier Tongue. The ice had formed arabesques like carvings in the slender windows of a mosque, and through them light fell, diffused through glimmering blue caverns. Had it been rock, it would have been a landscape painted by Leonardo, the pinnacles yielding to dreamy vistas of ice. If our landscapes were canvases, they were conceived by a mind raised above the troubles that afflict the human spirit.

In late September we saw our first seals, illuminated by a gibbous moon. Four Weddells lay on the ice between Erebus and its glacier tongue, resembling, from Sea View, mouse droppings on a dinner plate. Until then we had been living in the silence between movements of a symphony. Lying in the bag at night, I heard seals calling to one another under the ice.

When it was clear, during the day the skies were diaphanous, frosting the Transantarctics in pinks and blues, the faces of each peak as sharply defined as the cuts of a diamond. And then, suddenly, Antarctica would shut down. The winds roared across the frozen sea, battering the glacier tongue and tossing walls of snow into the air. We were trapped inside for days, the windows sheets. At night, a particularly violent blast might shake the hut and jolt us upright, our hearts beating, like a volley of artillery fire. Then it would abruptly drop into silence, as if it had been turned off. "At last!" we would murmur and settle back into the bags. But it was just building up to a fresh attack.

When the storm ended, the world seemed new, and the huts shed their cladding of ice like the ark dripping water. The snow had been blown from the foothills of Erebus, revealing polished blue ice stuck fast to the rock that protruded like an elbow below the treacherously seductive crevasse fields. A thin band of apricot and gasoline blue hung over the Transantarctics, and the pallid sun shed a watery light over thousands of miles of ice. We could have been in the silent corner of savanna where man first stood upright.

The storms seemed to have bleached our interior landscapes

too. We sat outside in the evening calm. Often we saw nacreous clouds, drifting high up in the infinite reaches of the sky.* There might be twenty-five of them, in twenty-five variations of opalescent lemons and reds and reedy greens. As Gertrude Stein said, "Paradise—if you can stand it." The dignity of the landscape infused our minds like a symphony: I heard another music in those days.

1995

THE SOUTH POLE

"Great God," Captain Scott wrote in his diary in 1912 when he reached the southern axis of the earth. "This is an awful place."

In the death throes of the twentieth century, the American government maintains a scientific base at 90 south, and in a typical summer season up to 130 people work in it. About 40 are scientists, the rest support staff: cooks, electricians, engineers, and so on. I lived with them for several weeks.

South Pole workers make the eight-hour trip in a military Hercules C-130 from Christchurch, New Zealand, to McMurdo on the fringe of the Antarctic continent. From there another C-130 conveys them 850 miles inland, up over the Transantarctic Mountains and across the polar plateau. Planes land on skis on blue ice, and to avoid frozen paralysis, the pilots keep the engines turning while the crew refuel.

The heart of the station is a sapphire-blue geodesic dome, a fifty-five-foot-tall harlequin aluminum structure shaped like the

*High-altitude, low-temperature formations. Nacreous clouds are the most dramatic manifestation of polar stratospheric clouds but are rare in the warmer Arctic. They are typically visible in September. Ozone reduction only occurs when polar stratospheric clouds are present, which partially explains why ozone depletion is significantly lower in the north.

lid of a wok. On top, a Stars and Stripes flaps among a small forest of antennas, and underneath a tunnel leads to half a dozen simple heated buildings with freezer doors. I cannot say that the station is ugly. It is too small and insignificant in that landscape to seem anything but vulnerable.

The mean annual temperature is minus 120°F. Nothing works in that kind of cold. Metal snaps. I have seen scientists in tears when the humidity barometer flutters between zero and one and all their instruments die. Yet many people at the pole work outside, bulldozing ice to make water or maintaining equipment.

The U.S. Antarctic Program lent me state-of-the-art gear. You know you're in a man's world when the long johns have willy slits. During my stay at the pole, 29 out of the 120 residents were women. Not until 1969 did Americans send their first women south—though that was years ahead of the British Antarctic Survey, and even then it incited the newspaper headline POWDER PUFF EXPLORERS INVADE THE SOUTH POLE. Liaisons inevitably develop, especially as relationships at home crumple under the strain of separation. On-station anxiety was concealed behind a mask of humorous resignation and encapsulated in the apocryphal e-mail message from home the blokes had pinned on the wall of the computer room: "Yours is bigger, but his is here."

The Amundsen-Scott South Pole Station doctor presides over a field medical facility. When I arrived, like many I suffered mild altitude sickness: the pole is at ninety-three hundred feet, which means you're standing on a layer of ice almost one-third of the height of Mount Everest. The combination of altitude and an exceptionally shallow atmosphere means that the human body receives about half its normal oxygen supply. The doctor put me on oxygen for two hours. I remember being marooned in a consulting room hung with posters of Neil Armstrong wobbling about on the moon. I asked the doctor if she'd be able to repeat the feat of the Soviet Antarctic doctor who, in 1961, removed his own appendix. "I've trained the others to do mine," she said. You have to use your initiative. Forty years ago a Swedish doctor took out a man's eye. He had never even seen an eye operation, but he was coached over the wireless by an ophthalmic surgeon in Sweden.

To minimize the risk of another ghoulish drama, everyone who goes south must undergo rigorous medicals. Before I went to the Antarctic, I created British fiscal history by claiming a syphilis test against tax.

My stay coincided with Christmas. A long-established tradition at the pole involved "A Race Around the World," a mile lap around the spot marking 90 south. We all did it, and we all got out of breath. Afterward we ate turkey in the galley.

The winter population shrinks to twenty-five. During eight months of darkness, temperatures plunge to the minus 100s. Until four years ago, when budget cuts prevailed, the U.S. Antarctic Program carried out a midwinter resupply airdrop. A C-141 plane flew over from Christchurch, refueled twice in midair, and tossed out boxes the size of upright pianos to twenty-odd people waiting in darkness on the polar plateau. One year they pushed out twelve hundred individually bubble-wrapped eggs, and only two broke.

Isolation and continual darkness hammer the psyche. American shrinks identified a "winter-over syndrome" in the Antarctic in which 72 percent of the sample reported severe depression and 65 percent had problems with hostility and anger. During one Antarctic winter, a Russian at Vostok Station killed a colleague with an ice ax during a row about a game of chess. To ensure it didn't happen again, the authorities banned chess.

It can be awful. But when the sun reappears and spring unfurls over the gleaming plateau, Antarctica isn't an awful place at all. Out on the ice the silence is so dense that you can hear the blood pumping around your head, and you look around and realize that this is the only place on the planet that nobody owns. "The stark polar lands," wrote Shackleton, "grip the hearts of the men

who have lived on them in a manner that can hardly be understood by the people who have never got outside the pale of
civilisation."

1999

POSTSCRIPT

The dome was sinking fast and has been decommissioned since I wrote this
piece. The sixty-five-thousand-square-foot modular station that replaced it sits
on thirty-six special hydraulic jack columns that raise the structure in ten-inch
increments as snow and ice accumulate. To build it, the National Science
Foundation flew in forty thousand tons of construction materials. New facilities include the IceCube telescope, a revolutionary search tool for the hypoth-
esized dark matter that might clarify the currently anomalous accounts of the
origins of the universe. IceCube is on the lookout for neutrinos, the subatomic
particles created by deep-space events such as exploding stars, gamma ray
bursts, and cataclysmic phenomena involving black holes and neutron stars.
I wish I could go back.

FROZEN TEN YEARS

*February 10, 1996. Mackay Glacier, Antarctica. Whiteout con-
ditions.*

Spent most of the day supine in the tent, and was really looking forward to dinner. Anxieties about fuel running out resulted
in me undercooking the pasta, then I had to spend ten minutes
breaking up frozen lumps of Parmesan with a geology hammer.
The label on the Parmesan tub says, "Matured ten months," and
someone has written underneath, in red Biro, "FROZEN TEN
YEARS." All five of us had a carrot for dessert—one each. A week
ago, when the resupply helicopter came, we got a small sack of
fresh food from New Zealand. I kept five carrots back, for a treat.

Food assumes a role of abnormal importance in this abbrevi-
ated environment. A naval commander who wintered over in

Antarctica in the 1970s reported a group obsession with food and said his men cared desperately if meals weren't up to scratch as food had become a substitute for sex.

The first explorers fixated on culinary ingenuity. One man assured himself of lifelong popularity by producing minty peas, revealing later that he had squirted toothpaste into the pot. During the hard times out sledging, when meals were doled out, men played the game Shut-Eye, or Whose Portion Is This? Someone named the recipient of each plate with his eyes closed so the cook couldn't be accused of favoritism. It wasn't a game, of course: it was a peacekeeping mechanism. When rations dwindled, everyone had food dreams, and the man who actually got to eat in his dream, rather than waking up just as a steaming plate of Irish stew was placed in front of him, was threatened with short rations by his colleagues. They were hungry all the time in those days, and in the long hours holed up in the tent, a man would speak bitterly about the second helping of treacle sponge he had turned down years before.

Eight thirty, and no meals until tomorrow. Maybe I'll have a dried fig. Find myself obsessing about the fig scene in *Sons and Lovers*. Food is a poor substitute for sex on a number of fronts, one of them being that all the food down here is frozen. Someone living on base brought a plastic bag of ice cream out to our camp two weeks ago. We had to warm it up on the Primus stove before we could eat it. You couldn't act out a Häagen-Dazs ad in Antarctica. By the time you'd achieved anything like smearable consistency, everyone would have frozen to death. As for that scene in *9½ Weeks* in which Kim Basinger and Mickey Rourke do rude things to each other with ice cubes—I find ice ceases to be sexy when you're sitting on fifteen thousand feet of it and there's a foot more lurking in your sleeping bag.

1996

None of these pieces mention the Cro-Magnon Walkman I carried throughout my Antarctic career. I massaged its batteries as lovingly as a baby so I could take refuge in Beethoven's late strings when storm clouds gathered literally, metaphorically, or, as sometimes happened, both at once. I do think music teaches us the thing we most want to know: that we are not alone. On the other hand— I reserve the right to be inconsistent—surely the only truth is that we are, in the end, alone. An Inuit at an ice hole means all that humanity means, so long as he is solitary. Add more figures and the picture becomes less human, not more so. Belonging is an illusion. Chesterton said something similar. Though not involving Inuit.

But here come some Inuit now.

When I wrote about the Antarctic in *Terra Incognita*, my life was ahead of me. I was closer to thirty than to forty. When, many years later, I tackled the Arctic in *The Magnetic North*— and this is not intended to be negative—my life as I perceived it was behind me: I mean that the die was cast, that the big decisions had been irrevocably taken, for better or worse. I was never going to be anything but a writer; I was never going to have a strong backhand or translate Rabelais or ice a Christmas cake. I say this without regret (well, with a touch of regret; who could say that she does not miss her younger self?), but perhaps it explains the distant melody of a requiem in that book, and in these two pieces too, works in progress that appeared in *Vanity Fair* and *Condé Nast Traveller*.

NO, NO, NANOOK

It was one of those Arctic nights when ocean and sky compete to achieve the most vulgar blue. Fog shimmied off the pack ice, and close to the ship platelets turned slowly in the current. The light had a washed, renascent cleanliness. I last observed the particular qualities of polar light in the Antarctic long ago. That had been a love affair of youth, one that lived on in the imagination, unresolved and unrequited. The Antarctic, after all, is an ineffable superlative: not just the only unowned continent, but the only one never to be inhabited or divided. The Arctic is the opposite. Owned, peopled, fragmented, and clogged with the prosaic troubles of the north rather than heady southern romance. And who, I had asked myself, could want that?

But the years went by, and youthful optimism had yielded to the restless melancholy of middle age. I started thinking about the Arctic. In my mind's eye, I glimpsed elegiac qualities that suited the uncertainties and doubts that are the chaperones of age. At the same time, the Arctic infiltrated the zeitgeist. One could barely open a newspaper without uncovering a fresh squabble over who owned what, or apocalyptic data foreshadowing global inundation. I stewed over it, not wanting to contaminate my Antarctic memories. In the end I went and found a new polar light. This is the story of my journey.

The Antarctic is a continent surrounded by oceans, the Arctic an ocean surrounded by continents. Which meant I needed a ship. And as more than half the Arctic Basin is frozen in summer, it had to be a ship that chews ice. In the days of a command economy, the Soviets had their reasons for commissioning the best icebreakers, and in the struggling market economy that followed the disintegration of the U.S.S.R., a modest travel trade took up the baton. I settled on the *Kapitan Khlebnikov*, a fifteen-thousand-tonne warhorse with a blunt bow, six diesel-electric engines tanking out 24,200 horsepower, and fifty-four cabins stacked in a coffee-colored castle. A plucky American tour operator had leased the *Khlebnikov* and its Russian crew from a Vladivostok shipping company, bringing in an English-speaking team to handle passenger logistics.

Following an east-to-west curve that started at Murmansk, our 3,256-nautical-mile, sixteen-day route took in the remote Russian archipelago Franz Josef Land; the Norwegian-owned Svalbard island group; and the practically unpopulated east coast of Greenland, before dropping anchor in Iceland's Reykjavík.

Foul weather and unexpected sea ice constitute the chief hazards of Arctic travel, but in our case another menace queued up for attention: Russian bureaucracy. Having boarded our ship along with ninety-odd other passengers, I waited thirty hours in Murmansk for "customs clearance," the international maritime term for a wad of large ones. All we could do was cool our heels, marooned among ziggurats of coal and the low elephant grief of other ships' horns.

Once out, finally, of Murmansk and the Kola Bay Fjord, the *KK* battled north through the heaving cyclone zone of the Barents Sea. Like everyone else, I clung to the stair rails as we plunged in and out of the rollers, reflecting miserably that this was not quite the same as trekking over a flat and stable Antarctic ice sheet. But on the third morning out we woke alongside the glittering rock faces of Franz Josef Land. The sky was streaky, like bacon, and the channel between ship and land was calm. Crouched along the north rim of the Barents Sea, the two hundred uninhabited islands of Franz Josef are among the most extraordinary geological formations on the planet, their sequence of high crystalline basalt cliffs and rearing sedimentary tableland spliced by narrow, deep channels. Heavily ice covered, the archipelago wasn't even discovered till 1873.

Once the crew had lowered Zodiac inflatables, we were able to begin our explorations on Jackson Island. The air was a balmy

43°F. (In fact, the mercury never once dipped below zero.) Despite a latitude of 81 degrees, on the beach terraces purple saxifrage and lemon snow buttercups flourished alongside cushiony moss campion and white poppies—the Arctic at full tilt. At that latitude in the Southern Hemisphere, not a single flower grows, even in the short burst of Antarctic summer, but the Eurasian Arctic benefits from the warm waters of the North Atlantic Drift, the last gasp of the Gulf Stream. We motored across a channel, toward fast ice extending off a headland. There we made the first of our eight polar bear sightings. A mother and first-year cub were prowling the ice edge, poking their noses into a soupy layer of grease ice. Sunshine in moteless shafts highlighted the newly molted sheen of their hollow guard hairs. A mile off, a heap of female Atlantic walruses had hauled out on the pack, thirteen hundred pounds apiece with skins of cinnamon suede. When one twitched, a tremor eddied through the mound.

Bears and flowers: the Arctic was more engaged with life than the Antarctic, and where there is more life, there is more death. Approaching fifty, one thinks as much about death as about romance (it was that fifty-fifty kind of age). Decay and imperfection were part of the natural cycle up here. At the end of our first landing I stood on deck squinting into the midnight sun as frost flowers formed on refrozen leads in the pack. What, I asked myself, had I ever seen in the Antarctic?

At Cape Norway, a shingle beach on the western extremity of Jackson Island, I paid homage at one of the most sacred sites of Arctic history. In the giddy era when the North Pole was still the geographical grail, Fridtjof Nansen, the polar explorer's polar explorer, had an idea about how to reach it. If Arctic ice drifted in the direction of the pole, why not allow a ship to freeze in and drift with it? When he tried, the ship refused to come unstuck. After two years imprisoned in ice, in August 1895 Nansen and his shipmate Hjalmar Johansen set out for help on skis and in kayaks. They traveled over the ice for six hundred miles, and when they reached Cape Norway, they built a subterranean refuge. To celebrate, Johansen changed his underwear for the first time in four months. The pair lived off bear and walrus and spent the winter huddled in the same sleeping bag. When the thaw came in May, they paddled for a hundred miles on the wildest of outside chances that they might reach Spitsbergen. Walrus destroyed the kayaks, and food was running out. On June 17, Nansen heard dogs barking. Three hours later he skied around a hummock on Cape Flora in the southwest of Franz Josef Land and saw a man in a tweed jacket. It was the English explorer Frederick Jackson, who happened to be on the spot, having set off from England in 1894 leading an expedition sponsored by the press baron Lord Harmsworth (Nansen later named the island after Jackson). The two men shook hands.

"Aren't you Nansen?" asked Jackson, scrutinizing the shaggy face of the world's greatest living explorer.

"Yes, I am," came the reply.

"By Jove," spluttered the Englishman. "I'm damned glad to see you." The whole world thought Nansen had perished. The two Norwegians went home on Jackson's ship and reached Norway at the same time as their own vessel, which in the end had unfrozen of its own accord. The refuge at Cape Norway remains, a troglodytic memorial to what men can endure. "Polar exploration," wrote one of the pioneers, "is at once the cleanest and most isolated way of having a bad time which has been devised."

Not on the *KK*. We had an exceedingly good time. When we weren't galumphing over the tundra or cruising the pack, I looked out for wildlife, either from the flying bridge or from Steel Beach on deck 7 (it was next to the engine vents). There were always birds in the sky. Every day we saw northern fulmars, black-legged kittiwakes, and Brünnich's guillemots, and most days red-throated divers, creatures so highly adapted to ice that they can barely walk on land. There were occasional sightings of Lapland longspurs and snowy owls, and on the most westerly outpost of Russian territory, the sucrose-white Victoria Island, we actually saw ivory gulls nesting on a shingle spit. And I heard birds sing! There are no songbirds in the Antarctic. The environment is too harsh. Song suggested a place where people belong.

The ship's Mi-2 helicopters, double-engine Russian beasts built for the polar regions, offered the best view of the *KK* actually breaking ice. As the two-inch steel ice skirt smashed into the pack, it either pushed the sheets up until towers of shattered portions tottered sideways or jammed them under the hull, where they met an ice knife that pulverized them into white rubble. The waves formed by the breaking process were, as Sylvia Plath wrote about waves somewhere else, "mouthing icecakes." As old ice is thicker than young, its dispersal requires increased horsepower. Snug in my cabin at night, I learned to calibrate the blows. But we enjoyed a smooth journey west to Svalbard. A brisk five hundred miles from the tip of Norway proper, the Svalbard islands, of which the largest is Spitsbergen, cover 24,300 square miles (approximately the size of Ireland or West Virginia). There has never been an indigenous population, but there was a human dimension. Svalbard was once the center of the whaling industry, and on Amsterdam Island we walked among the graves of Dutch whalers and the remnants of their labors in seventeenth-century Smeerenburg, or Blubbertown. The strand was overlaid with Siberian driftwood, swept from the great rivers as they froze and spun around in the circular currents of the Arctic Ocean before being blown onto the beaches of these islands. In the sky, big wind-sock-shaped clouds hung below a layer of cirrostratus. At the tryworks, hardened residue traced the outlines of the copper cauldrons in which men rendered blubber as soon as the whale was flensed. A medium-sized bowhead yielded twenty to thirty tons of oil, as well as hundreds of the horny keratin strings called baleen that hung in their mouths to filter food (they made ideal corset stays). By the end of the seventeenth century all the coastal whales were dead, along with many of the whalers, and from then on flensing and rendering took place on floating factory ships in the open sea.

The whalers were the first of many to threaten the fragility of the Arctic environment. I had taken my place on the list now. My journey raised the old question of personal responsibility in a fresh and awkwardly acute form: there was a terrible irony in our absorption in the wonders of the natural world, having burned up hydrocarbons by the ton to reach them. In the Antarctic, I had imagined, as young people do, that the beauty surrounding me would last forever. On this trip, feverish talk of climate change attenuated the anxieties of age. Would all this be here for my children's children?

When it comes to climate change, the Arctic has been vested with the canary's role in the coal mine. However scientists interpret data, the most significant climatic warming has unarguably taken place north of the Arctic Circle. Sure, the Antarctic is melting. But the Arctic is melting faster. When we sailed into Svalbard's Kongsfjord, I marveled at the dazzling immensity of the glaciers. Yet climate scientists harvesting data for forty years have found that all are in retreat: the Midtre Lovénbreen has lost 40.4 feet in average thickness since 1977. Old glaciers shrink as part of a natural cycle, and anyway the Midtre Lovénbreen still extends farther than it did fifteen hundred years ago. But these glaciers are melting faster than ever before—much faster. Even factoring in Svalbard's surge glaciers (those that still lurch forward), climatologists have measured a negative trend in mass balance overall, this latter being the crucial annual difference between accumulation at the center of the ice sheet and melt at the edges. In addition, the Arctic Ocean is likely to influence climate change through alterations in temperature and salinity induced by a higher influx of glacial melt into the circulation of its cold, south-moving currents and by the loss of reflective properties as its ice lid melts. (The cold water is exchanged for warm water surging north in a process called the meridional overturning circulation, a crucial factor in the engine of winds and ocean currents that generate weather.) The distinction between natural methods of readjusting the earth's energy balance in these ways and anthropogenic interference in the same processes—this might be the greatest scientific conundrum of our time. The answers lie under Arctic ice. Can they be found? Nobody knows. But only a fool would say we shouldn't be looking.

On open-sea stretches like the 370-nautical-mile Svalbard-to-Greenland leg, the ship's remorseless three-meals-plus-a-day regime threatened calorie-induced paralysis. But in a gym in the bowels of the ship, I joined iron-thighed Russian sailors as they thrust and flexed to blaring Siberian rap, the crash of waves on the bow directly above adding tympanic rhythm to the pounding from the boom box. The session concluded with a birch-twig thrashing in the sauna. A girl can have a worse time at sea.

As we crossed, on our way to Greenland, from the Eastern to the Western Hemisphere (00 degrees of longitude), the *KK* met unforeseen, unbreakable ice. Captain Pavel Ankudinov has cut thousands of miles of ice at both ends of the earth. "In the satellite images we receive," he explained as he and I peered out the bridge window at the solid white ocean ahead, "fog obscures the ice cover, so to a large extent we sail blind. The Antarctic is easier than the Arctic, as the ice down there is softer. It has snow on top, so cuts more easily. Up here I sometimes see pressure ridges forming and rising before my eyes." Puffing his Troika cigarettes, Ankudinov manfully maintained the ship's Russian flavor despite its international clientele. Like all Vladivostok natives, he was a fast talker, even in staccato English. Managing to smoke, talk, and inspect ice all at the same time, he told me he had joined the *KK* straight out of his naval academy in 1985 and worked his way up, learning on the job the chaotic complexities of sea ice. Years ago he discovered that the key to polar travel is flexibility, and the day we reached the unbreakable ice, he changed our course, heading back out to sea and skirting the frozen barrier in order to hit Greenland farther south than planned.

Four times the size of France, Greenland has more ice than anywhere except the Antarctic: its abiotic ice blanket, in places ninety-eight hundred feet thick, covers 80 percent of the interior, with the result that the fifty-seven thousand Greenlanders huddle on the coastal fringes. From the air, ice prairies bent in every direction. As I looked down from the chopper, the land ice, hatched with crevasses, resembled cellulite. (I used this analogy in *Terra Incognita*. In red pen in the margin, my editor Tony Colwell—a myopic, bow-tie-wearing relic of the old school who taught me all I know—wrote, "Cannot find *cellulite* in the *OED*.")

In the Northeast Greenland National Park, the least accessible park on the planet and at 375,000 square miles also the biggest, deep channels scoured of ice by katabatic winds enabled the *KK* to make landings around the intricate fjord systems of King Christian X Land. Beyond the bosomy hills of the coastal tundra—here were yellows and grays, after so much white and blue—we hiked below a waterfall unwoven by a polar wind and watched musk oxen truffling for sedge, relics of the ice ages blinded by curtains of black hair. It was a landscape of ancient resonance. Paleo-Eskimo, immigrants from North America, followed the musk oxen migration routes down the Greenlandic coasts. One only had to look over the berry-bearing hills with their shards of bone and feather to glimpse a heaped-up human past.

We made a final landing at Ittoqqortoormiit in Scoresby Sound, the most isolated settlement in Greenland. The municipality is the size of Great Britain, its population 562. Brightly painted houses sprouted satellite dishes, and sledge dogs yanked at their traces, the snow crust friable beneath our boots. In one of the many ironies of a warming climate, the loss of ice that has deprived Greenlanders of their hunting grounds may yet usher in foreign investment, and jobs, as newly exposed rock yields up its minerals. A trial dig by Hudson Resources of Vancouver recently unearthed a 2.4-carat diamond at Garnet Lake in the west of the island, prompting the arrival of diamond hunters from all over the world. Prospectors have found gold, zinc, and lead, and oil multinationals are negotiating licenses to explore tracts of open water around the coast. And so it goes on. Like many indigenous peoples around the circumpolar north, in two generations Greenlanders have made the leap from subsistence hunting to a developed, technology-dependent society. In Ittoqqortoormiit, I saw seal ribs pegged out to dry alongside a child's nylon Batman suit. People really do belong here. Whalers, hunters, black-haired boys—they invest the ice with meaning.

Both polar regions appeal to something visceral in the spirit, especially in an era when we seem to have lost contact with the natural world. But I was pleased to end on a human note. The Antarctic, when it comes down to it, is a metaphor for the terra incognita beyond the earthly realm: an image of an alternate and better world. The Arctic, on the other hand, deals in realism rather than romance. It is intimately connected to us—to our future, our crises, and our dreams. It is an image of the beautiful world we are destroying.

2008

Solovki: Russia in Miniature

I have a bad case," said the pilgrim conspiratorially, "of *govo-rukha*." I said it sounded painful. In fact, *govorukha* describes a mix of garrulousness and taciturnity, an endemic condition in the Russian far north characterized by bursts of direct speech alternating with the silent reserve bred into those who live in geographical isolation. But once victims start to talk, they can't stop. Even the salty waves of the White Sea, hurled over our small boat by a polar wind, failed to dam the conversational flood.

Hard by the Finnish border, the White Sea, or Beloye More, forms the most southerly gulf of the Barents Sea and Arctic Ocean, a three-pronged embayment sheltered by the motherly arm of the Kola Peninsula. Between the Karelian coast and what Russians call the summer coast, the islands and islets of the Solovki archipelago lie half a degree south of the Arctic Circle, and according to generations of true believers they cradle the national soul. (Look at a 500-ruble note. It has an engraving of Solovki on the reverse.) The medieval monastery on the main island represents the endurance of hope and faith and the survival of the human spirit against what once looked like unwinnable odds. But the price had been so high. In 1923, Red Guards threw the monks out after four centuries, tore down the icons, and set up a prison, shipping in foes by the ten thousand. As Solzhenitsyn wrote, from the one cancer cell in that White Sea outpost a tumor spread all over Russia.

To reach the White Sea, I had boarded a Number 22 sleeper train at Petersburg's Ladoga station for a sixteen-hour rock through the birch forest, though sixteen hours is a hop, in Russian railway terms. The rivers were wide and the landscape flat; God, it was flat. At Petrozavodsk the Number 22 stopped for half an hour, and women in knit berets hawked smoked fish on the platform, plucking each one, stiff like a board, from a rope necklace. One seller had an eel in a basket. It was that heady period of White Nights, when the sun never sets, and at midnight apricot rays flashed off miles of porcelain telegraph insulators.

Overnight, the birches grew shorter and the air colder. Cars also shrank as the train raced north: rust-bucket Ladas instead of the BMWs of metropolitan mobsters. A sway at the curve before Begeza; gabled snowmobile lockups on the shore of Lake Vyg; and at last the White Sea port of Kem, halfway between the

Kandalaksha Gulf and Onega Bay. The landscape had just hung on through winter and was browned out and exhausted. There were no ruined factories here and no toppled statues of Lenin sneering skyward in Ozymandian reproach. Just the noble rot of the backwoods and a woman in a housecoat milking a goat. As I rode a bus from the railway station to the coast, it was difficult not to notice that, like the birch trees and the cars, the people were smaller. These were a short, stubby lot, compared with their stringy Petersburg compatriots. But the paved road was a good one, and the bus pressed on, through miles of more snowmobile lockups and depleted fences that swayed in the wind. Presently the road collapsed at a jetty. When the bus emptied, the wind dropped suddenly, as if it had been switched off. Four or five fishing boats lay still on the water like sledges on snow. On the churned-up mud of the empty shore, two German shepherds nosed around a motionless Caterpillar truck, its bucket frozen in mid-maneuver. And there was my boat: an old trawler.

At the jetty, ninety Karelian pilgrims had already squeezed into the modest cabin. As soon as the captain weighed anchor, a priest and his assistant began intoning a service, each brandishing a large crucifix. The other women whipped head scarves out of their string bags (everyone had a string bag). I like to think of myself as a well-prepared, culturally sensitive traveler, but I had not anticipated an act of worship on a ferry. A polar balaclava wasn't quite the ticket when it came to the Orthodox head-covering rule. But it was all I had. So I put it on. Outside the porthole, the water sparkled in the morning sunshine. As the mainland shrank to a thin line, the rhythmic rise and fall of the ritual words, mirroring the swell of the sea, invoked the longing for God that played such a living role in old Russia, a country still recognizable up on the fringes of the federation. The pilgrims intoned, a framed photograph of a saint was passed around to be kissed, and mobile phones trilled again, like the dawn chorus after the stillness of night.

After two hours, perhaps longer, a dark sequence of turrets and domes rose from the distant waves, a tightly self-contained silhouette pulling the currents into its own magnetic field. It seemed wondrous: it must have seemed a miracle to a medieval pilgrim. My own pilgrims reached into their string bags for bulky Horizon cameras and streamed on deck to start snapping.

Although a microclimate sustains cherry trees and cabbages, as well as six hundred lakes and swamps, Solovki winters are still nasty, brutish, and long. On Big Solovki, where we disembarked, a thousand civilians inured to hardship live alongside the holy fathers, servicing the pilgrim trade, harvesting salt, and struggling to maintain a power supply. Beyond the coastal sorrel and Siberian cedars, violet mists curled through the larches, the scent of hagberries cut the air, and lakes shone through vertical slits between the forest trunks. The ubiquitous dun-colored mud of the north spread inland in what Dostoevsky called "a sort of pea jelly."

A pair of monks first moved to uninhabited Solovki in 1429 to settle as hermits, their models the desert ascetics of Christianity's first centuries. The White Sea islands offered exceptional anchorage, plentiful freshwater, berries, and limitless fishing. But the monks could only cross from the mainland between June and August, and then it took two days of rowing. Despite the hardships, others followed, and in time the settlers founded a monastery. What Mount Athos and the Plateau of Tibet offered in height, Solovki had in latitude. The sixty-five monks currently in residence maintain the isolation of their predecessors. A religiously minded friend in Moscow told me that when Putin visited in 2001 as president of the federation, the abbot had to gather his flock in advance and explain who Putin was. This strained the limits of the credible. But it was an attractive notion of unworldliness. Putin had gone to Solovki to mark the tenth anniversary of the collapse of the Soviet Union. He used the visit to laud the achievements of the state and the contribution of Orthodox Christianity, "without which Russia could hardly exist." Then he said that all peoples were equal before God and that Russia had always guaranteed that equality. Now Solovki really had heard it all.

A translator-archivist had agreed to accompany me on a tour. But first, a liturgy. At five hours' duration, standing up to boot, a service at St. Filip's was not for the fainthearted. Monkish chanting floated around the cupolas like wind in the sallows, and I shifted from foot to foot.

"From his time," Anna said, gesturing at an icon of Ivan the Terrible as we at last left the church, "Solovki was the focal point of economic, religious, and cultural life along the White Sea coast. Hundreds of craftsmen worked in sheepskin, copper, and timber. But the salt trade was the most lucrative." Without its salt production, Solovki would have remained a minor monastery with little influence on Russian history. Even the name Solovki derives from the Russian word for salt. Annual production peaked at twenty-two hundred tons, all of it extracted from highly salinated brine deep in the earth, a natural occurrence around the White Sea, which is itself exceptionally salty.

After the revolution, Bolshevik supporters locked the churches, packed off the monks, and crated up the monastic icons and jewels. The islands had been a convenient dumping ground for undesirables for centuries: Peter the Great had dispatched his enemies to prison cells within the monastic walls. But now the leaders of the newly minted Soviet Union chose the archipelago as the prototype for its first gulag, hanging Lenin's portrait in place of Christ's on the cathedral altar. In time, doomed collectivization policies expanded the gulag system. By 1930, the prison population at Solovki had swollen to an obscene twenty-eight thousand, and 44 percent of them had typhus.

The tortures enacted there have entered the mythology of the northlands. But clandestine religious life persisted. In the 1920s a priest-prisoner known as Father Nikodim kept a small cup on a string around his neck with which to celebrate the Eucharist. A prisoner who gave birth in the camp remembered: "We walked together into the forest, to where there was a small wooden chapel, some benches, and a spring. There the priest, who had a cross and was wearing a cassock, baptized my son."

The salted herring Anna and I had eaten at lunch in the steamy café seemed miraculous in its ordinariness. When we had finished, she had asked if I would care to accompany her to collect a box of archive material from Sekirka, a hill church about seven miles away on the east of the island. We were to travel in the old museum Land Rover, virtually an exhibit itself. The mud road was exceptionally bumpy, and we hit our heads numerous times on the (fortunately canvas) roof of the vehicle. Loons were feeding on the lakes in the softwood forest. We could see the Sekirka belfry above the treetops long before we arrived at the foot of the hill. The church there is the only one in the world with a lighthouse on top. Three monks lived in the cloisters. One of them came out to greet Anna when we walked up. I asked him if the lighthouse still functioned. "Oh yes!" translated Anna. "It's used ten months a year—August to May." The forest there was fragrant with bilberries, and winds had bent the ashes and birches into shapes Anna called "dancing trees." As we went into the church, she said, "Solovki used to be the most revered name in all Russia. Then it became the most feared. But when you actually got to the island, there was a name that was more feared. It was Sekirka. Nobody came back from this place." A spy hole had been clumsily drilled in the door so guards could observe their prisoners. It would have been an obscene image anywhere, but it was in a church. After a guard spotted him celebrating the Eucharist, Father Nikodim arrived at Sekirka. He slept at the bottom of three layers of other men, piled in the church like firewood, and it was there that he died of asphyxiation. At the same time, naked men were made to sit on a pole for hours high in the unheated nave. When they fell, they were beaten. Prisoners went to desperate lengths to avoid this torture. One inmate wrote, "I saw how people deliberately burned their mouths or sex organs to simulate syphilis . . . people swallowed pieces of glass or nails to get into the hospital . . . the number of deaths was enormous here." On a small patch of a corner wall, faces on a fresco had been scratched out. "One generation destroys what the previous ones have created," I said as we walked out into the sunlight of a vegetable garden. "But they didn't destroy it," said Anna fiercely. "The spirit lives."

Outside the church, the early monks built 365 steps as part of their *podvig*, or "ongoing spiritual struggle." But the steps were made for going up. During the gulag, guards tied prisoners to logs and rolled them down, their bodies bouncing on the frosted wooden treads. Anna and I descended in silence and continued along a narrow path cut through the birch forest. "In the mosquito season," she said, "they tied men tightly to trees, naked, and left them there all day." The mosquitoes, according to Anna, who had seen photographs of these events, were "like a moving carpet." The crunch of my boots on iced mud released the resinous scent of bog rosemary. But I knew I was walking on bones.

Countrywide, 1937 was the worst year. It was the start of the Great Terror. "That was a time," wrote Anna Akhmatova in an unforgettable poem, "when only the dead/Could smile, delivered from their struggles." In Solovki some *zeki* escaped into the forest and took their chances. According to one source, "The killing and eating of human beings was not considered something extraordinary above the 65th parallel, as it was a matter of survival and was considered a more or less original way to procure food." Many of the other prisoners were deliberately worked to death or murdered; at Solovki, in August, the administration announced a death quota: twelve hundred prisoners had to be executed. A witness recalled: "Unexpectedly they forced everyone from the open cells to a general count. At the count they read out an enormous list of names to be taken on transport. They were given two hours to prepare . . . a terrible confusion ensued . . . columns of prisoners marched out with suitcases and knapsacks." They died near the village of Sandormokh, and the killers threw their bodies into a pit. "I should like to call you all by name," Akhmatova ends the poem, "but they have lost the lists."

At least two millennia before the first monks cast anchor, about the time Celtic people brought ironworks to Britain and an elite emerged among the trading peoples of the lower Mississippi delta, the bountiful catch and safe harbors of the White Sea islands attracted nomadic fishermen and hunter-gatherers. Besides tools and burial mounds, they left a mysterious sequence of labyrinths, most of them on Bolshoi Zayatski, a turbulent forty-minute boat journey from Big Solovki. Anna had arranged for us to join a tour on a small motorboat. Six Russians pressed indecorously into the cabin while she and I leaned against the bow rail and shouted over the dyspeptic growl of the engine. Cheerful and lively, and formerly a military lawyer, Anna was born in Petrozavodsk and had been brought up speaking Karelian at home. (In the 1937–1938 campaign against non-Russians, Karelia was among the nations that virtually ceased to exist.) "What made you decide to come here?" I shouted. "God decided!" she yelled back with a warm smile.

A tint of sage and cadmium overlay the scene, as if the landscape had been washed. Boulders, juniper bushes, lichen—even the cranberries blushed green and yellow. Entirely different from its forested neighbor, the island was all tundra, the horizon a swath of merged land and sea; the landscape was apocalyptic in its broad scope. Wanderers in the far north often write of being on the edge of the world, and of life. I could have laid out a cosmic labyrinth myself.

Across the open land, the aspen boards of a church had silvered in the fine rain, and brown juices from the swampy earth seeped up the lower rows. Inside, stacked timber rose above my head. It was exceptionally cold that day, and the loons on the lakes had taken refuge in the sedge. A bank of cloud obscured the sun, but toward the end of the afternoon a thin line of orange light appeared along the lower edge of the cloud, like the line that glows after the flame on burning paper. The Bronze Age spirals we had come to see spread over the plain. Their fat mossy whorls— essentially rings of concentric circles—ranged from three feet in diameter to about eighty feet; the moss and lichen that formed the rings had grown over carefully positioned stones, and rough pyramids of bare stones lay in random piles. Did the first fisher- men lay out the stones as a way of reaching toward some un- obtainable transcendental truth? Or did the stones mark the edges of a Bronze Age rubbish dump? Experts agree only that early nomadic hunter-fishers laid circular patterns to fulfill the re- quirements of customs, rituals, or beliefs. Either way, the mossy whorls revealed the human spirit at work, stretching back across oceans of time. They were manifestations of the human need to make order. Anna picked out a route back to the tiny wharf. Before reboarding our boat, we both looked back over the tundra. Vaporous drafts of air blew in from the east and hung over the labyrinths. Anna had finished her history lesson and stood in silence. The meaning of the patterns lay in a country beyond words. Like poetry, or music, or the aspen wood cross of a Chris- tian ascetic, the sturdy stone rings ratified the transcendental impulse, that dark grope toward truth that lies at the heart of being human.

On my last day I walked from lake to lake, following whortle- berry outcrops and the flight paths of the loons. Close to a dammed reservoir marked on my rudimentary map as St. Filip's Pool, knotweed was making progress over a grid of concrete struts, remnants of an abandoned plan to throw a ring road around the forest. When the economy collapsed, the infrastructure went with it, and Solovki was not immune to the problems experienced across the disintegrating Soviet Union. Public money simply stopped, like the water behind the dam; the hospital was heated just enough to stop the drips freezing, and as in the end it was the only building that was heated at all, the administration moved onto the wards. The Polish journalist Mariusz Wilk went to live in Solovki at that time. He wrote that when he arrived in 1990, you could buy sixty loaves of bread for the price of a bottle of vodka. When he left in 1996, it had gone down to three loaves per bottle.

As the afternoon ended, I hurried to the public sauna for a final roasting. I had been attending women's sessions at the *banya* behind the monastery, a decrepit brick building with an exterior colonized by milky fungus. After a brisk bout of sweating to the locomotive hiss of liquid on hot stone and excruciating plunges in a trough of iced water, I swaddled up and took my place among the women in the rest room. At first, nobody spoke. By the end of the week, they wouldn't stop talking. When I could edge in a word, I reflected that with its Bronze Age relics, monastic sanctity, and gulag ghosts, Solovki opened a window onto the sweep of Russian history. "Yes," said my neighbor, heat radiating from her crepey skin. "On Solovki you see Russia in miniature, like the tiniest *matryoshka* doll." The island even reflected the shrinking awareness in Russia of the need to condemn the crimes of the gulag ("Say what you like about Stalin, he revived the economy . . ."). Above the quiet chants in the churches and the muttered prayers in the hermitages there was no tone of sober repentance—the "Never again" of Dachau or Auschwitz. But the spirit lived in the quiet chants and the muttered prayers; they plucked new life out of death, as they always had. It was easier to believe in when you weren't tied to a tree, but it was a kind of humanity that eluded articulation.

2007

POSTSCRIPT

Among Arctic peoples I confronted human misery and degradation at close range and over a sustained period. This was not, for the Inuit, a psychic landscape: it was real. Besides all the other issues, the experience presented a challenge. It is the writer's duty to find redemption, to glimpse the evidences of the unseen world in the debris of our human hopes. Borges wrote somewhere that humiliation, unhappiness, and discord "are given to us to transform, so that we may make from the miserable circumstances of our lives things that are eternal, or aspire to be so." Finding hope—that has been the way through, the solution.

A word in this context on Barry Lopez, the American writer from the Pacific Northwest whose 1986 *Arctic Dreams* remains the best contemporary book on the polar regions. In natural things and human gestures Lopez perceives "the illiterate voice of the heart." He is the most literate of writers, but that small unfathomed voice informs every one of his paragraphs. In *Arctic Dreams* and his many essays (collected in *About This Life: Journeys on the Threshold of Memory*), Lopez examines two of my own recurring themes: the effect of landscape on the imagination, and the relationship between character and landscape. Indeed, this latter might be, throughout Lopez's oeuvre, the dominant motif. His keen ecological awareness permeates many of the essays. He is attracted to the rift that has opened between human society and nature, and he laments, overtly or by implication, the ways in which we have lost touch with the natural world. This regret crops up in the work of so many nature writers (one thinks of Richard Mabey). I have always felt that this theme—our separation from the natural world—should be closer to my heart than it is. I am too involved, I think, with the shifting inner landscapes of the individual.

More specifically, Lopez champions the theory that art can close the gap between us and the natural world. I would so like to believe that. "It is through story," Lopez writes in *About This Life*, "that we embrace the great breadth of memory, that we can distinguish what is true, and that we may glimpse, at least occasionally, how to live without despair in the midst of the horror that dogs and unhinges us." "At least occasionally": a title for my autobiography.

The fight against despair lies underneath all of Lopez's writing. Darkness is never far off; at the heart of it all Lopez sees "our beautiful and infernal complexity." He has said that his aim as a writer is to contribute to a literature of hope and that through writing and reading he seeks a reprieve from the "wild conflict that defines life." My sentiments entirely. We look to him as we struggle for meaning in a world gone wrong. In the meantime, we write off our losses on the page. For what is writing if not to avenge oneself on life?

II | ROLE MODELS

0 Miles   1   2

0 Kilometers   2

What makes a travel book work? A pattern in the carpet: the book must be fundamentally about something other than the journey (taking for granted style, insights, a core of human sympathy, and the ability to give a snapshot impression of a whole life from a fleeting but revealing angle. Oh yes, and the novelist's willingness to let the obscure remain obscure). The canon— *Naples '44, Old Calabria, A Pattern of Islands*—who could say that these are just about a particular place at a particular time? Apsley Cherry-Garrard's *Worst Journey in the World* is not only about what happened at the South Pole in 1912. It is about me and you and here and now; it is about leaky taps and finding the money to pay the gas bill and discovering that perhaps one isn't quite the person one thought one was. You could say the same about *The Iliad* or *The Nun's Priest's Tale*. In his 1950 Nobel acceptance speech Faulkner reminded everyone that "problems of the human heart in conflict with itself alone can make good writing."

Jonathan Raban once wrote, "As a literary form, travel writing is a notoriously raffish open house where very different genres are likely to end up in the same bed." I couldn't agree more. Insisting on separation—this is to be designated travel writing, that something else—has always seemed pointless, like the nonsmoking section in the restaurant, itself as much use as a non-pissing section in a swimming pool. Indeed, I fell in love with travel writing not through the printed word but at the theater. As a schoolgirl in Bristol, I worked for several years selling ice cream bars in the lobby at the Bristol Old Vic. Perks included free tickets, as well as access to the parties thrown every weekend by students at the Theatre School. I was fifteen when I saw a production of Somerset Maugham's *Letter*, and I was mesmerized at the way Maugham deployed the torpor of the plantation outside Kuala Lumpur and the scents of the Chinese markets of Singapore. Walking out after the play across the cobbles of King Street, I felt a door had opened. I went on to read all Maugham's nontheatrical travel writing (most of it from the golden interwar period) and from him progressed through everyone else. I noted that in all the best books, association counted for as much as facts.

The pieces assembled in this section are all about writers who engage with the spirit of place. I have chosen people whose views of the world fire me up and to whom I feel linked by a correspondence of belief. Their struggles to weather the psychic landscape, often, are what most attracted me; by engaging with the bigger topics, albeit often fleetingly, they take readers not only out of themselves to another place but into themselves as well, to another other place. And, above all, I was interested in the ways in which they negotiate the delicate relationship between the two. Mary Kingsley is the first example. This piece was written as an introduction to a new edition of her book *Travels in West Africa*.

Mary Kingsley: Travels in West Africa

Mary Kingsley was not unique, though hers was a rare breed. She belonged to that tribe of tweed-skirted Victorians who battled through malarial swamps, parasols aloft, or scaled unnamed Pamirs trailed by a retinue of exhausted factotums. History has tended to write them off as benignly mad eccentrics, but the best among their volumes have stood the test of time: Isabella Bird's *Lady's Life in the Rocky*

Mountains, Harriet Tytler's *Englishwoman in India*, Kate Marsden's *On Sledge and Horseback to Outcast Siberian Lepers*. But Kingsley heads the field.

She was born in London in 1862, high noon of imperial splendor. Her uncle was Charles Kingsley, canon of Westminster and author of the bestselling fairy tale *The Water-Babies*. His brother, Mary's father, was a doctor, though he practiced little, instead roaming the world as personal physician to a succession of languid aristocrats. Mary's mother was his cook; he married her four days before Mary was born.

The Kingsleys were neither rich nor poor. As a child Mary lived with her mother and younger brother in a smallish house in Highgate in north London; her father appeared every couple of years, brimming with tales of foreign lands (he was a keen naturalist, and Mary longingly fingered the crumbling spiders and ferns he carried home in leather cases). Amazingly—given the sophistication of her publications—she never went to school. Blue eyed and slender, with a long face and hair the color of wet sand, she led a sequestered life even by Victorian standards. "The living outside world," she wrote later, "I saw little of, and cared less for, for I felt myself out of place at the few parties I had ever had the chance of going to, and I deservedly was unpopular with my own generation." But she had "a great amusing world of my own other people did not know or care about—that was in the books in my father's library."

Her mother was an invalid, so Mary ran the house. The family moved to Kent when Mary was seventeen, and five years later they shifted again, this time to Cambridge. When her father was no longer able to travel on account of poor health, Kingsley looked after him too. She described these years as "a losing fight with death all the time." In 1892, both parents died within six weeks. Mary Kingsley wore black for the rest of her life. She later confided in a letter to a friend that she would have liked to exchange her relations, advertising them perhaps in *The Exchange and Mart* "for fire irons or anything useful." But she also acknowledged the bondage of "duty, the religion I was brought up in." She moved back to London to keep house for her feckless brother, Charley.

Kingsley had been to Paris once and to Germany once, and after her parents' deaths she took off on a short holiday to the Canary Islands. There she made a couple of trips across to Africa. Contrary to the impression she gives in *Travels in West Africa*, she had been obsessed with the region for years, reading voluminously in the field and absorbing her father's tales. When she set off on her first proper trip there, in August 1893, she was thirty. The glory days of Livingstonian exploration were already over. The Berlin Conference in 1884–1885 had marked the final stage of the parceling out of the dark continent by the Great Powers, and West Africa was essentially being run by a sketchy network of colonial administrators, few of whom had much of a clue as to what they were supposed to be doing. *Travels in West Africa* tells the story of Kingsley's second, eleven-month voyage, though she draws on material gathered in the first. Her ship reached Freetown, Sierra Leone, on January 7, 1895, and she set off southward through those countries now known as Ghana, Nigeria, Cameroon, Equatorial Guinea, and Gabon. The whole region was known to traders and missionaries alike as "the White Man's Grave."

The trip involved almost unimaginably hard travel. Approaching the Remboué—an episode recounted in chapter 7—our heroine wades through swamps for up to two hours at a time, up to her neck in fetid water, with leeches around her neck like a frill. She marches twenty-five miles through forest so dense that the sky is never once visible, and she falls fifteen feet into a game pit laid with twelve-inch ebony spikes. "It is at these times," she writes, "you realise the blessing of a good thick skirt." I have traveled through parts of the world where terrain and climate conspire to make the journey challenging. But I have never done it in a long trailing dress with a tight waist and a high collar, trussed up in a corset and lace-up boots that let in the water; nor have I trawled through feculent swamps without a whack of prophylactic in my blood and a batch of industrial-strength antibiotics in my pack. Kingsley is apparently imperturbable, whether uncovering the detritus of cannibalism in her bedroom, deploying a shoelace in her corset, or being stalked as game. And her diaries reveal that she leaves out some of her most epic adventures. Her feats of seamanship, for example, when she thrice took a two-thousand-ton vessel over the Forcados Bar and up the creeks. Or the time she was shot in the ankle by a muzzle-loader (it took months for the iron fragments to work their way out of the wound).

Kingsley responds profoundly to the African landscape. "I believe the great swamp region of the Bight of Biafra is the greatest in the world," she writes, "and that in its immensity and gloom it has a grandeur equal to that of the Himalayas." If you have sat on the deck of a cargo ship and floated down the coast of West Africa in all its mesmerizing luminosity, you will recognize the scenes Kingsley describes in this volume and its sequel, *West African Studies*. "You automatically believe that nothing else but this sort of world, past or present, or future can ever have existed," she says, "and that cities and mountains are but the memories of dreams." Here, as elsewhere, the sheer joy she takes in her journey leaps off the page. "To my taste," she writes, "there is nothing so fascinating as spending a night out in an African forest, or plantation . . . And if you do fall under its spell, it takes all the color out of other kinds of living." Agreed.

Her favorite words are "uproar," "palaver," and "skylarking," phenomena significantly absent from her English life. Kingsley's travels liberated her from the bondage of self—a bondage from which, in the drawing rooms of London or Cambridge, it was impossible to escape. She felt whole and authentic in Africa. Back in England she inevitably fell ill with a range of illnesses, many of the neurasthenic variety. In this book she claims she went on her long journeys in order to continue her father's study of early religion and law, but surely it was more complicated.

Kingsley brilliantly conjures a landscape. The reader can *see* the silver bubbles of Lake Ncovi as the canoe carves a frosted trail; the rich golden sunlight of late afternoon; or the wreaths of indigo and purple over the forest as day sinks into night. Crucially, and unlike most of her peers, Kingsley also has an eye for the comic detail, and it is wry humor that maintains the narrative drive throughout *Travels in West Africa*. A man who contracted a bad case of west-coast fever, the author notes, shook so violently that he dislodged a chandelier, which in turn smashed a valuable tea service and a silver teapot in its midst. She has too an uncommon instinctual sense of the right moment to leaven the mix with a dash of dialogue. And her adjectival clauses seldom hit the wrong note. Who fails to shudder when reading of the smell of rotting elephant "strong enough to have taken the paint off a door"? And who can forget the cook on the Mungo Mah Lobeh expedition who "yawns a yawn that nearly cuts his head in two"?

Yet Kingsley was not a natural writer. Her unofficial editor, Dr. Henry Guillemard, wrote of an "undammable logorrhea of Kingsleyese" and advised her that "when a crocodile is coming over the stern of a canoe . . . he must not take six pages to do it." In its unexpurgated form, *Travels in West Africa* runs to six hundred pages—which is too long. This edition uses the text excellently abridged by Elspeth Huxley, herself a doughty traveler and wonderfully gifted writer on foreign parts. The charm of the book, I think, lies in Kingsley's blend of high seriousness and whimsical wit, a combination people generally did not like in a woman— still don't—and the fact that she pulls it off makes her success all the more admirable. The whimsy derives in no small measure from the author's relentless tendency to anthropomorphize— thus fireflies converge "to see if our fire was not a big relation of their own," a canoe proves itself to be "weak-minded," and a counterpane deployed as a sail longs to become a counterpane again. A susurrant row of coconut palms is "behaving badly," the branches "gossiping" so loudly close to the telephone wire running alongside them that "mere human beings can hardly get a word in edgeways" (even lumbered with the cliché at the end, the joke works).

Like many, she used wit as her armor—she acknowledged it. Her letters reveal that inside she was an inchoate mass of doubts, fears, and regrets. Who isn't? Mary Kingsley never had a boyfriend, never had sex. One can only wonder what she was thinking as she sat by the campfire watching oiled and naked limbs flashing, or as the Fang in chapter 6 presses himself alongside her at dinner wearing only a loincloth. "I know nothing myself of love," she told her first biographer. "I have read about it . . . I have never been in love, nor has anyone ever been in love with me." She went further in a letter to a male friend. "The fact is," she stated bluntly, "I am no more a human being than a gust of wind is. I have never had a human individual life. I have . . . lived in the joys, sorrows and worries of other people . . . it is the non-human world I belong to myself. My people are mangroves, swamps, rivers and the sea and so on—we understand each other." The most important relationships in her life were with places, not people. She said once, in a letter, that she went to West Africa to die—as opposed to the published reason for the voyage, the one about continuing her father's studies. There is no doubt that she recklessly courted danger, even death (one thinks in particular of the journey to the Remboué). There is an element of high-Victorian self-mortification.

At the heart of her lies a painful paradox—painful, that is, to admirers. Vaunted in both her own time and ours as a role model for women, Kingsley opposed female suffrage, and when a journalist lauded her achievements as "A New Woman," she announced huffily, "Every bit of solid, good work I have done has been through a man." What is one to make of it? I think she was just ahead of her time. Intellectually unable to think herself into a different world in her homeland, she was used to fighting to do what she wanted in a man's way—which was the only way, if what you wanted was to paddle a canoe with a semi-naked hunk, and who wouldn't want to do that? Subscribing to some vague female collective suggested the frightful prospect of a locked drawing-room ghetto. (That's the best I can do.) Although she was an antifeminist, Kingsley had an enlightened attitude to the African, at least by Victorian standards. I believe she genuinely saw him as an equal. Different, but equal. "I confess," she writes in chapter 10 of *Travels in West Africa*, "that the more I know of the West Coast Africans the more I like them. I own I think them fools of the first water for their power of believing in things; but I fancy I have analogous feelings toward even my fellow-countrymen when they go and violently believe in something that I cannot quite swallow." She naturally respected tribal beliefs; when standing in front of a huge tree that one tribe worshipped, she said she wasn't surprised that they did, it was so beautiful. Almost alone among white travelers of her time, Kingsley was in favor of African nationalism. "It is the black man's burden that wants singing," she wrote in a short book called *The Story of West Africa*. She was particularly wary of the missionary. "Ah me!" she writes. "If the aim of life were happiness and pleasure, Africa should send us missionaries instead of our sending them to her."

She often comments on the deleterious effect that so-called progress has already had on West Africans. "Nothing strikes one so much, in studying the degeneration of these native tribes," she snorts, "as the direct effect that civilisation and reformation has in hastening it." (And what horrors to come!) She was ahead of her time and is consistently good on the gulf between white ideas on Africa and the reality she observes. In her long discourse in this book on local ideas and philosophies, she writes that "the difficulty of the language is, however, far less than the whole set of difficulties with your own mind."

Some have suggested that Kingsley was economical with the truth. Although the physical hardships of her journey are not open to doubt, there are exaggerations in these pages. Did she really take a Fang canoe in the dead of night and paddle out alone, as described in chapter 5? I doubt it. Several episodes border on the farcical, for example, the scene in chapter 2 in which she falls through the roof of a Fang house. But what does invention matter, in literature?

When she reached home after her second journey, she again lived with her brother in London. She lectured widely on her travels, quickly becoming what we would call a celebrity, though it was a more dignified business then. In 1897, *Travels in West Africa* was published, and it was an immediate success, as was *West African Studies*, which Kingsley published in January 1899. The Boer War was ravaging southern Africa, and that same year she sailed down to the cape in order to nurse Boer prisoners of war in a camp in Simonstown (she said in a lecture prior to departure that she felt "homeward bound"). This was the immolation she sought. "All this work here," she wrote to a friend, "the stench, the washing, the enemas, the bed pans, the blood, is my world. Not London society, politics, that gateway into which I so strangely wandered—into which I don't care a hairpin if I ever wander again." She started smoking and drinking wine, allegedly to ward off illness. But the fags and booze failed. Don't they always, in the end? Kingsley died of typhoid on June 3, 1900, aged thirty-seven, and was buried at sea with full military honors.

Alone on a riverbank at night, leaning against a rock, she writes of the majesty and beauty of the scene. "Do not imagine it gave rise," she warns, "to those complicated, poetical reflections natural beauty seems to bring out in other people's minds. It never works that way with me; I just lose all sense of human individuality, all memory of human life, with its grief and worry and doubt, and become part of the atmosphere." Lucky her. With characteristic paradox, she concludes the passage with a poetic touch of the very kind she has just disclaimed. "If I have a heaven," she reflects on the scene, "that will be mine." I hope it is.

2006

POSTSCRIPT

Kingsley's assertion that she identified more closely with places than people made a profound impression on me when I researched this piece. Other writers and artists have made similar claims. Stanley Spencer, a hero of mine, told his first wife that all his significant love affairs had been with places, not people. (Did it really have to be her that he told?) Betjeman said he often felt more for buildings than he did for human beings. My interest in the theme sprang from a deep fear that I too might be like that. But in the end, it is the human drama that grips me. Place is a backdrop against which that human drama unfolds. It plays the role of a stage set. That doesn't mean that the words "Kashgar," "Samarkand," and "Zanzibar" don't make my heart beat faster, or that I don't dream of the boom of shifting sand caused by sharp temperature change (what Marco Polo called "the tramp and clash of great cavalcades at night"). It's just that those things are not enough on their own. But why not use them to leverage the harder stuff? As I indicated at the start of this section, so much in literature rests on the relationship between the inner journey and the outer one. In the best travel writing, the outer journey expresses the inner. The following piece pays homage to a master.

Norman Lewis

I crunched up his spruce-lined drive, the front door sprang back, and the upright figure of Norman Lewis, aged ninety-three, stepped into the sunshine to greet me. He wore slacks, an open-necked striped shirt, and a sky-blue cotton jacket. His hangdog face, punctuated by a salt-and-pepper mustache, opened into a smile. He looked wonderful, but later, leaning across a copy of *The Times Atlas* lying open on a coffee table, he cupped his ear. "In a small way," he said apologetically after asking me to speak up, "none of the bits of me quite work anymore."

Lewis is the author of thirteen novels and as many works of non-fiction. Graham Greene considered him "one of the best writers, not of any particular decade, but of our century." He still publishes a book a year, the most recent, like Frank Sinatra comeback albums, agreeably reordered compilations of familiar classics with the odd new piece thrown in that has lain at the bottom of a drawer for some decades, with good reason. He says—and I believe him—that he couldn't care less that nobody talks about the novels anymore. He stopped writing fiction in 1987 with *The March of the Long Shadows*; he can't quite remember why, but he thinks it was because he got into the habit of travel books and loved doing them too much to stop.

Together with his wife, Lesley, a handsome Australian some decades his junior, Lewis settled forty years ago deep in rural Essex. Their village has an ancient church, a pond, and a souvenir shop called Hansel and Gretel. Lewis says he bought his sixteenth-century farmhouse—once a brothel—because when he went to view it a green woodpecker was digging up a worm on the lawn.

Every room, including the flagged entrance hall with its cavern-
ous fireplace and bread oven, is crammed with artifacts and
souvenirs carted back from far-flung lands. "That," Lewis says,
pointing to a large oil of the Bay of Naples hanging in the sitting
room, "was given to me at the end of a Soviet tour I made as a
guest of the Writers' Union in lieu of royalties for my novel *The
Volcanoes Above Us*. In the National Gallery of Moscow, I was
told to choose a painting from the wall as a going-home present."
The Russian translation of the novel went on to sell six million
copies.

Lewis was born in 1908 in Enfield, a north London suburb proliferating with semidetached houses, aspidistras, and monkey
puzzles. He still speaks with a whiny Thames valley accent,
though it is enlivened now—so I fancy—by an antipodean twang
that he must have absorbed from Lesley. His Welsh father was a
disillusioned chemist of the dispensing variety, and fond of the
bottle. The first three Lewis boys died in mysterious circumstances before reaching adulthood, and in an attempt to keep
Norman alive, his parents dispatched him, at the age of nine, to
lodge with three aunts in Carmarthen, a grimly astonishing experience recounted in detail in *Jackdaw Cake* (the aunts baked a
special dish for the jackdaws, which was tastier than the fare they
served up to their young charge). When I asked him about this
period in his life, his indignant tone indicated that the wounds
were still raw. "I was beaten at school in England for being Welsh
and beaten at school in Wales for being English. But it did me a
great service: I understood that the world was a very hard place."
When he was allowed back to the Elysium fields of Enfield, he
discovered that his parents had become spiritualists.

Despite winning a scholarship to the local grammar school,
he abandoned formal education at seventeen to work in the family
photography shop, subsequently developing the business into a
chain of his own, installing managers, and flitting back inter-

mittently for three decades to collect "pocket money" until he finally sold out to the respected camera chain Dollond's. In the early years he also turned his hand, with some success, to a variety of small-scale buying-and-selling schemes of the kind routinely undertaken in the pinched and colorless 1930s. ("The experience of those years," he has written, "fostered resilience—possibly even, of necessity, a sense of adventure.") The work financed a bit of travel, and in 1937 Lewis was approached by the Colonial Office to undertake a photographic espionage mission into Yemen, a journey that forms the title piece of his latest collection, *A Voyage by Dhow*. (Like all masters of nonfiction, he is a champion recycler. Some pages of *Dhow* have already appeared not only in color supplements of the 1970s and 1980s but also in previous books.) Although his work needs a lot of editorial tidying these days, Lewis has not lost his eye for the telling detail. Stranded on the tiny island of Kamaran, at that time occupied by the British, he deftly evokes the lonely futility of the remote colonial governor, homing in on "a garden in which a single rosebush had struggled to survive under the protection of a small tent."

He never made it into Yemen, but the voyage produced his first book, *Sand and Sea in Arabia*. He had already married Ernestina Corvaja, a Sicilian whose parents had settled in Bloomsbury. The family had Cuban roots, and in July 1939 the young couple moved to Havana with their son. The sojourn was interrupted—for Norman, at any rate—by the outbreak of World War II. He sailed home and reported to the War Office, which sent him for Arabic lessons. With time to spare, he learned Russian too and has subsequently added other languages to his arsenal.

Service with the Intelligence Corps took him to Algeria, Tunisia, Italy, Austria, and Iraq, and he admits to enjoying the war a great deal. But the years of enforced separation did in his marriage, as he describes in *The World, the World*, the fifth book in his autobiographical cycle. He moved back to Britain, and in the spring of 1948 his first novel, *Samara*, was accepted by Jonathan

Cape. Shortly after, the publisher backed a journey through In-dochina during the precarious last years of the French colonial regime. *A Dragon Apparent* (1951) was the result, an engaging and vivid book revealing the honed prose shaded with tenebrous humor that was to become Lewis's trademark. It was a commercial coup, although the author noted that in-house "enthusiasm in my presence was kept under control." *Golden Earth* swiftly followed, about travels in Burma, when insurgent armies were to the fore. "Mr. Lewis," Cyril Connolly wrote of this book, "can make even a lorry interesting."

His health was poor, so he moved to Spain and became a fisherman in the village of Farol on what is now the Costa Brava. And so it went on: more journeys, another marriage, more children. For decades he sped off to the Mexican sierra at forty-eight hours' notice, hired a mule, and vanished. Time had a different quality then: in *A Voyage by Dhow* he remembers kicking up his heels for six weeks in Aden before the vessel was even loosed from its moorings.

The defining theme of the new collection is a Lewisian regular: the relentless homogenization towed in the wake of change and progress. He catches Lahej at the very moment of transition, the ancient tented settlement immobilized by brick as the authorities force its inhabitants to live in buildings. Lewis's sensibility has always revolted against breaches with the past: the poverty of the modern experience, as he sees it, is rooted in our lack of contact with our own past. He despises above all the "cultural nothingness" of contemporary society. "Now is the time to see South Mexico," he wrote in *The Observer* in 1980 after describing how the ancient pottery center of Amatenango was churning out Disney kangaroos. "Nothing can dim the glory of the great pre-hispanic ruins and the great colonial towns, but outside that, in ten years it will all be Amatenango."

Lewis's reputation now rests on his limpid prose, but it was as an investigative journalist that he made his name. He has no hesitation in citing a long article called "Genocide in Brazil" that appeared in *The Sunday Times* in 1968 as his major achievement. The piece led to a change in Brazilian law and to the formation of Survival International, the charity—still flourishing—dedicated to the protection of aboriginal people. We know a lot more about ethnocide now. It is difficult to remember just how groundbreaking it was when Lewis opened the subject up, and not just in Brazil either. It was he who read the Lloyd's economic monthly report stating complacently that the Mexican economy showed a 7 percent growth in real terms, and saw children dying of disease and malnutrition, and wondered about the conflicting evidence. What a tragedy that those heady days of the twelve-thousand-word essay have vanished from British journalism.

His eye falls in particular on the role of missionaries, and several of the pieces in the new book return to the territory covered in devastating detail in *The Missionaries* (1988), a heart-breaking indictment of collusion between governments and missionary organizations in their campaign to "sedentarize" aboriginal peoples. "The great human tragedy of the missionary conquest of the Pacific is being repeated now in all 'untouched' parts of the world," he wrote in that book. "In another thirty years no trace of aboriginal life anywhere will have survived." Crucially, he is sparing with the tragic detail, understanding (instinctually, I think) the perils of compassion fatigue. He plays to the gallery. In *Dhow* he recounts how missionaries translating the Bible into the Panare language were stumped to discover that the tribe lacks any word for guilt. The only solution (plainly) was to reedit the scriptures in such a way as to implicate the Panare in Christ's death. Gone were the Romans, the Last Supper, the trial, and Pontius Pilate turning away to wash his hands. "The Panare killed Jesus Christ," read the new gospel, "because they were wicked."

A sense of connection with the past attracted him to the Mafia, a subject he has used time and again in his work. His bestselling novel *The Sicilian Specialist*, published in 1974 and incorporating at that time undisclosed facts about the Kennedy assassination, was removed from sale in some American cities following a Mafia ban. "The story of the Mafia," he says now, "is about the development of a human being who defends the cultures of the past. The Mafia has been vulgarized: any petty criminal now is referred to as a mafioso. But the true Mafia revolves around a specialized reorganization of society. I admire facets of it, just as it is possible to admire facets of a person. To a certain extent a mafioso defends a medieval culture in a modern world."

After talking in the living room, we moved outside, the freshly mown stripes of lawn gleaming with a mosquey-blue shimmer from Islamic tile work on the back wall of the house. Lewis brought the tiles from North Africa after secretly entering Algeria during its war under the code name Bismuth. Like all European travel writers, he has been drawn to the south rather than the colder landscapes and temperaments of the butter-eating north. Spain and Italy are among his most regular destinations. His masterpiece—and his own favorite among his books—is *Naples '44* (1978), the diary of his year as an intelligence officer attached to the U.S. Fifth Army. The city was so destitute when he arrived that its denizens had eaten the tropical fish in the aquarium. Yet at the end he can say, "A year among the Italians has converted me to such an admiration for their humanity and culture that were I given the chance to be born again, Italy would be the country of my choice." In Naples one glimpses Lewis the romantic, longing deeply for what he calls "human solidarity." He was last there five years ago. "Yes," he told me, "it had changed, of course, but people still walk the streets singing at dawn."

His style evolved little as the decades unraveled, though one detects, in later work such as *An Empire of the East*, his 1993 volume on Indonesia, a gloomy undertow. He has always reveled in understatement without indulging in the juvenile self-deprecation of contemporary blokeish travelogues. "The plane was a little discouraging," he once wrote when taking off from a perilously tiny bit of landing strip in the high Andes, "with significant patches in its fuselage and a small oil-drip from the engine, and the American pilot lopsided like an arthritic horseman, due as he admitted to crash-landing in the remote past."

He is not a man for the confessional. Even in his autobiographical cycle one sees him but dimly. It is a trait learned in his childhood: he writes in *Jackdaw Cake* of "long practice of self-concealment." But the inner man is there, of course, because we see the world through the prism of his vision. The situations he enjoys most—those that inspire him as a writer to his greatest creative flights—are when he finds himself a silent and almost invisible observer among a small group of temporarily immobilized foreigners. "The moral atmosphere on board," he notes of one riverine journey, "was perhaps similar to that of a medieval pilgrimage."

Above all, he has a rare ability to conjure a place. Turbaned Uzbeks "move like chess pieces through the morning mist" while a bus "rampaged on through the long hot day, and then into a haggard nightscape of cactus and flints." And here he is toiling up into the Guatemalan hinterland: "We trudged through great palisades of shadow thrown down by the morning sun. Birds chuckled and hooted. A deer started up and raced away into the mist. Tiny, scarlet flowers had opened everywhere overnight in the close grass, and beads of watery condensation sparkled among the quartz seams of the rocks." He remains the most filmic of writers: I wish someone would turn his books into movies. The scripts would be easy, as Lewis has always had a perfect ear for dialogue.

He is not as famous as certain of his peers, or indeed as many younger men; he is not as famous as he should be. This is partly because he has never been a member of a literary coterie. Apart from a description of his friendship with Jonathan Cape in the early days (he calls the publisher's offices Heartburn House, as burned Irish stew was invariably served), he has written little of the hothouse literary world. His aloofness has meant that he has, compared with, say, Patrick Leigh Fermor, been somewhat ignored by the literati; more positively, it has lent him a remote, inscrutable quality. In the 1980s he was even in danger of being forgotten, and those who sang his praises most loudly were journalists such as Auberon Waugh, Dick West, and Patrick Marnham, rather than conventional travel writers of the Theroux-Raban axis. Waugh once wrote that Lewis was "outstandingly the best travel writer of our age, if not the best since Marco Polo."

Lewis is currently finishing a book about his first father-in-law, Ernesto Corvaja ("I loved him until he died, and he treated me like his son. I regarded him in greater esteem than my own father"). It is shaped around a journey, largely on foot, to Seville Cathedral in 1924. As we moved back into the house, he told me that he has spent longer over it than he has over any other book, mentioning the word "research" and waving an arm toward the 2002 *Lonely Planet Guide to Spain* lying alongside a yellow folder containing the typescript. Does he have his notebooks from the journey? "No." Is he cavalier with the truth? He looked offended. "Do you," I stumbled on, "like the rest of us, burnish the hum-drum?" After all (I thought but didn't say), he has a startling ability to remember verbatim conversations that took place half a century before. "No," he said again, looking me in the eye. "I don't care enough to make things up. I'm not at all ambitious."

When he talks about the new book, he comes to life. He still has things to say, is still fighting. He claims to have no hope for the future ("everything gets worse"), but surely if this were the case, he wouldn't still be cranking it out. He no longer reads, except the paper, but he still travels. He was about to fly off to the Costa Brava, though he had rejected the first hotel Lesley found, appalled, above all else, by the sun umbrellas depicted in the brochure.

"These days," he said, squinting into the late-afternoon light pouring through the window, "travel writers have to go a lot further, try a lot harder, and endure a lot more." After a moment's reflection he added ruefully that he regrets not going far enough himself. "I did it the easy way," he murmured. But few authors have left such an infinitely beguiling canon; few have so consistently freed themselves from the shackles of their period and entered the immortal zone. Greene described Lewis as a great writer "of our century." That, of course, was the last century. But here he is, the wily old master: still at it.

2000

POSTSCRIPT

Lewis died at home in Essex three years later, leaving fifteen novels, sixteen works of nonfiction, and a body of literary journalism. He has still never broken through the mysterious barrier that separates the admired from the famous.

The more I thought of him over the years, the more it seemed that, like many writers, Lewis spent the best part of himself on the page, leaving the scraps for daily life. In 2008 a rather brilliant authorized biography appeared to mark his centenary, and it confirmed my view. *Semi-Invisible Man* by Julian Evans is almost as gripping as its subject. Evans was Lewis's friend and sometime editor, and he made deeply thoughtful use of the archive, from letters to unpublished typescripts and water-stained notebooks stretching back over six decades. The man who emerges is a figure of mandarin manners (though quick to take offense), of modesty and reserve (though he had a penchant for fast cars), and of outbursts of enthusiasms. Everyone said his stories were mesmerizing, if you could get him to start talking. Married three times, Lewis had five children by three women, his record dubious in the paterfamilias department. When he visited the maternity hospital to see one baby for the first time, his wife looked out the window to spot the proud father in a sports car with a blonde. He was always restless and had the physical stamina to gratify his escape reflex. At eighty-one he could drink a whole bottle at lunch, then bound up a steep hillside like a mountain goat.

What makes him so good? He always found the right phrase, whether confronting the "bitter, withered reality" of Mandalay, the air of the Pyrenees "limpid with nightingales," or the dawn fisherman-archers of old Chiang Mai. I once followed his footsteps through the tribal foothills of Orissa, using his book *A Goddess in the Stones* as a guide. The subtle, complex way in which he had speared the scene onto the page was extraordinary, even down to the face of a villainous Domb fleecing a Dongria Kondh farmer bringing a single pumpkin down to market. His prose is characterized by restraint and musicality, his approach by tolerance and detached sympathy. Detribalization preoccupied him, whether it was happening to Moïs of Vietnam, to Panare on the Orinoco, or to Ayoreo fugitives in Bolivia. He saw romance going out of the world. But the most salient stylistic characteristic of the travel books, and the one that elevates Lewis above his competitors, is his own absence from the pages. The narrator is an agent of the material, not a character in the story.

It was a book about the Mafia, *The Honored Society*, that established Lewis's reputation in the 1960s. But the travel books are better than the novels. Too much of Lewis's fiction is characterized by a lack of engagement and a preference for action and atmosphere over human complexity. Although for many years he desperately wanted to be viewed as a novelist rather than an author of travel books, he never was. Almost every significant travel writer of the past half century has expressed a similar belief in the higher position of fiction in the literary hierarchy of their imagination. Yet were any of them as good, as novelists, as they were as writers of nonfiction? Perhaps Bruce Chatwin, but I do not think he will stand the test of time as a travel writer (more of that later). Lewis will.

Semi-Invisible Man reads in parts like the best kind of social history. Evans shows his protagonist meeting a sweetheart in a Lyons Corner House in the 1930s ("Xanadu as far as either of us was concerned"); serving in the Intelligence Corps after landing at Salerno in 1943 ("She said she would pray for me, if I would get her some louse powder"); gulping Benzedrine and

booze in the Soho of the 1950s ("Take a benny, Dad," the Lewis children ordered Father if he started to slow down). The 1970s see our man purchasing
wine-making kits in the Braintree branch of Boots. At one point Ian Fleming
got Lewis recruited into the Intelligence Services. The subterfuge appealed to
the hidden observer that was such a large part of Lewis's writing self, and he
remained involved for thirty years.

Throughout the first half of his biography, Evans wrestles with the discovery that Lewis manipulated facts to suit the prose and that apparent artlessness conceals magisterial reshaping and, er, invention. In an essay in his
1959 collection, *The Changing Sky*, Lewis describes himself cutting free a mal-
treated dog in Ibiza. His daughter Karen, who was there, tells Evans it was
her mother who freed the hound. Even *Naples '44* turns out to be "more a
portrait of creative recollection . . . than of events." Much hand-wringing en-
sues as Evans attempts to understand what went on. "We can never get a perspective on ourselves," he asserts manfully over one blatant piece of Lewisian
self-reinvention. "It is not misleading as such. It is just easy to be misled by it."

I think a Norman Lewis book works like an El Greco painting. Author and
artist subordinate reality to a higher truth. In an El Greco, perspective, proportion, and anatomy are less important than a mystical interpretation of
Christian subjects. The viewer is encouraged to transcend the physical world
in order to focus on the subject's spiritual essence and to experience a direct
connection with God. In Lewis's case, the striving is for a truth that's truer than
the truth: the poetic truth.

Through meticulous analysis of the evolution of Lewis's style, Evans has
written a book about the turbid relationship between life and art. He is
deeply interested in the mechanics of creativity. When something happens
apparently accidentally in the story, Evans comments, "in the deep narrative
of a writer's interests there are probably few accidents." I would so like to
believe that. But it cannot be so.

It is amusing to learn from Evans that in the early 1980s Lewis became
obsessed with the popularity of an upstart called Paul Theroux who was selling more books than he was. So the feet were of clay after all. Whose aren't?
Lewis continued writing almost to the end, and if the material was thin, as
Evans puts it, "the music lingered on."

Domestic Manners of the Americans

D omestic Manners of the Americans is a traveler's account of the newborn republic between the Revolution and the Civil War. An enchanting blend of topographical description, social commentary, and robust rebuke, the book fizzes with the energy, fun, and righteous indignation of a dumpy, middle-aged Bristolian called Fanny Trollope.

What an inspiration is Fanny! She has the essential reporter's curiosity, insisting on being lowered into Ohio coal mines or hoisted onto Pennsylvania factory platforms. A radical by temperament rather than ideology, she is determined to uncover the truth about the fabled American democracy. Voyaging through the slave state of Kentucky, Fanny notes with unease that all men are not as equal as had first appeared. "You will see them with one hand," she later writes of her Cincinnati neighbors, "hoisting the cap of liberty, and with the other flogging their slaves." Above all she despised "the total and universal want of manners," the manifestation of which ranged from eating foot-long slices of watermelon in public to tossing pigs' tails into flower beds and vomiting in the theater pit (this happened in Washington, "appear[ing] not in the least to annoy or surprise" the rest of the audience).

When I was finding my own feet as a writer, Fanny Trollope was my role model. She was after all a Bristolian of modest origins, like me. She was one of the first travel writers, making an artistic form accessible long before the men usually cited as the first practitioners of the genre. I so admired the way she refused to submit to defeat, battling on through catastrophe, bankruptcy, and heartbreak. Her son Anthony once declared that "of all the people I have known my mother was the most joyous, or at any rate, the most capable of joy." And to top it all she was a fine and intuitive writer—stylish, pithy, elegant, waspish. Fanny is still a role model—living proof that there is life after menopause.

Her refusal to acknowledge any taboo made people call her vulgar. Few nineteenth-century writers would have mentioned that Thomas Jefferson sired children "by almost all his numerous gang of female slaves," or complained about the Pennsylvania Academy of the Fine Arts covering up the penises of its statues. In her prose and her life, Fanny moved with eighteenth-century ease from battlefield to boudoir. She is associated with the Victorians, like her famous son, but really she was raised in the world of rakes and Hogarthian vulgarity, unafraid of confronting both in print when she had found them in life.

Domestic Manners has not been out of print for 178 years. Trollope's prose has outlasted its age because it touches universal themes: gender, race, religion, liberty. It is hard to remember now just what a pioneer Fanny Trollope was, observing the United States before Tocqueville, let alone Dickens. She remains incomparable. Mark Twain took all the European commentators up the Mississippi, and on the last page of his copy of *Domestic Manners* he noted, "Of all these tourists, I like Dame Trollope best."

2009

Tété-Michel Kpomassie

first encountered Tété-Michel Kpomassie in a tent on the top of the Greenland ice cap. The temperature was 20 below, and I had burrowed into my sleeping bag to read in the small pool of light cast by a miner's lamp strapped to my forehead. Every so often, like a soft-shelled crab, I poked my head from the bag to take a gulp of air. The tent was brightly lit by the midnight sun, the sky outside the plastic pane the fabled Arctic blue. But it was impossible to read without being sealed into the bag. One's fingers froze, otherwise, while turning pages.

Nighttime in the polar latitudes provides a robust test of a book's capacity to take one's mind off the horror of the moment (surely one of the functions of literature). From the first page, Kpomassie revealed himself as the man for the job. His superb volume, *An African in Greenland*, not only drove out the cold. It did what I most like a travel book to do. It held up a mirror, and the Arctic reflected back the world.

An African in Greenland was first published in Paris in 1981, a period in which Lévi-Strauss and exotic ethnology had captured the imagination of French intellectuals. In Kpomassie's book they got two for the price of one, for the first chapters deal with the author's childhood in rural Togo. It was a long journey from Togo to the Arctic Circle.

The author records how, as a small boy, he fell out of a tree while gathering coconuts and, following a purification ceremony by the high priestess of the python, was destined to be initiated into her cult. The prospect was so terrifying that he dreamed of escape—to Greenland, which he had read about in a missionary bookshop in Lomé. Greenland was, to the young Kpomassie, the antithesis of the jungle—white, frozen, and python-free. When he was sixteen, he took off. The journey to the distant unknown is among the oldest stories ever told, but in his book the self-educated Kpomassie makes it his own. It took him eight years to get to Greenland, working his passage up the west coast of Africa port by port and taking jobs in France and Copenhagen. But his real break came when he found a wealthy mentor in Paris.

In 1965, aged twenty-four and an Arctic greenhorn, Kpo-massie arrived at Julianehåb, now Qaqortoq, in the south of Greenland. At five feet eleven he towered above the Inuit, and, of course, he caused a sensation. The national broadcasting station announced his arrival on the evening news. "I had started on a voyage of discovery," he wrote, "only to find that it was I who was being discovered."

Kpomassie was a man for whom the interior and the exterior life converged, and he recorded his observations and responses with the same artless ingenuity, combining comicality, like all the best writers, with a sense of the sad absurdity of life. As an African, he did not carry the white man's burden, and it would not have occurred to him to romanticize Inuit lives. He describes a baby suffocated by drunken parents; a meal of rabid dog; a group conversation in someone's front room that continued as each person took his or her turn squatting over the shit bucket. More significantly, he notes more than once, "the crying lack of mutual help in a Greenland village, and the villagers' profound contempt for their poorer countrymen." But he took everything in his long stride. When his drunken host pissed in his rucksack, soaking all his clothes, he was unperturbed. In his book he perfectly captures the pared-down existence of Greenland and the grace of its people under pressure.

The Inuit competed to host him, and he immersed himself in their lives, learning both language and customs. Greenlandic society was on the cusp in 1965—or, rather, had just teetered over the edge of the slope that led to Westernization. Qaqortoq already had a cinema, though the projectionist halted the film every ten minutes for a muffled voice to translate the last batch of Danish subtitles into Inuktitut over a megaphone. (There was still no bank in the country, however.) In the populated south the old customs had already vanished. "Children are sent to school," Kpomassie observed, "but are not taught anything about the traditional activities. Even worse, that way of life is disparaged to their faces, although it is their own. When they grow up, they can't even paddle a kayak." Like many white men before him, Kpomassie relished the Inuit Greenlanders' enthusiasm for casual sex and for loaning out wives. Until, that is, he found his special girlfriend snuggling up with another. "I was quite willing to share other men's girls," he notes, "but not my own." But endemic boozing and gonorrhea eventually lost their appeal. "Greenland morality was beginning to disgust me," he writes (no wonder: he had just done a long stint in the hospital with a suspected dose of the clap), and so he made his way up the west coast in search of the pure white land he had read about in the Togolese jungle.

Denmark laid claim to Greenland, a landmass fifty times its size, as early as the seventeenth century, and at the time of Kpomassie's visit the islanders had not yet won home rule. But as our Togolese Odysseus moved north, Danes faded away. He wintered in a turf hut entered through a tunnel on all fours. "The house," he wrote, "vaguely reminded me of an African mud-walled hut." (In fact, it was an *iglu*. Contrary to Western belief, an igloo is a traditional, turtle-shaped house made of stone and peat, entered by a tunnel—*katak*—and ventilated by a hole in the ceiling— *qingaq*.) Kpomassie's host was Robert Mattaaq, a destitute paterfamilias who wore trousers tied up with string that he did not take off for the entire winter. Mattaaq had papered the walls of his igloo with pictures torn from magazines; he referred to the collage as his library. Under his supervision Kpomassie learned to drive dogs, perched alone in the darkness on a mound of frozen fish, and he came to see the patterns that had governed Inuit life for centuries. Even wife loaning had a practical significance, as, if a man was killed hunting, his wife's lover provided for the dead man's family (so there was some mutual help after all). It was a survival mechanism. Above all Kpomassie immersed himself in the spirit world. In the inner life of the Inuit, not only did all living creatures have souls, but so did inanimate objects. Each rock, lamp, and sealskin had its *inua*, or "owner." "These *inué* [plural form]," he writes, "are not exactly souls but manifestations of the strength and vitality of nature." They are spirits that walk around at night and talk. For the Inuit, it made their empty land less lonely. Rituals designed to appease the spirits governed every aspect of life, from hunting to mourning the dead. "In the eyes of an Eskimo hunter," marveled Kpomassie, "the arctic world with its vast, frozen expanses, its barren, snowy peaks and great, bare plateaux—all that drab, white, lifeless immensity of little interest to an African like me—becomes a living world."

Once the forces of what we call civilization set about the dismantling of Inuit culture, there was little chance for those myriad spirits that had been roaming the hunting grounds for two millennia. Shortly after Kpomassie's visit, the Danish government pursued the now infamous G60 policy. To facilitate administration, civil servants decided to concentrate Greenland's population in the bigger communities of the south, and as a consequence they relocated the occupants of villages with fewer than five hundred inhabitants. In larger settlements the Grønlands Tekniske Organization bulldozed turf dwellings and replaced them with flimsy wooden houses. Mattaaq was shifted south like a piece of furniture, still with the string holding up his trousers, but without any of the less tangible things that warded off despair.

Forty-five years after Kpomassie first drove a dog team across a starlit ice field, the future of the Arctic remains notably uncertain. The grubby compromises are even more visible. Here in the foothills of the twenty-first century the Arctic reflects the twisted human muddle we have made, a sink of degradation and beauty. Many authors kept me company in the sleeping bag when I made my own circumpolar journey. But Kpomassie came closest to capturing that ambiguous polar truth which is, after all, at the heart of being human.

2009

Involvement with the polar regions drew me into the literature of exploration. I mean, by this term, proper books of universal aspiration, not accounts by men with frozen beards, the latter featuring prominently on the cover, showing how dead they could get, or how much faster they were than the next guy, who anyway cheated in a manner that would surely soon be unmasked. I mean books that reveal through subtle modulations of prose the surpassing beauty of extreme environments and that try to put into words the human desire to see what lies on the other side of the mountain. Many examples crowd the shelves, a good proportion out of print and forgotten. The next piece was commissioned as an introduction to a new edition of Frank Worsley's classic, *Shackleton's Boat Journey*.

Shackleton

The heroic age of Antarctic exploration began in 1895 at the Sixth International Geographical Congress at London's Imperial Institute. It followed many years of discovery elsewhere: during the nineteenth century the white man had penetrated most of Africa, and he was running out of places to go. On August 3 the delegates to the 1895 congress passed a resolution "that this Congress record its opinion that the exploration of the Antarctic regions is the greatest piece of geographical exploration still to be undertaken."

In Britain polar fever ran especially high, as the conquest of the last white spaces had become a metaphor for the triumph of imperialism. When, in 1908 and 1909, two men claimed to have reached the North Pole, all eyes turned south.

Ernest Shackleton had been to Antarctica twice before the expedition described by Frank Worsley. He served as a lieutenant on Scott's 1901 *Discovery* expedition and sledged to the 81st parallel with Scott and Edward Wilson before being invalided home with scurvy. Before that trip, he had never used a tent or sleeping bag. In 1907, Shackleton returned to Antarctica aboard *Nimrod* as leader of his own expedition. That time he marched to 88°23' south, ninety-seven miles from the pole. Turning back then, without losing a man, may have been his greatest decision. He returned a hero.

When Shackleton set out for the third time, aboard the three-hundred-ton *Endurance*, with Worsley as captain, his farthest-south record had been beaten. The Norwegian Roald Amundsen had reached the pole, and so had Scott, though the latter had perished with four companions during the return journey. A new goal was required, so Shackleton cooked up a daring plan to lead the first fifteen-hundred-mile march across Antarctica. The pole was only halfway. Shackleton was going to cross the whole continent.

Endurance sailed from London's West India docks on August 1, 1914. It was heading for the Weddell Sea, where Shackleton planned to set up base camp. A support ship, *Aurora*, was proceeding to the other side of the continent. Its men were to establish a base on Ross Island and lay a trail of depots in the direction of the pole for Shackleton and his team, who would be approaching from the opposite direction. Shackleton called his ambitious operation the Imperial Trans-Antarctic Expedition.

The ship anchored off South Georgia on November 5, 1914, with twenty-eight hands: eleven scientists and seventeen seamen. A month later it pushed south to the Weddell Sea and almost immediately encountered pack ice. It rattled through it for three hundred miles, a period Worsley described as "fine, hard, open-air life." On January 19, 1915, the ice froze around the ship, which zigzagged for a thousand miles beset in the pincers of a floe and was crushed after a long fight. *Shackleton's Boat Journey* begins at this point.

On October 27, 1915, the men abandoned the paralyzed ship at 69 degrees south and tried to haul supplies over the ice ridges to land. The plan, not mentioned by Worsley, was aborted. Resigned to the fact that sledging to safety was not an option, the twenty-eight men camped on floating ice for five months. During that time they drifted six hundred miles. They shot the dogs and the carpenter's cat. On April 9, 1916, the floes broke up, and the men were forced to launch the three lifeboats they had saved from *Endurance*.

They reached Elephant Island, an outpost of the South Shetlands, but there was no hope of a chance rescue in that remote spot, so on Easter Monday six men set sail in one boat—the *James Caird*—for the whaling stations of South Georgia eight hundred miles away. This seventeen-day ordeal forms the heart of Worsley's book. What they endured beggars belief. But it was not over when they landed. Worsley goes on to describe a climb over unmapped mountains from King Haakon Bay to Stromness. After that, they had to rescue the men growing blubbery underneath a pair of upturned lifeboats on Elephant Island.

I have always considered *Shackleton's Boat Journey* the greatest story ever told. When I get to the part where the three men arrive at the whaling station, and to the quiet line "My name is Shackleton," my stomach takes a turn every time. I never tire of this book.

Worsley published a serialized account of the boat journey in 1924 in the magazine *The Blue Peter*. He first told the story in book form in a volume called *Endurance*, which appeared in 1931. It is an expanded version of *Shackleton's Boat Journey* and continues many years beyond it. The shortened version was first

published by Hodder and Stoughton in 1940, and that edition
was reset in 1959 in a two-shilling and six-pence edition with a
fabulously garish comic book cover. In 1974 the Folio Society is-
sued a hardback in a slipcase with an introduction and notes by
Duncan Carse, himself an Antarctic pioneer and arguably the
man who knows South Georgia better than any other. (Carse later
played the detective Dick Barton in the cult radio series *Dick
Barton: Special Agent*.) Three years later an American edition appeared with an introduction by Sir Edmund Hillary. The subsequent British version of that was called *The Great Antarctic Rescue*.*

Of the six men aboard the *Caird*, only Shackleton and Worsley published accounts of the journey. Shackleton was mired in
debt when they got home. He had to get his book out before the
story went off the boil, so he employed a ghostwriter. His book
South came out in 1919, twelve years before Worsley's *Endurance*
and twenty-one years before the first edition of *Shackleton's Boat
Journey*. Worsley had time to consider what had happened, and
he produced the better account. In places, *South* is curiously
stilted. "Earnestly we hoped," wrote Shackleton or his ghost, "that
never again would we encounter such a wave." Perhaps it was an
inevitable consequence of getting the book done quickly. Shackleton was also drawing on a range of other people's diaries
(members of the expedition were contractually obliged to hand
over their diaries when they reached home), and to a certain
extent his is a composite account lacking a single narrative voice.

---

*In *Shackleton's Boat Journey*, Worsley says that the *James Caird* is clinker-
built, which means made of overlapping bits of wood. This is a mistake. In
Endurance he had written, correctly, "The *James Caird* was double-ended and
carvel built." The mistake appeared in the 1940 first edition of the shortened
book and has never been corrected. If you look at the *James Caird*, it is plain to
see that the planks butt on top of each other—that it is carvel-built, in other
words. It seems inconceivable that Worsley could have made this blunder,
knowing the boat intimately (and it had been built to his specifications, too).
The error may have been the work of an editorial gremlin.

It is stylistically inconsistent. Worsley's book, on the other hand, has both the common touch and a unified narrative voice.

Flashes of Shackletonian rhetoric survived the ghost of *South*. Arriving on South Georgia, Shackleton describes how they flung the adze, logbook, and cooker down on the beach: "That was all, except our wet clothes, that we brought out of the Antarctic, which we had entered a year and a half before with well-found ship, full equipment, and high hopes. That was all of tangible things; but in memories we were rich. We had pierced the veneer of outside things. We had 'suffered, starved, and triumphed, groveled down yet grasped at glory, grown bigger in the bigness of the whole.' We had seen God in his splendors, heard the text that Nature renders. We had reached the naked soul of man."

The twenty-two-foot six-inch *James Caird* was named after a Dundonian jute manufacturer who had sponsored the expedition. After the journey to South Georgia, Shackleton had it sent to Birkenhead, whence Worsley brought it to London in a goods truck hitched to a passenger train. It was the focus of various fund-raising efforts, including a spell on the roof of Selfridges. After Shackleton's death his school friend and benefactor John Quiller Rowett presented the boat to their alma mater, Dulwich College in southeast London. In 1967 it was lent to the Maritime Museum in Greenwich and restored in a display that included rocks collected on South Georgia by men from the modern HMS *Endurance*. The museum eventually grew tired of it, and in 1986 it returned to Dulwich, where it was stored among the lawn mowers.

The boat was resurrected in 1990 by another Dulwich alumnus, Harding Dunnett, who made it his mission to rehabilitate both it and Shackleton's reputation. He got the boat properly displayed in the North Cloister of the college, wrote a book, and set about founding the James Caird Society, which swelled to five hundred members and still meets twice a year to dine around the boat and toast Shackleton. I had seen many pictures of the *James*

Caird, but when I went to Dulwich to pay homage, I was shocked at its littleness. Its height above the water is not much greater than a bath. Was it really possible that they had sailed it eight hundred miles across the unforgiving Southern Ocean?

As *Endurance* slid down the English coast, Britain declared war on Germany. Shackleton offered his ship and all hands to the war effort, but the first lord of the Admiralty, one Winston Churchill, replied with a one-word telegram: "Proceed."

In *South*, Shackleton writes that once they had left home, "The war was a constant subject of discussion . . . and many campaigns were fought on the map during the long months of drifting." He adds a detail to Worsley's account of the meeting with the Norwegian manager of the whaling station after the crossing of South Georgia. The first question Shackleton asks the man is "When was the war over?" It was May 20, 1916. Like Scott, during the war years Shackleton was deployed as a symbol of British endeavor. Sir Arthur Conan Doyle said in a speech, "We can pass the eight Dreadnoughts, if we are sure of the eight Shackletons." Most of the twenty-eight signed up or were conscripted when they got back from the Antarctic, including Shackleton and Worsley. The contrast between their struggles in Antarctica and the slaughter in Europe punctuates their accounts like a refrain. Shackleton dedicated his book "to my comrades who fell in the white warfare of the south, and on the red fields of France and Flanders." Frank Hurley, the expedition photographer, ends his book *Argonauts of the South* with the words "Emerged from a war with nature, we were destined to take our places in a war of nations. Life is one long call to conflict, anyway." In *Shackleton's Boat Journey*, Worsley reports that he sold Third Officer Alfred Cheetham one match, to be paid for with a bottle of champagne when Cheetham opened "his little pub" in Hull. "He never paid the debt," states Worsley, "for he was killed fighting the Germans in the North Sea just before the Armistice."

After the war, Worsley went south with Shackleton again, aboard the wooden sealer *Quest*. On that journey, on January 5, 1922, Shackleton died in his cabin at South Georgia. Worsley ends *Endurance* with a moving account of the death of his friend. "For seven and a half years we had been the closest of friends," Worsley writes, "and for the greater part of that time we had been in daily contact. We had passed together through many valleys of shadow, and each time that we had won through the bonds which united us had been strengthened. I knew that I should never look upon his like again."

"Surely," he went on, "there is no end with such a man as Shackleton: something of his spirit must still live on with us."

Perhaps it was with one eye on commercial success that Worsley or his publishers called this account *Shackleton's Boat Journey*. Worsley was skipper of the *James Caird* and, as navigator, the man chiefly responsible for the boat journey's success. But Shackleton was the national hero, and he lies at the heart of the book. Written after his death, a loss Worsley felt keenly, it is a threnody to his leadership. His talent in this department is a leitmotif of the text. Worsley notes that no man under Shackleton's command ever suffered from scurvy, a fact he ascribes to his "constant care." The description in the first chapter of Shackleton saving Ernest Holness "by instinct" has the flavor of an Old Testament miracle. Indeed, there is something of the prophet about the Shackleton who emerges from these pages.

"We were full of hope and optimism—feelings that Shackleton always fostered," writes Worsley at a time when their situation looked its most hopeless. "He seemed to keep a mental finger on each man's pulse," he continues, noting that if Shackleton saw that a man was going down, he ordered hot milk all around without revealing for whom it had been ordered so the man would not feel ashamed. "So great was his care of his people," he writes, "that, to rough men, it seemed at times to have a touch of the woman about it." This was praise.

He was not a saint, thank God. Worsley writes in part 3 that the Boss, as they called him, was often irritable. In *Endurance*, Worsley said that on one of the rescue journeys back to Elephant Island, Shackleton appeared to blame him, Worsley, for the gale that blew up. Worsley took it nobly. "I was glad that he should have some little outlet for his misery."

Frank Wild, who served on all Shackleton's expeditions and took over as leader of the *Quest* expedition after the Boss died, said this at a meeting of the Royal Geographical Society on November 13, 1922: "I am in the unique position of having served with *all* the British Antarctic explorers of repute since my first voyage with the *Discovery* and of having an intimate first-hand knowledge of their work in the field. My opinion is that for qualities of leadership, ability to organize, courage in the face of danger, and resource in the overcoming of difficulties, Shackleton stands foremost, and must be ranked as the first explorer of his age." Apsley Cherry-Garrard, who went south with Scott, made a comparison that has been hijacked by almost every explorer since. "For a joint scientific and geographical piece of organization, give me Scott; for a Winter Journey, Wilson; for a dash to the Pole and nothing else, Amundsen: and if I am in the devil of a hole and want to get out of it, give me Shackleton every time."

Shackleton was the poet of the south. Hurley recounts an episode that took place when the men were leaving the crushed ship. They had removed some possessions, but a strict weight restriction was imposed on what they could carry. Just as they were about to set off, the Boss spotted an edition of Browning's poetry on the ice. He put his hand in his pocket and tossed a few sovereigns onto the floe. "I throw away trash," he said as he picked up the book, "and am rewarded with golden inspirations."

Worsley was born in Akaroa, New Zealand, in 1872. He was apprenticed at fifteen in sailing ships of the New Zealand Shipping Company and subsequently served as mate, then master, on government schooners in the South Pacific. After the transition to steam, he became a member of the Royal Naval Reserve. This is how he ends *First Voyage in a Square-Rigged Ship*, a *Boy's Own* tale of his early life, published in 1938. "Carrying our portmanteaus we were tramping toward the railway station when I saw a well-remembered figure approaching. I forgot that I was a full-blown sailor-man who had sailed round the world; I only remembered that I was a boy and that this was my father."

In *Endurance*, Worsley says that he joined Shackleton's expedition as a result of a dream. In this dream he was navigating a ship along London's New Burlington Street, which was full of ice. The next day ("Sailors are superstitious") he hurried off to Burlington Street and found the expedition offices. Displaying characteristic impulsiveness, Shackleton immediately engaged him as master. "Remembering this in that dim cold twilight," Worsley wrote in *Endurance*, "surrounded by a world of snow and ice, I silently breathed a prayer of thankfulness that I had gone to Burlington Street that morning that seemed so long ago, for whatever befell, I was living a great adventure, living side by side with a great man."

After the *Quest* expedition Worsley went north with the British Arctic Expedition and thereafter continued to go to sea in various trading vessels, including a spell treasure hunting on the Cocos Islands. By then he was a Royal Navy commander and the holder of an OBE. In the war he got a Distinguished Service Order and Bar and had three submarines to his credit. He died in 1943 in Claygate, Surrey. Worsley was a seaman in his bones, and his obituary in *The Polar Record* noted, "It was as a navigator that he stood supreme."

I would like to say a word about Worsley's feat of navigation in the *James Caird*. It was he who got them to South Georgia, not Shackleton. He was using dead reckoning, a method of establishing one's position using the direction and distance traveled rather than astronomical observation. This system involves taking the sun's position, but on the boat journey the sun made a brief appearance once or twice a week. Dead reckoning, writes Worsley, became "a merry jest of guesswork." In addition, the map he had of South Georgia was incomplete and inaccurate. His achievement is almost without equal in the long history of seamanship.

He emerges from the pages of his short book as an immensely likable figure, quick to praise his colleagues and sensitive enough not to name weaker men such as the frostbitten one who dropped the oar when they moved camp on Elephant Island. Worsley says he was sorry for the twenty-two when he was busy on the rescue mission—a largehearted sentiment, given the horrors he endured aboard the *James Caird*. His unpublished diaries, presented to the Scott Polar Research Institute by his widow the year he died, are consistently informative and jolly. On the day they abandoned ship, Worsley switched from ink to pencil, and eleven days later, camped on an ice floe, he wrote this: "While looking ahead and planning to meet all possible dangers, I do not worry about those dangers, which will probably be very great, but live comfortably and happy in the present, and can truly say that at present I am enjoying myself far more than I would in civilisation."

He is a natural storyteller. Like an old pro, he leavens his account with direct speech and breaks the relentless roll call of flannel-white skin and frozen toes with a beautifully written description of the albatross. In another moving passage he describes a beach littered with the debris of ships wrecked by the Southern Ocean. All the way through his book, the beauty of the Antarctic functions as a counterpoint to the men's ordeal. "Suddenly," writes Worsley, "the clouds parted, and the roseate cliffs of a great glacier shone high above the storm-tossed waters of the bay."

His prose style is measured and sparingly decked with imagery. In part 1, the ice creeps north "with its human freight." When Holness tumbles into the sea after the ice has split beneath him, Shackleton finds him in his sleeping bag in the sea "like a full-grown Moses." If the book has an emotional focus, it is the description of Worsley and Shackleton "snuggling" together at the helm of the *Caird*. "While I steered," writes Worsley, "his arm thrown over my shoulder, we discussed plans and yarned in low tones. We smoked all night—he rolled cigarettes for us both, a job at which I was unhandy. I often recall with proud affection memories of those hours with a great soul."

In part 3, Worsley twice writes that he sensed a fourth presence as he, Shackleton, and Tom Crean crossed the mountains of South Georgia. Shackleton had already made a meal of this in his own account. "When I look back at those days," he wrote in *South*, "I have no doubt that Providence guided us . . . I know that during that long and racking march of thirty-six hours over the unnamed mountains and glaciers of South Georgia it seemed to me that often we were four, not three. I said nothing to my companions on the point, but afterwards Worsley said to me, 'Boss, I had a curious feeling on the march that there was another person with us.' Crean confessed to the same idea. One feels 'the dearth of human words, the roughness of mortal speech' in trying to describe things intangible, but a record of our journeys would be incomplete without a reference to a subject very near to our hearts."

The fourth presence was assured its place in history when T. S. Eliot acknowledged that Shackleton's account had inspired a stanza in *The Waste Land*. Eliot's narrator asks, "Who is the third who walks always beside you?" Eliot didn't know that the fourth-presence story was a later fabrication to boost sales of *South*. All very Shackletonian.

For decades history favored Scott. Shackleton won fame in his lifetime, but Scott entered the national psyche. He not only reached the pole but also died a hero's death at a critical juncture in the country's history. Scott was relentlessly mythologized, and, perhaps for that reason, in recent years he has been put through the mill of historical revisionism. The two men were not friends. Scott was a Royal Navy man, whereas Shackleton—the difference explains a good deal—was in the merchant navy. Scott was very English, whereas Shackleton, who once stood unsuccessfully as a Unionist MP, was Anglo-Irish. Shackleton often acted on impulse. He is alleged to have recruited Ernest Joyce after he spotted him passing the expedition office on a bus. His personal and financial affairs were a muddle, and the phrase "long-suffering" could have been coined for his wife, Emily. It is not a surprise that he had run-ins with the Admiralty: he was too colorful for an institution. Sir Ernest was a showman. He drank too much, smoked too much, and slept with other men's wives: that's why we like him. He's like we'd like to be. Poor old Scott, on the other hand, was shy, and discreet, and prone to depression as we are.

But how likable Shackleton is. His star is again in the ascendant. The *Endurance* expedition in particular is at last recognized as the epic of survival that it was. Its memorabilia are fetching astonishing sums. In September 1996, Christie's auction house decided to try out a few Marston watercolors. George Marston was the *Endurance* artist; Worsley mentions that he caulked the seams of the *James Caird* with his paints. A picture of the three boats on a floe with a catalog price of £8,000–£10,000 went for £29,900. Marstons began tumbling out of attics up and down the land.

Vivian Fuchs finally crossed the continent more than forty years after Shackleton's aborted attempt. Earlier this decade the Norwegian Børge Ousland man-hauled across alone and unsupported. When I was at South Pole Station in 1994, the Norwegian skier Liv Arnesen poled in from Hercules Inlet on Christmas Day and sat down to roast turkey with us in the galley.

The Imperial Trans-Antarctic Expedition was a failure, in that it did not meet its goal. But as Roald Amundsen wrote in *The Daily Chronicle*, "Do not let it be said that Shackleton has failed . . . No man fails who sets an example of high courage, of unbroken resolution, of unshrinking endurance." *Shackleton's Boat Journey* is about the nobility of the human spirit. It is a timeless enough theme, whatever your personal pole. I have read a fair number of diaries kept by the early explorers, and when I was in Antarctica, I often thought of those pioneering souls. They seemed to dwell in some Homeric age of Antarctic exploration, their figures bestriding the bergs like crampon-clad colossi. An American geologist asked me one day, as we chip-chipped away at a patch of the Nansen ice sheet, whom I would have chosen to go with. Although I admired many men, it was an easy decision.

It would have been Shackleton.

1998

Apsley Cherry-Garrard: Bad Trips

The Worst Journey in the World is a masterpiece, and its author is a hero—a true hero, I mean, not one of those tin-pot adventurers who crowd the front pages in our own gruesomely unheroic age. He was a vital protagonist in a feat of exploration, survived against what seemed like insuperable odds in the middle of heartbreaking beauty and crucifying hardship, and lost his two best friends, his health, and his peace of mind to boot—then he went and redeemed those losses by transforming them, on the page, into an allegory of hope that will uplift the human spirit till the next ice age. What more can you ask of a hero?

He was born Apsley Cherry in 1886, still a cloudless era for the English landed classes. The roar of technological progress could barely be heard in genteel Bedford: the streets were lit by gas, the cabs were drawn by horses, the swollen tribes of domestic servants had not yet shrunk, even in the redbrick street where baby Apsley mewled. His father, a fifty-three-year-old colonel also called Apsley, had recently returned from more than twenty years' soldiering in India and Africa. The walrus-whiskered veteran was enjoying a peacetime post in command of Kempston Barracks on the outskirts of Bedford, and there he had met and married Evelyn Sharpin, the daughter of an eminent local doctor. Apsley senior was descended from a prosperous line of lawyers and colonial civil servants who had lately settled in Berkshire. When, in 1887, his elder brother died without issue, the colonel found himself the owner of Denford Manor, near Newbury, and other properties besides. He promptly retired from the regiment with the rank of honorary major general and shifted his family— Apsley junior already had a sister—down to leafy Berkshire. Five years later, when the general's aunt Honora Drake Garrard also died without issue, he inherited a much bigger estate up in Hertfordshire and a minor fortune to go with it. As a condition of the inheritance he was obliged to take his aunt's name in addition to his own. And so, in 1892, the name Cherry-Garrard came into existence.

The burgeoning family—two more girls had arrived—duly installed themselves in their new home, Lamer Park, just outside Wheathampstead. The house was a model of eighteenth-century architectural chastity (it was always said, in the family, that Robert Adam had been employed there), with well-stocked parkland landscaped by Humphry Repton in the golden age of the English country house estate. Apsley junior shortly submitted to prep school in the bracing air of Folkestone, and after that seven modestly unhappy years at Winchester College were followed by a more satisfactory stint as an undergraduate at Christ Church, Oxford, where his father and grandfather had preceded him. His eyesight was poor, and the difficulties this caused him were compounded by shyness and paralyzing anxiety. He read classics at first, but soon switched to modern history. He was not an especially gifted scholar and was awarded a third-class degree.

Sisters persisted, and Cherry, as he came to be known, was finally outnumbered by five to one. When his father died in 1907, he became a substantial landowner and head of the family, a responsibility he took seriously but did not enjoy. After graduating, he went off around the world on a cargo ship. He was tall (five feet ten), slim, and handsome, with dark brown hair, brown eyes, and well-proportioned features. The trouble was, he didn't know what to do with himself. When he traveled up to Scotland in the early autumn of 1908 for a shoot on a moor owned by his cousin Reginald Smith, he was at a loose end. But there he met Edward "Bill" Wilson, the doctor and naturalist who had accompanied Scott to the Antarctic on his first journey, in 1901. A committed Christian with marble-blue eyes and a raking stride, Wilson walked with his new friend through the mists of the grouse moors and told him stories about long marches and lonely camps in the snowfields of the south. Cherry had grown up with his father's tales of bivvying on the veld and, like all schoolboys, had pored over images of little wooden ships in the pincers of ice floes inching their way up the Northwest Passage or of doughty Britons battling their way through the broiling, malarial heart of Africa. He determined to apply for a position on Scott's second expedition.

Here *The Worst Journey in the World* takes up the baton. Cherry explains how he came to be appointed zoological assistant and how the *Terra Nova* steamed out of Cardiff in June 1910 among a flotilla of tugs. He was twenty-four when he sailed south, and two and a half years later he came back a different man. England was different too. Those years—1910 to 1913—turned out to be the most tumultuous of the twentieth century for Britain. The certainties of Cherry's youth ("God in his Heaven," as his exact contemporary Siegfried Sassoon put it, "and sausages for breakfast") had vanished as if in, it seemed to the young polar explorer in his bewilderment, a single national gulp.

In the first weeks of 1914 the denizens of the committee in charge of Scott's expedition, busily ensuring that its reputation was molded by their hands alone, asked Cherry if he would write the official narrative, setting down for posterity the story of the whole show (as Scott's deputy, Teddy Evans was first in line for the job, but he was too busy advancing his naval career). Cherry was delighted, and with characteristic diligence began interviewing scientists and seamen, writing to firms that had supplied equipment, and amassing piles of paper listing exactly what had gone south with the *Terra Nova*. Essentially, he was planning to compile a guide for future explorers. Then the war came, and he hurried off to command a battalion of armored cars in Flanders. After a few months, having seen little action, Cherry was invalided home with ulcerative colitis, a debilitating condition associated with anxiety and one for which there was no effective cure. His convalescence was long, and painful, but through it his thoughts on his book matured. In his attitude to writing he was influenced in no small measure by a friendly neighbor whose land abutted his own. He was the most famous author in the world, and his name was George Bernard Shaw.

A fugleman for those out of step with the times, Shaw was an ideal companion and mentor for Cherry. I do not think *The Worst Journey* would be so wonderful had the two men never met. Shaw helped Cherry realize that he did not want to write the standard expedition narrative, a wooden affair lacking psychological light and shade. By the start of 1920, Cherry had severed his links with the expedition committee and turned himself into an independent author. His working title was now "Never Again: Scott, Some Penguins, and the Pole" (he had briefly considered calling the book "To Hell: With Scott"). Although "Never Again" survived at the top of his powerful final chapter, Cherry realized that the title was a weak one for a whole book. In a letter drafted, but never sent, to the Arctic explorer Vilhjalmur Stefansson, Cherry later revealed, "It was objected that it [the title] was too much like, 'Christ, Some Coppers, and the Cross.'" This last has a Shavian ring.

In December 1922, *The Worst Journey in the World* appeared in a two-volume edition financed by the author and distributed by the publishing firm Constable. Together the books tell the story of the expedition from beginning to end, but Cherry draws a landscape, not a map. The winter journey to Cape Crozier lies at the heart of the narrative, literally and emotionally; this is the journey that was the worst in the world. In the blackness of a polar winter Cherry and his friends Bill Wilson and Henry "Birdie" Bowers trekked across Ross Island to the Cape Crozier rookery to collect the eggs of the emperor penguin. At that time it was thought that emperor embryos, if examined at a sufficiently early stage of development, would provide a vital link in the evolutionary chain (a theory subsequently disproved). The three men did not take dogs: they pulled their own sledges for five weeks, often over ice ridges that were six feet high. The temperature fell to minus 76°F, their teeth shattered in the cold, and the tent blew away. But they were still friends when they staggered back to the hut. "In civilization," Cherry wrote, "men are taken at their own valuation because there are so many ways of concealment, and there is so little time, perhaps even so little understanding. Not so down South. These two men . . . were gold, pure, shining, unalloyed."

The following February, after marching more than halfway to the pole, Cherry took a team of dogs out from the hut as winter shouldered in across the polar plateau. He drove them 130 miles south to a food depot in order to wait for Captain Scott and his four companions, expected home from the pole any day. Cherry tells the story, in *The Worst Journey*, of the decisions he made on this abortive trip and why he made them. But he could have made other decisions, and they might have led to other outcomes. He could never forget it. In November of that same year he pushed back the cambric flap of a small tent buried in drift fewer than 13 miles from where he had made his last camp on that dog journey—the last camp, that is, before turning back. In the gloom he made out Birdie and Bill, frozen solid, like wood, and lying on either side of Scott. All three had perished on the return march from the pole. "That scene," Cherry wrote, "can never leave my memory." Many years later he said that his book— this book—was a memorial to Bill and Birdie. "It is hard," Cherry wrote, "that often such men must go first when others far less worthy remain."

So what about the book? It is a blend of narrative, reflection, and anecdote threaded with literary reference and allusion and the occasional historical digression. Cherry is a most English writer, his prose characterized by quizzical detachment, a fine sense of irony, and a capacity for gloom tempered with elegiac melancholy. The bitter brilliance of his sentences glimmers with dignified skepticism. As a stylist he is Mozart rather than Wagner, eschewing the tempests in favor of harmonious quadrilles and sonatas. The words of *The Worst Journey* are as plain as crotchets on a stave.

It was instantly recognized as a modern classic, a few dissenting voices notwithstanding. The London *Evening Standard* reviewer called it "the most wonderful story in the world," and Shaw announced that its success "has exceeded all expectations." As the double-decker cost three guineas, the price of a weekend at the seaside, the books hardly raced off the shelves, but to Cherry the thought that he had put the record straight was more important. "It has done what I specifically wanted it to do," he wrote to his printer, "get the business into some kind of perspective and proportion." But he did want the book read, and to his unending delight, throughout his lifetime many editions followed the Constable original, both in foreign lands and in Britain. (The work first appeared as a single volume in 1937.) After a hesitant start in the United States, a country Cherry profoundly mistrusted, in the spring of 1930 the Dial Press finally brought the book out. "Where shall the likes of it," asked the *New York Times* reviewer, "be read for sheer strength, clarity and beauty of phrase in the literature of polar exploration?" Dial's timing was flawless. Antarctica had been on the front pages for months, as the young Virginia naval pilot Richard Byrd had just claimed to have flown over the South Pole in an aluminum airplane—the first man there since Scott. But *The Bookman* was far more impressed with Cherry's story. "It makes Byrd's journey," the review read, "seem no more harassing than a train trip from Albany to Troy." ("He [Cherry] is plainly far more intelligent than most explorers," wrote H. L. Mencken in *The American Mercury*, though this was not a hotly contested field.) Back at home, in June 1937 two smart sixpenny volumes appeared as numbers 99 and 100 in Allen Lane's revolutionary Penguin series. A poster was printed depicting a penguin with a cricket bat tucked under one flipper bowing to a distant crowd. "We celebrate our centenary," read the caption, "with Mr. Cherry-Garrard's *Worst Journey in the World*."

Many officers and scientists on Scott's team also wrote books about the expedition. None have lasted: all take a factual approach that ignores the gloopy layers of emotional and imaginative experience that make us human. The Antarctic committee rushed out an edited version of Scott's diary in 1913, and it is rightly recognized as a significant contribution to the literature of exploration. But Scott has lost his mythic status, and the diary reads now more like a historical document than a work of art. And of course, the world has shrunk: even young women writers find their way to the South Pole these days, and the bookshelves are jammed with tales of contemporary polar antics. But *The Worst Journey in the World* has endured. Why? Because, like all great writers (and he is a great writer), Cherry frees his story from the confines of its time and place. Yes, he conjures a specific landscape. Who can forget his descriptions of the pleated, blue-shadowed cliffs of a glacier, the patter of dogs whooshing across the snow crust, and the friendly smell of tobacco at the end of a long day on the trail? Yes, he writes about crampons and snow goggles. But his description and detail are a means to an end. The book is a parable, which is what he most wanted it to be. It is about not the winning or the losing (or being the fastest or the first without oxygen or any other superlative); it is about "the response of the spirit": a notion as valid today as it was in 1922 or in 1322. "We did not forget the please and the thank you," Cherry noted in his account of the trek to Cape Crozier. "And we kept our tempers, even with God." After all, as Cherry acknowledged, we all have our winter journeys, sooner or later. And if you march them, he concluded—you see there really is hope there, at the bottom of it all—"you will have your reward, so long as all you want is a penguin's egg."

The book was published in the same year as *The Waste Land* and *Ulysses*, works that epitomized the new wave of literary modernism. Both Cherry and *The Worst Journey* are at first glance deeply traditional. Yet a central preoccupation of each, the notion of the sterility and fragmentation of postwar Western culture, is also a vital modernist theme—as in Eliot's "heap of broken images." So Cherry wasn't entirely out of step.

Cherry married Angela Turner in September 1939, a popular time to wed. She was a land agent's daughter from Ipswich and thirty years his junior. Theirs was a happy union, though there were desperately bleak periods when Cherry submitted to nervous breakdowns and what would today be diagnosed as clinical depression. Again, like his contemporary Sassoon, Cherry combined acute self-awareness with an inability to act on it. He was like Robert Graves's cabbage-white butterfly, which, having "never . . . /[m]aster[ed] the art of flying straight, . . . /[L]urches here and here by guess/And God and hope and hopelessness." As his biographer, I am often asked whether his experiences in the south, above all his loss of his most loved friends and the vague sense that he might have been able to save them, "caused" his mental collapse. Of course, I do not know. I think Cherry was genetically predisposed to depression, and he might well have entered his tunnels if he had never been south of Brighton. After all, many do. But events in the Antarctic did not help him cope with his anxiety. In short, I think a toxic combination of genes and events set off a dysfunctional reaction in his neurotransmitters that brought him down.

He died in 1959 at the age of seventy-three, of congestive heart failure and bronchopneumonia.

Who was Cherry? He was a cynic and a committed pessimist. He responded deeply to literature and was not very interested in God. Like many authors, he found writing easier than speaking. He liked ice cream and strong coffee, enjoyed bird-watching and book collecting, and was determined never to have children. In middle age he was a curmudgeonly reactionary: he complained a lot, had an obsessive hatred of vicars and income tax, and was convinced that the world was going—had gone, rather—to the dogs ("This post-war business is inartistic," he wrote in the little-read preface to the second edition of *The Worst Journey*, "for it is seldom that anyone does anything well for the sake of doing it well.") But in his heart he was a romantic: he believed in the redemptive powers of both nature and art. How can you resist a man who wrote of the Antarctic photographs taken by Scott's "camera artist," Herbert Ponting, "Here in these pictures is beauty linked to tragedy—one of the great tragedies—and the beauty is inconceivable for it is endless and runs through eternity"? Somewhere in the deeper recesses of his consciousness, Cherry believed (I believe) in the perfectibility of the human spirit. In an introduction to George Seaver's 1938 biography of Bowers, Cherry wrote of Birdie's "spirit without boundaries." He went on to say that Birdie and his companions "have left something behind in men's minds; it is shadowy and intangible and perhaps a little fanciful, but it is something greater than all the pyramids in the world, and much more important."

Cherry was thirty-six when *The Worst Journey* was published. In many places his book—he only wrote one, as he had nothing further to say—reads like a restless threnody for lost youth; the disquiet of a man approaching middle age sings through the clear prose. There are moments of pure Chekhovian longing as he contemplates the dear distant days ("And the good times were such as the Gods might have envied us") and mourns the grubby superficiality of the present ("For we are a nation of shopkeepers"). It is this strand of lyricism that gives the book poetry. As a writer Cherry had flawless instincts, however, and he recognized that the tone of wistful recollection and sorrow had to be leavened with humor. "Polar exploration," he began robustly, "is at once the cleanest and most isolated way of having a bad time which has been devised." He smuggled in a lot of jokes.

The greatest adventure book of all time? I think so. None other combines such a thrillingly gripping story with such heartbreaking prose: no, I cannot think of a single one that comes close. *Seven Pillars of Wisdom*? As a writer, Lawrence is a lightweight next to Cherry. Maurice Herzog's *Annapurna*? Fabulous, but in the end it's just about mountains. *Arabian Sands*? A classic, but it lacks the godlike touch. From the crucible of suffering, Cherry fashioned a great work of art. Like all writers, he goes on talking after his death—and we should listen. *The Worst Journey*, as its author wrote, "is a story about human minds with all kinds of ideas and questions involved, which stretch beyond the furthest horizons."

2003

Freya Stark

I first encountered Freya Stark twenty years ago, when I was beating my first book into submission. I had made a six-month journey around the Greek island of Euboea (known as Evia in Modern Greek), and I wanted to write about the island's ancient past as well as my own adventures. But nothing seemed to make the runny typescript bind together. Should I give up? Browsing the travel shelves in a secondhand bookshop one desperate afternoon, I pulled out Stark's 1956 volume, *The Lycian Shore*.

She traveled widely in Loristan, Palestine, Lebanon, Iran, Syria, and Iraq, and she was the first Western woman to travel through the Hadhramaut, that part of the Arabian Peninsula which is now Yemen. She located the long-fabled Valley of the Assassins halfway between Tehran and the Caspian Sea, a gripping adventure recounted in 1934 in her first travel book. (The Assassins were a Persian Shia sect.) A woman traveling alone is a suspicious figure even in 2010. But seventy years ago?

Stark was a gifted linguist, an accomplished ethnographer, and a useful unofficial diplomat. During World War II, she undertook valuable work for the Foreign Office in Baghdad and Cairo. Her journeys and her books (there were more than thirty) were a heady mix of hardship and luxury, scholarship and mischief,

loneliness and intimacy: all perfect combinations, and the op-
positions give her prose its tensile strength. In *The Lycian Shore*,
Stark describes a journey down the Aegean coast of Turkey in
the thirty-foot yacht *Elfin*. Like all true writers, she recognized
that the present is above all else a continuation of the past, and
on Turkish shores she found tangible evidence of the unity of
landscape and history. Picking her way among ruins abandoned
by Greeks and Persians, Stark writes of "a bond of past and future, with us between them." She was reading about the campaigns of Alexander the Great as *Elfin* sailed by those very spots
where he had addressed his armies. Reflecting that Alexander's
notion of unity throughout Asia Minor had quickly evaporated,
she concludes nonetheless, "It left behind it in the barbarian
night—like a touchstone, or Cinderella slipper on the steps of the
Greek palace—the civilization by which we live today." Not an
original thought, but the expression gives it new life.

Making the connection: that was the key.

If I had to pick a favorite from her oeuvre, it would be *A Winter
in Arabia*. Although the book describes the 1937 journey through
the Hadhramaut, Stark wrote it in 1971, by which time she had
digested a lifetime of experience, both of foreign lands and of
that more hostile territory, her own heart. A guest of the tribes,
she conjures little girls in magenta silk trousers, their silver anklets
frilled with bells, the drumbeats of the sultan's procession, and
veiled women at her sickbed bearing gifts of salted melon seeds.
A Winter in Arabia is also Stark's funniest book. A set piece
at the races—only one horse competed—ends in farce, with Stark
the stooge. What a wonderful film this would make, though it's
hard to see anyone but Peter O'Toole in drag playing the heroine,
reprising his Lawrence of Arabia.

A Winter in Arabia is an intimate book, less freighted with
history than *The Lycian Shore* and more the expression of a
woman who has come to terms with it all. Stark no longer had to
write about the continuing past: it had become part of her, and of

her vision of the world. I learned a lot from the mature Stark. How much can one put in of oneself? Very little—but one well-chosen sentence can season a chapter with personal flavor. There is no such thing as a natural writer. But there is an instinct to keep reworking until the thought is married to the words. Stark had it. She was especially good when deciding whether a fine topographical description had a deep thought behind it or was just showing itself off. The older she got, the more she made sure that her prose sprang from a true consideration of essential meaning. In *A Winter in Arabia*, as in other late works, she switches from distant shot to close-up in half a sentence, as Chekhov does in the plays. The effect is dynamic. It's hard to think of a writer in the travel game who most closely demonstrates the merits of Flaubert's three rules for good writing: clarity, clarity, and finally clarity. When I reread her now, her restrained powers of description, husbanding the lyrical moment, shine as brightly as they ever did, and they will continue to shine for all eternity.

By the 1950s she was famous, as a writer and a traveler. She glittered in the drawing rooms of London and loved a party; then, having drunk her fill, she ran off to peek out at the world from a solitary tent. Isn't that the best kind of life imaginable? Although she was small and unprepossessing, she loved clothes and once had a pheasant made into a hat. "There are few sorrows," she said, "through which a new dress or hat will not send a little gleam of pleasure, however furtive." Indeed. Stark also had a penchant for soldiers. (Who doesn't?) But she was unhappy in love, and it was travel that got her out of the hole; then she wrote off her losses on the page. I wish I didn't understand that quite so profoundly.

Stark once wrote to her editor in London, John Murray, asking him kindly to send a tin bath out to her in the wild interior of Yemen: more than one could expect of one's publisher today. But her books are more relevant than ever. Besides sheer enjoyment, one should read her for a fresh perspective on the intractable issues dogging Christian-Muslim relations. She was able to see both sides, and what she found was similarity, not difference. In *A Winter*, reflecting on a row between a British archaeologist and local laborers, she wrote, "One is always coming upon these mutual and identical criticisms from East and West." The greatest woman traveler of the twentieth century? I think so, though Gertrude Bell, a fellow Arabist twenty-five years Stark's senior, runs her a close second. (Stark considered Bell overrated, accusing her of never staying anywhere long enough to get to the heart of things.)

"One can only really travel," Stark once said, "if one lets oneself go." My sentiments entirely. But I must give her the last word. "As we walked through the welter of civilizations, layer upon layer," she writes in *The Lycian Shore*, "the moonlight made the poplars bright like waterfalls and the marble seats of a small odeum shone through them . . . [T]he rich light . . . mixed with lamps that shone from cafés, where only a few fishermen now lingered; and lay warm and soft on the decks of caiques pulling at their hawsers by the quay; and on the castle towers in the water, where a shadowy gate was roofed with shafts of horizontal columns, green stone carried from Halicarnassus over the bay."

2010

Four Biographies

A word about book reviewing. The literary editor in Cyril Connolly's *Enemies of Promise* was called Mr. Vampire, because he sucked the young reviewer's blood by diverting his talents from proper work—the writing of his own books. There is an element of truth there, but still, I always liked reviewing and can't kick the habit—though I regret the days have long gone when reviewing financed other, less overtly commercial work.

The following four pieces are reviews of authorized biographies, each of a travel writer I admire. I first read Martha Gellhorn when I was eighteen. I chanced on a paperback copy of *The Face of War* in a secondhand bookshop and devoured the first thirty pages standing there among the shelves. It was Gellhorn's blend of fact and fiction that ensnared me. The inscription on the flyleaf read, "To Joyce, from Mother. God Bless. And Happy Travels." Others had followed Martha before me. I still feel the same way about her. I wish I had met her. In 1998, aged ninety, Gellhorn decided she had had enough. The light had gone out, so she swallowed what she needed.

Not only do I think she is a marvelous writer—at her best, one of the best—I also identify with Gellhorn the woman. "The open road," she wrote, was "my first, oldest and strongest love"; elsewhere she recorded that "only work gives shape and sanity to life"; and she once wrote to a friend to say, "I have only to go to a different country, sky, language, scenery, to feel it is worth living." I feel and think all those things. Like Martha, I loathe domesticity (she called it "the kitchen of life"). She was obsessed with her weight; so am I, and I hate myself for it as she did. When a love affair was going well, her biographer Caroline Moorehead writes with acuity, "It was not in Martha's nature to feel safe, and nothing gave her a greater sense of unease than her own character." Golly, yes. But besides being by far the greater writer, Gellhorn had so many qualities I lack: she was utterly without self-pity and contemptuous of self-indulgence.

CHEWING CEMENT: MARTHA GELLHORN

Martha Gellhorn, who lived from 1908 to 1998, was a feisty, fastidious American war correspondent. She was writing about the fighting for six decades, and although each conflict was different, her message was the same: "There is neither victory nor defeat; there is only catastrophe."

She was born in St. Louis, her father a doctor, her mother an early suffragette and social reformer. After a happy childhood she went to the prestigious Bryn Mawr College but did not graduate. In 1930 she turned up in Paris with two suitcases, a typewriter, and $75. She was off. And what a life it was. Lovers, almost all of them married; abortions; assignments; books, usually greeted with mixed reviews; a rape—Caroline Moorehead documents the lot with zest and insight (*Martha Gellhorn: A Life*). Gellhorn settled on various continents, obsessively fixing up houses (houses are a leitmotif of this book). Then of course there was Hemingway. They covered the Spanish Civil War together: when fascist shells hit their hotel, the prostitutes came scuttling out of the foreign correspondents' rooms "crying in high voices like birds." Gellhorn married the old dog in 1940, and the pair stayed together for seven years. Moorehead does not have much time for him. "I'll show you, you conceited bitch," he shouted at his third wife. "They'll be reading my stuff long after the worms have finished with you."

When she was forty-two, Gellhorn adopted a son in Italy. The pages in which she finds her baby boy are intensely moving and brilliantly done. The adoption was not without its difficulties: Moorehead handles this with sensitivity. Gellhorn went on to get married once more, in 1954, that time to Tom Matthews, an amiable, patrician American living in London.

An experienced biographer whose previous subjects include Bertrand Russell and Freya Stark, Moorehead knew Gellhorn for decades: the older woman was a friend of her parents'. She is scrupulous in her insistence on context, striving, almost always successfully, to conjure the topography and zeitgeist against which her mesmerizing protagonist moved. This is especially important in the early years, a time when, as Moorehead has it, "the Coolidge prosperity under which Martha had grown up had seen young women for the first time earn decent salaries, move around freely and unchaperoned and live in apartments on their own."

Moorehead is chiefly preoccupied with two sides of her subject: the writer and the lover (what else is there?). Like almost all really good writers, Gellhorn found writing excruciatingly hard: she called the bad times, when words didn't come, "chewing cement." Her trademark, as Moorehead says, was "her ability to weave the daily scenes of war into an infinitely larger picture." She wrote short stories and novels as well as hundreds of nonfiction pieces and several nonfiction books; her best-known book, the autobiographical *Travels with Myself and Another*, appeared in 1978 and still sells steadily. She was a hard worker, and a conscientious one, and she had no regard for scoops. For sixty years she wrote about the poor, the weak, and the dispossessed, whether in the textile mill towns of North Carolina or the bombed-out villages of South Vietnam.

She was blond and tall with very long legs, one of those women who aren't especially beautiful but can be fantastically good-looking. There was no shortage of lovers. At the close of a single year of her thirties she noted that in twelve months she had had three major love affairs and four minor ones and had got pregnant by an eighth man. But she didn't get much out of sex and said she never knew complete love, except for that she felt for her mother, whom she called her "true north." In respect of the individual love affairs, Moorehead notes rather wonderfully at one point, "she had never crossed that odd line between affection and addiction." God, she was tough. "I want you," she wrote to one married lover. "Find out for yourself whether you want me."

To keep her demons at bay, she took off. She thrived on hardy, solitary travel and was never afraid, she said; she felt instead "angry, every minute, about everything." She covered her first war when she was twenty-eight, long before the American military was prepared to accredit female correspondents. One sunny day in May 1945 she went to Dachau. "I do not really hope now," she wrote to a friend afterward. "Not really; I only feel one can never give up." She was hollowed out by the misery of that war, of all wars. It is here, halfway through Moorehead's account, that the book takes root, and one believes in Martha Gellhorn.

This is a deeply sympathetic portrait, which is not the same of course as a hagiographic one. As a biography it is a model of what Hugh Kingsmill called "the complete sympathy of complete detachment." Moorehead had abundant sources for most of the years under scrutiny, as Gellhorn was a committed letter writer, and there are many people alive who have memories of the last decades. The narrative drive never stalls as the action zigzags between Europe and the Americas, with forays into Asia and a longer one into East Africa, which Gellhorn discovered relatively late. A starry cast of walk-on parts ranges from Eleanor Roosevelt, a mentor and confidante from the early 1930s, to H. G. Wells, who pretended Gellhorn slept with him, and Sybille Bedford, who said that meeting Martha was like being exposed to a 1,500-watt bulb.

"I do not wish to be good," Gellhorn wrote, "I wish to be hell on wheels, or dead." My own sentiments exactly. She could be a monster. "It is impossible not to feel sorry for Matthews," Moorehead notes as the second marriage goes off the rails. Although Gellhorn does not emerge from these pages as a likable figure, she is a deeply admirable one, and in certain essential ways desperately attractive. I took away from the book above all an overwhelming sense of what it is to be human. You can't ask much more of a biography than that, can you?

2003

Gellhorn attracts me; the Bruce Chatwin who steps from this next book repels me. First, though, I admire Chatwin as a writer—hence his inclusion here. I learned a lot from him when I was starting out, absorbing his aversion to the subordinate clause and his commitment to the wastepaper basket. Lesser travel writers colonize a territory; the best ones, like Chatwin, never do. He was a stylist above all else. I don't care for his ideas. The phrase "the worst of all tragedies is the plight of the semi-educated" recurs in his famous notebooks. The worst? I don't think so, Brucie. The worst of all tragedies is seeing your children roasted alive in a small African war, or being part of a whole population of ordinary people rendered extinct by a crazed demagogue. Here was a man who dealt with the shadows by refusing to entertain doubts about anything at all. Admirers of the poise, sanity, and balance of, say, *In Patagonia* can't help thinking of the author as poised, sane, and balanced. Chatwin, it turns out, was none of those things. Readers of *Eugene Onegin* would be forgiven for making the same mistake about Pushkin. In the case of both Pushkin and Chatwin, genius died young and so attracted sentimental sympathy. In this book Nicholas Shakespeare gives us a monster, sometimes unwittingly, I think. But what is that, in literature? Writers are only truly alive in their work.

FUCKING THE TEA COZY: BRUCE CHATWIN

Bruce Chatwin is the first full biography of an influential, even cultish modern writer who famously blurred the boundaries between fiction and nonfiction. Published in twenty-seven languages, as a writer and a human being Chatwin was a maverick. One lover, Miranda Rothschild, said, "He's out to seduce everybody, it doesn't matter if you are male, female, an ocelot or a tea cosy."

Chatwin presents a particular challenge to the biographer as he worked ferociously hard to create a mythical persona only distantly related to himself. Under the circumstances, Nicholas Shakespeare has done a splendid job (*Bruce Chatwin: A Biography*). An accomplished writer himself, like his subject he tells a gripping story. Adroitly manipulating the threads of Chatwin's life—"the uncanny good luck, the speedy in-and-out, the all-suggestive fragment, the speculative theory, the fascination with provenance and the origin of things"—Shakespeare describes books "cooking" in the writer's head and conjures sentences like this one to portray Chatwin's prep school: "After the war, the shortage of well-trained teachers explained the presence of some characters who would have found a comfortable billet in Evelyn Waugh's Llanabba." The text rattles along, its emotional highs and lows magnified by the author's eye for the dramatic moment. One chapter opens, "A little after 9.30 p.m. on 15 October 1958, Sotheby's new chairman Peter Wilson raised his gavel to auction seven Impressionist masterpieces. He had staked his career on this moment."

Often, though, in these 550 pages, I caught the whiff of the laundry list. There are too many interpolated comments from the garrulous cast of walk-on parts who knew Chatwin, as if Shakespeare were determined to move as far as possible from his subject's elliptical, pared-down prose. He is similarly heavy-handed with the background material: Does anyone care about the prep school headmaster's brothers? It would have been a more successful book if, after the years of diligent research, Shakespeare had distilled the material down and down and down until *Bruce Chatwin* were half its present length.

———

Born in 1940 to a prosperous Sheffield family, his father "a wise old sailor and a sound lawyer," Charles Bruce Chatwin "was a typical war baby, coddled by an anxious mother, fussed over by a team of elderly, mostly female relatives for whom he was the hope of the tribe." After public school he became a bright star at Sotheby's, enrolled late at university to read archaeology and flunked out, became another star at the *Sunday Times*, abandoned that too, and wrote some very, very good books. He was an uneasy bisexual, married once ("to stop myself going mad"), didn't have children, although he wanted to, and went to absurd lengths to conceal the fact that he had AIDS. He never settled anywhere and had some unusual habits like sitting on the toilet and defecating with the door open, no matter who might already be in the bathroom. At the end, he converted to Greek Orthodoxy.

What an unattractive person he was. We learn that he "never tolerated being teased," that he liked posh people, that he never washed up in twenty-three years of marriage, and that once, when he and his wife arrived at a restaurant with some *Sunday Times* cronies to discover that there wasn't a table big enough, Chatwin told his wife to clear off (she did). His lover Jasper Conran said, "Probably there was no one Bruce loved more than himself." One friend—a *friend*!—says in this book that "he [Chatwin] saw himself as a sort of present to mankind." He was horribly affected. V. S. Naipaul (limbering up in the wings in this book) reckoned he was trying to live down the shame of being the son of a provincial lawyer. At Sotheby's, Chatwin liked to go around pronouncing this and that to be a fake; many of his colleagues thought he was a fake. Anthony Powell wrote in his diary, "I always feel there was something a bit phoney about Chatwin."

He worked fantastically hard at the mythmaking, desperate to make himself fascinating. The individual details are trivial—who cares if he told people that his dad had to sell a Stradivarius to pay the school fees? But they add up to a failed person. As

Shakespeare's chapters unfurled, I was so repelled by this handsome man that I began, irrationally, to wonder if the books can really be that good after all. So I reread *In Patagonia*, went straight on to *Utz*, and reassured myself. He was a great writer, and his stories put a torch to the imagination. The most famous first line of any travel book ever written belongs to him. The 1977 minor masterpiece *In Patagonia* opens, "In my grandmother's dining room there was a glass-fronted cabinet and in the cabinet a piece of skin." (Was there? Of course not!) Chatwin's prose is cold, knuckle hard. "In the complete works of Bruce Chatwin," comments Salman Rushdie, "there is not a loving fuck."* The warm person Rushdie perceived behind this sepulchral prose does not leap from Shakespeare's pages. Chatwin charmed many people, but it is difficult to convey charm on a page.

Did the biographer succumb to the myth? He opens the first chapter with the Chatwin quotation "He was all things": well, so are we all, in our way. Shakespeare regurgitates some pretty unpalatable comments that don't contribute much to his portrait. Professor Zampini, who knew Chatwin in Patagonia, says he was "in the tradition of Drake, Cavendish, Darwin, Bridges. For a long time the only way to be universal was to be English." I wonder. "He was a Rupert Brooke," says James Ivory. I don't think so. But at other moments, Chatwin springs to life like a mosaic splashed with water. Shakespeare does not recoil from Chatwin's personal failures, and he tries to decipher the man behind the masks. He thinks that Chatwin's ambivalence about his sexuality and his fear of AIDS were bound up in the same energies that drove him to travel and write: "a case, perhaps, of a deficiency on one side of the balance producing the fruit of the other." Others called Chatwin a moral coward.

---

*Though there is a noisy one. Chatwin concludes somewhere that in his experience, unless you've had sex in a tent with a lion roaring outside, you haven't lived.

It is so difficult to have any sense of another person's inner life, but in this vastly enjoyable book Shakespeare successfully shines the beams of his torch onto a psychic landscape peopled by fearful monsters that Chatwin kept mostly at bay by continually moving and reinventing himself. His brother, Hugh Chatwin, reckons that about 60 percent of the content of the books is true. "It was the story that counted," he told Shakespeare.

1999

FICTION NEVER LIES: V. S. NAIPAUL

Born to the descendants of indentured Indians in colonial Trinidad in 1932, V. S. Naipaul rose to become one of the greatest writers of the twentieth century. The world was his subject: apparently stateless, he observed through a wide-ranging and narrow-focusing lens and turned what he saw into heartbreaking prose of almost unparalleled force and clarity. "In England I am not English," he wrote in a letter in 1954; "in India I am not Indian. I am chained to the 1000 square miles that is Trinidad; but I will evade that fate yet." And he did.

Patrick French, whose previous work includes a distinguished biography of Sir Francis Younghusband, has produced the first volume of the authorized life; the second will be published after the subject's death (*The World Is What It Is: The Authorized Biography of V. S. Naipaul*). One of the many strengths of his deeply impressive book lies in its analysis of the evolution of the master's style and the development of the themes and anxieties that shaped his writing over half a century. Naipaul left the Caribbean before he was eighteen when he won one of the coveted "island scholarships" and read English at Oxford. (French paints a charming picture of assorted Naipauls crowding around the television in Port of Spain straining to hear the words of Vido's early stories as they crackled over the BBC World Service.) From the 1957 novel *The Mystic Masseur* to the unclassifiable *The Enigma of Arrival* three decades on, race, sex, and deracination float remorselessly to the surface, and later, especially in the peripatetic journalism, so do the development of Islamic radicalism and the suggestion that it might be a serious threat to the world. In the 1980s the quickening impulse was replaced by what French calls "a technical brilliance," and Naipaul came to rely less on intuition and more on thought. The best of his books straddle fiction and nonfiction, and in this he is almost unique in our time.

In 1955, Naipaul married fellow Oxford graduate Patricia Hale. French read Pat's diaries in the voluminous Naipaul archives at the University of Tulsa, the first person to do so. She emerges as a kind of willing Paschal Lamb. A vital helpmeet, Pat supported her husband financially until it all came good. She was distraught at his twenty-four-year relationship with Margaret, the Argentinean mistress with whom Naipaul traveled openly on lengthy research trips and enjoyed what French discovers to be a sexually violent union. When her husband installs Margaret in the marital home in Wiltshire when Pat is in the London flat, the diary records, almost unbearably, "the awfulness of them handling my things, my kitchen things." Margaret, meanwhile, draws pictures of Naipaul's penis wearing sunglasses and a lime-green cowboy hat. Much later, when Naipaul famously revealed to *The New Yorker* that he had been "a great prostitute man," Pat was undone. "It could be said that I had killed her," Naipaul told French. "It could be said. I feel a little bit that way." When she got breast cancer, her husband continued traveling. Pat died on February 3, 1996. Six days later, Vidia's Pakistani fiancée moved into the marital home. Naipaul sent his literary agent to pay Margaret off. The headlines ran, A SPOUSE FOR MR. BISWAS.

With the instincts of a storyteller, French establishes a complicity with the reader by loosening up his text with humor. "The only Blacks he associated with now were Conrad and Barbara," he writes as his quarry's star rises. Naipaul learns he has "one" the 1971 Booker from an illiterate note by the publisher Carmen Callil. At a writers' symposium in Sweden our hero and Michael Frayn try their first sauna. When Kurt Vonnegut finds them naked on a bench ("It seems to be getting hotter"; "It's quite hot now"), they are mistakenly still in the changing room. Pity we couldn't have had this as a jacket image.

This is a gripping book, one of the most compelling biographies I have ever read. Like most good things, it is not perfect. At 550 pages few will wish it longer; we did not need to know the wartime occupation of the head porter at Univ, Naipaul's Oxford college. The prose changes gear with uncomfortable clunks as the story enters a new era. "In the days before mobile phones, email or texting," French explains, "everything had to be done by hand."

Faithless Hindu, unyielding mandarin, and fastidious Brahmin, Naipaul enjoyed presenting himself as a monster. Africa had no future, Islam was a calamity, France was fraudulent, and the Gold Coast remains just so, solely to annoy the liberals. The author's dismissal of his homeland became part of his persona. As French notes, he became "a phenomenon . . . a cultural purgative and an applauded pantomime villain." He justified his actions by portraying himself as a figure controlled by irreducible needs. A prodigious worker—what great writer isn't?—Naipaul wrote so densely in his notebooks that the word "cigarette" takes up less than a centimeter. Prizes piled up, as did financial rewards (Naipaul's income rocketed from an annual average of £7,600 in the 1970s to £143,600 in the 1980s), honorary doctorates, and the knighthood, though the phone will not ring from Stockholm until volume 2.*

*When Wole Soyinka won the Nobel in 1986, Naipaul said, "There they go, the Nobel committee, pissing on literature again." Fifteen years later he went to

French is too rigorous an analyst to succumb to the biographer's need to impose coherence. But a coherent picture does emerge from these pages. It is a picture of humanity, of an intellectually incorruptible man battling to make sense of it all while failing as a human being. "An autobiography can distort; facts can be realigned," Naipaul told French. "But fiction never lies: it reveals the writer totally."

2008

POSTSCRIPT

You have to admire someone who doesn't give a shit. A few years ago I did a stint on the Council of the Royal Society of Literature, and when a revered Indian sage died in Oxford, we asked Naipaul to write his obituary for the society's magazine. To our surprise, he agreed. The piece came in, to length and on time. It began, "Nirad Chaudhuri was an old fool."

Many consider Naipaul the greatest living writer in English—the first to say it being V. S. Pritchett (Philip Roth pips him, in my book, but that's a high bar). Patrick French pronounces *A Bend in the River* Naipaul's greatest novel, and, presumably in homage, its first line furnishes the title of the biography. My vote goes to *A House for Mr. Biswas*, a loving fictional tribute to Naipaul's father and the first book in which the author entered what Pritchett termed "the determined stupor" out of which great books are born, as the writer becomes consumed by the writing. Though one cannot forget the way in which the India books glitter with pessimistic intensity. *An Area of Darkness* (1964) recounts the author's first visit to his ancestral homeland, a country until that point "out in the void beyond the dot of Trinidad." There was a certain asceticism about Naipaul's sensibility on that journey, pierced only when he talks admiringly of a girl's breasts, or keeps visiting the lavatory on a plane to pat on free eau de cologne, or rants about the horribleness of Americans.

Stockholm to collect his own Nobel Prize, and nothing was said in the urination department. I just love that about him. It makes me feel good to be alive just thinking about it.

As is often the case, one sees how good he is all the more clearly when one notices how bad he can be. And he didn't stop in time. I make no comment on *The Masque of Africa* (2010). French does not say so, but I suspect Naipaul has never been much of a reader himself. It all came from within.

I love the way Naipaul is more interested in failure than success. He is right. Failure is more attractive. The recurrent theme of exile in all the books is consistently convincing: an exile that was literal in his case, metaphoric in mine, and yours, and everyone's. Naipaul was almost always on nobody's side. And although nothing of the self is ever overtly present in the prose, the strong narrative center of reserve never weakens. It holds everything together, like a centripetal force. There is some kind of integrity at the heart of him.

When he accepted the post of writer in residence at Makerere University in Uganda in 1966, Naipaul arrived to inform his hosts that he took the title at its word: he intended to remain in his residence and write. But he did go out to jog. His partner was Paul Theroux. Ah yes, Theroux. French refuses to admit the brilliance of *Sir Vidia's Shadow*, Theroux's memoir of the ultimately failed friendship, thinking instead that if he shows some of it was made up, as he does, he will diminish its value. French goes to some lengths to show that Theroux was a servile pest who wouldn't leave Naipaul alone. ("He wrote tourist books for the lower classes," comments the master.) But Theroux comes out on top. Why? Because *Sir Vidia's Shadow* offers a master class in the power of detached irony married to acute observation, and Theroux smuggles in a killing base note of regret.

I admire Theroux. I might be the only person still standing who does. I can't say why his popularity has waned, except to acknowledge, first, that all tides turn and, second, that readers got fed up with Theroux the narrator being so irritable on the road. *The Great Railway Bazaar*, Theroux's 1975 account of a looping rail journey between London and Asia, became an international bestseller and launched fleets of other people's travel books. It took him four months to make the journey and only another four to write the book. In *Bazaar*, as in all his best books (*The Old Patagonian Express, Dark Star Safari, Ghost Train to the Eastern Star*), the brilliance lies in Theroux's ability to deploy a sequence of close-up shots to form a semi-global panorama. In the detail, he recognizes that the man at the bottom of the heap tells the truest truth about his land. Noting that "luxury is the enemy of observation" (agreed), Theroux instinctively homes in—like Greene—on the seedy, the tired, and the second-rate.

Funny, informative, and lyrical, Theroux cannot be challenged in the field he reinvented. He has an almost perfect ear for the rhythm of his prose. "The century-old station at Haydarpasa," one chapter begins, "was floodlit and looked like an opera house on the night I crossed the Bosporus to take the night express to Ankara." Like almost all true writers, Theroux is a hard worker, and his output over a long career has been prolific. The whole of it is bound together by his strong clear voice, a unique voice. Unlike Naipaul and that other master, Norman Lewis, Theroux is omnipresent in his work, not an agent of his material: it is a signature of his style. In his observations he is true to his experience, and this commitment to the truth extends to himself. In *Sunrise with Seamonsters*—among my favorite of his books—he tells the story of an evening in Kampala under curfew in 1966. He was with a friend, and each of them had taken a girl back to Theroux's apartment. Late at night, Theroux suggests to his friend that they leave the sleeping girls and go for a walk. While they are out, Theroux reveals that he wants to swap girls: he would like to slip back into his friend's bed and enjoy a different companion in the morning. The friend agrees. "Habiba was amused when she discovered," writes Theroux, "awaking as the act of love began, that someone else was on top of her." This is a horrible story, but I like the fact that Theroux is honest enough to tell it.

His early books sold the best, but to my mind the mature Theroux is the one to read. In the later work he acknowledges lower expectations, a contempt for political promises, and—crucially, I think, for the creative imagination—the fact that "after a certain age the traveler stops looking for another life." My experience exactly. In comparing two European–Asian train journeys thirty years apart, he concluded that "the greatest difference was in me. I had survived the long road that leads to the present." Like me, Theroux celebrated being fifty with a book (he had rather more justification, but let that pass). In *Fresh Air Fiend* he summed up the experience. Turning fifty, he reckoned, is like being "marooned on a little island, from which there is no rescue, but only different kinds of defeat."

The 1970s tried to reinvent the 1930s in travel writing, if not in couture. The 1930s were the golden age: one thinks of Norman Douglas, Peter Fleming, Graham Greene, and Evelyn Waugh. But Robert Byron leads the pack. *The Road to Oxiana*, his most celebrated book, retailed the saga of the author's journey to Persia and Afghanistan with Christopher Sykes. In his book *Abroad*—published in 1980 and itself brilliant—the critic Paul Fussell so far forgets himself as to say, "What *Ulysses* is to the novel between the wars and what *The Waste Land* is to poetry, *The Road to Oxiana* is to the travel book."

ALMOST CASTRATED: ROBERT BYRON

Robert Byron is the travel writer's travel writer. Between the wars he motored across the Balkans in an open-topped Sunbeam and galloped over the central Asian steppe on a wooden saddle, a notebook in one pocket and a glass jar of Fortnum's chicken in aspic in the other. His books still dazzle. Like Alexander Kinglake, George Curzon, and Norman Douglas, he was an exponent of the fine English tradition that upheld travel as a learned pursuit.

He was born in 1905 in Wembley, hardly a cradle of the fine architecture he came to worship. His father, a civil engineer, was perennially short of cash, but still he managed to dispatch the boy to Eton. After Oxford (he was booted out, but right at the end) the young Byron moved to London and began a career in journalism, making a strong start by getting sacked from the *Daily Mail*. From then on, he traveled and wrote continually, producing a robust body of articles, many for *The New Statesman*, travel books, works on art, and even a jointly authored comic novel. He was also a stylish draftsman and a talented photographer, loitering among the ruins with a sketchbook and a cumbersome camera in a tin box.

The early journeys were unpromising. "How horrible most of Europe is," he complained to Henry Yorke, the only friend who was a better writer than he. But things looked up. He loved Mount Athos, where Byzantine frescoes in barrel-vaulted chapels fueled his gathering prejudice against classical art. The following year he motored around Spain in a green Bentley to study El Greco, Gavin Henderson at the wheel only slowing down from seventy to fifty to swig from a bottle of Vouvray. Byron looked like Queen Victoria—short, with a yellowish complexion, a pudgy face, and slightly popping eyes. Highly strung by nature, he was easily bored, often bad tempered, and regularly rude. He loved collecting beautiful things, had immaculate taste, and was fascinated by clothes and fabrics. Above all he had a passion for architecture that remained constant throughout his life. James Knox has a keen appreciation of the architectural zeitgeist, as any writer on Byron must (*Robert Byron: A Biography*). When the Duke of Norfolk insisted on pulling down Norfolk House, one of the masterpieces of London, Byron wrote in *The New Statesman*, "When noblesse ceases to oblige, it is not surprising that richesse should do likewise." In India, Byron thought Edwin Lutyens's Viceroy's House in Delhi "the first real vindication of modern architecture." (He was closely associated with *The Architectural Review*, the first magazine to engage with modernism in buildings.) Having led the Victorian revival, Byron awakened to the wonders of Byzantine art during a trip to Italy in 1923. "He was at the forefront of the rediscovery of Byzantine civilisation," according to Knox, looking to Oswald Spengler as a "powerful voice bestowing authority upon his own anti-classical prejudices." The decorated Timurid fragments he studied on the Persian trip led Byron to abandon his puritanical creed, but the highlight was the eleventh-century Gumbad-i-Kabus, "a tapering cylinder of café-au-lait brick" that "ranked with the great buildings of the world."

In his travel books, as Knox shows, Byron early on established the method of suggesting the spontaneity of speech through quick-fire and often unattributed dialogue. This was developed to great effect in the later works, notably in *The Road to Oxiana*, a work in which Byron artfully deploys the diary form to create the appearance of artlessness. (Bruce Chatwin always referred to this book as "a sacred text.") He never misses the chance to make a joke, whether describing a gallop through the bare highland landscape on wooden saddles ("at every rise almost castrated") or coining a cunning code word for the Shah to avoid arousing suspicion: Marjoribanks. On his day he was a heartbreaking writer, and one who, uniquely, treated ancient buildings and modern people as two facets of a continuing story. Of *The Station*, Knox comments perceptively, "He made Athos his own," which of course is what all the best travel writers do with the landscapes they love.

The story benefits from a lively cast of characters, including Nancy Mitford, Evelyn Waugh, who named Byron as one of five young writers to embody the spirit of their generation, and James Lees-Milne. Byron consistently and unsuccessfully tried to seduce the last, until they finally had a fistfight in a lift. (He had avoided lectures at Oxford because of the "horrible proximity of women undergraduates.") There is little on the affairs that did come off—one longs to know more about the "Japanese train attendant"—though Knox is good on Byron's greatest love, Desmond Parsons, brother of the sixth Earl of Rosse ("You remain the pattern, the zenith of all the world can give me," Byron wrote to him longingly before Parsons died of Hodgkin's disease at the age of twenty-six). In the end one has no real sense of the interior life, but perhaps this is a lot to ask.

This is a thoroughly researched book, solid in content. Knox is reluctant to form judgments, allowing instead the facts to speak for themselves. In the matter of style, he is less sure of himself. Much of the narrative is wooden ("And so his days at Eton drew to a close"), and he has a fondness for cliché (several characters are "bowled over," tempers "begin to fray," and friends appear "in hot pursuit"), which is ironic, in the light of what Anthony Powell called Byron's "obsessive repugnance for cliché."

Nonetheless, the prose warms up in the second half, and there are beguiling touches: we glimpse our man in Venice, "growling at waiters and German holidaymakers," and after Lord Jersey's sensational fête champêtre in 1939, Knox writes, "Illumined, thus, in the flashlight of notoriety, the Georgian Group took a final swaggering bow before the curtain came crashing down upon its world." Byron had been in on the founding of the Georgian Group, "a crusader in the battle to save Georgian London."

As the horror of the late 1930s unfolded in Germany, Byron became an obsessive opponent of fascism, appeasement, and anyone who supported either. When war finally came, he hurled himself with customary vigor into politics and in particular propaganda, arguing for the creation of a union of states to preserve world peace after Germany's defeat. In the guise of a *Sunday Times* war correspondent, he was commissioned to travel to Mashhad as an observer and sailed out of Liverpool in February 1941. A U-boat torpedoed his ship, and he was drowned two days before his thirty-sixth birthday. The last pages of this engrossing book are elegiac and beautifully done, a threnody for the talent extinguished by that war—by all wars.

2003

Jan Morris

'm *passionate* about sports cars," cried seventy-seven-year-old Jan Morris as she pressed a foot to the floor, clenched the steering wheel, and tossed her cloud of white hair. "This one has six gears. They advertise it by saying, 'Add a little danger to your life.' I like that." The dun-colored Welsh countryside raced by. Then Morris screeched to a stop, rolling down the window to indicate, with a theatrical flourish, the embowered grave of David Lloyd George, nestling in the live green shadows on a bank of the Dwyfor.

This was our third meeting. I had come to visit the home Morris shares with her former wife, Elizabeth, near Llanystumdwy in Caernarfonshire, in the northwestern corner of Wales. For many years the Morrises lived in the big house across the way, then, when their four children were grown (a fifth died in infancy), Jan and Elizabeth sold it and moved to its modest eighteenth-century stable building. After our supersonic excursion to Lloyd George, we lunched in its homey kitchen. While Elizabeth busied herself with the creamy Welsh cheeses—both women exude warm hospitality—the stately Jan flirted with me. After coffee she and I settled upstairs in her forty-foot work/living room overlooking Cardigan Bay. The chimney of a handsome old stove punctured the middle of the slate roof, and on one of the surrounding sofas purred Ibsen, a pointy-faced Norwegian hunting cat.

Like Alan Bennett, Morris is an institutional figure on the literary landscape—the queen mother of the book world. By any standards, hers is an impressive body of work. Comprising more than forty volumes, it embraces numerous portraits of cities and countries, most notably *Venice*, which first appeared in 1960 and is still revered as the classic work on that city; several collections of essays; two works of autobiography; two novels (one of which, *Last Letters from Hav*, was short-listed for the Booker); two biographies; a book about her house; and, by far her most ambitious literary project, the *Pax Britannica* trilogy charting the rise and decline of the Victorian empire.

In her latest offering, *A Writer's World*, a sequence of magazine essays tracks the progress of the planet over half a century. The early pieces read like dispatches from the Jurassic, and one is bound to reflect with awe at the whacking length of Morris's writing life. She was in Atlanta, notebook in hand, the day after the Supreme Court declared racial segregation in state schools illegal. She was filing from Sri Lanka when it was called Ceylon. And in 1961 she covered the Eichmann trial in Jerusalem. One delightful essay refers to the vexatious issue of snagging nylons in 1950s Manhattan (not her own nylons, at that point).

Which brings us to that business vulgarly known as a sex change.

From the age of three or four, Morris knew herself to be a girl in a boy's body. She had no trouble marrying ("to me gender is not physical at all, but is altogether insubstantial"), but after she had done so, her longing to live as a woman grew more urgent. Between the ages of thirty-five and forty-five she experimented with the idea, though she held off taking hormones until her children had been conceived. When the chop came, it was in Casablanca. She found this conclusion "inevitable and deeply satisfying—like a sentence which, defying its own subordinate clauses, reaches a classical conclusion at the end" (a fine analogy).

Rebecca West announced of Morris that "he was a better writer than she." Would she have been more of a writer if she hadn't changed sex? It's true that the best books came early—*Pax Britannica*, *Venice*, possibly her first American travelogue, *Coast to Coast.* Critics have claimed that the softer sensibilities associated with womanhood are apparent in her post-Casablanca writing, and in *Conundrum*, her 1974 account of her gender change, she herself wrote, "Just as I feel emancipated as a person, so I do as a writer." But one of the most notable things about this robust new collection, and about her oeuvre as a whole, is how little her work has changed, in both style and content if not quality, over half a century. When I put this to her, she quickly agrees.

It is difficult to imagine, in these times, the courage it must have taken to come out as a transsexual in the 1970s. Morris was a pioneer. She mostly enjoyed, she claims now, the social dangers, and likes to make a joke about being a member of two clubs at the time, one as a woman and one as a man, and about changing her clothes in taxis when traveling between them, but the price she had to pay, in social terms alone, must have been a high one, and not funny at all. We were talking of the fabled 1953 Everest expedition, of which she was a member, and of the crucial role of its leader—the often overlooked John Hunt. Morris admired Hunt a good deal. There was a long pause, and I thought she was remembering her old friend Hunt, who died in 1998. She spent some minutes stroking Ibsen, then she suddenly said, "It must have been very hard on the old boy. The sex change, I mean."

One wonders if she could have gone through with it without what she describes as "a constancy of love and personal happiness which was far more influential upon my style than any simple change of sex." She is referring to Elizabeth, the daughter of a Ceylon tea planter who was once her wife and is now "my partner in life." Jan once wrote—after the sex change—that her happiest moments were still played out on the forecourt of Terminal 3, when she saw Elizabeth again. As for Elizabeth herself, one can only wonder at, and envy, what Morris describes as her "fathomless understanding."

———

Jan was born James in Somerset in 1926, her mother English and her father a Welsh engineer. Hers was a happy childhood, except for the fact that every night, every week, every year, she said a prayer to God: let me be a girl. After choir school at Christ Church, Oxford, she went to Lancing College during World War II, not a happy experience, and one that led her to volunteer for the army at age seventeen. She was kindly treated in the Ninth Lancers, "stranger and impostor though I was." After being de-mobbed, she returned to Oxford to read English and has earned a living as a writer ever since, initially as a reporter and soon as a roving freelance essayist. In her thirties and forties she was hugely in demand on both sides of the Atlantic: as she puts it, "I had a world at my feet." Her great scoop as a reporter had un-folded on Everest. Against all the odds, Morris got the news of the ascent through, famously, in time for the coronation. Her book *Coronation Everest*, first published in 1958, is a perfect piece of historical romanticism, a style, or genre, paradigmatic of her work in general. She conjures the smell of wet leather, the taste of the *chang*, the sound of the tent bellying around the hap-less reporter as he battled to contain his carbon paper within his portable typewriter. When, lying in his sleeping bag three days after the ascent, Morris heard on his crackly radio that his dis-patch had got through, "I felt," he wrote, "as though I had been crowned myself."

Always preferring her Welsh side to its English counterpart, and long a member of Plaid Cymru, Morris announced in May during a speech at a gala event attended by the queen that she was a Welsh republican. In her doorstop tome *The Matter of Wales*, published in 1984 (and reissued, as *Wales*, in 1998), she talks about "the dream of independence," though now, she says, she has changed on that point. "I have grown out of the idea of nationhood—I don't believe in it anymore. I used to feel very strongly about the nation of Wales and the state of Wales, but now I think the only thing that matters is cultural independence."

Her stature in her adopted homeland is reflected in the dubious honor of being one of two Welsh people to get sent fake anthrax during the recent scare (the other was First Minister Rhodri Morgan). In 2001 she predicted that one day the idea of nationality will seem as impossibly primitive as dynastic warfare or the divine right of kings.

Morris does not analyze: she conjures a mood. Her prose is quaintly mannered. She favors, for example, that now rather absurd-sounding syntax in which the subject is relegated to the end of the clause ("Different indeed is the character of the gondola"), and she dauntlessly seizes near-obsolete phrases such as "many a": "ships sail through many a picture here," she writes in the romantic whimsy *A Writer's House in Wales* (2002). Her only direct stylistic influence, she reckons, is Charles Doughty's *Travels in Arabia Deserta*, that velvety rich slab of stately antique that stood so proudly in the imagination of the literary elite of Morris's generation. At the end of it all she is not a great writer (sorry, Jan). But at certain descriptive moments, she is nearly perfect: Leningrad becomes "an obituary of the European ideal"; Gary Powers in his oxygen helmet being dressed for the flight at Peshawar is "like a knight before battle"; supertankers supplied by helicopter with mail and medicines are "like passing sadhus accepting offerings." It's difficult to imagine that *Pax Britannica* will not be read in a hundred years.

The new collection confirms that she is, and has always been, irredeemably old-fashioned in her sensibilities as well as in her style. She prizes good manners, acknowledging ruefully that as a traveler "I am ingratiating almost to a fault" (an Australian critic once dubbed her "a literary Mary Poppins"). In her lectures I have heard her boast of stealing facecloths from expensive hotels; one senses that she longs to commit more serious offenses but just can't bring herself to go through with it. If she and Paul Theroux took a train journey together, he'd be insulting everyone else in the carriage while she dispensed Murray Mints.

The sweep of history is her forte. "To liberals everywhere," she writes in *Heaven's Command*, the first volume of *Pax Britannica*, "England had replaced Napoleonic France as the hope of mankind." She does not engage with contemporary issues: even in South Africa in the 1970s she glosses, "That seminal human conflict, the antipathy of color."

When she is describing extremes of evil or of suffering, this refusal to engage can diminish her writing, reducing her to a kind of Patience Strong of travel literature. She chuckles a little too benignly, for example, over the murderous foibles of the Albanian dictator Enver Hoxha, and the piece on Ireland in *A Writer's World* is vapid to a degree. What she likes is pageantry and the glint of gold letters on black marble. She writes fabulously of the grand gesture—"the Great Trek of the Afrikaner zealots, lurching in their ox wagons ever further into the harsh hinterland"—and about the detail (Cole Porter's "True Love" blaring from the radio of her rental car as she goes to meet a group of segregationist intellectuals), but the territory in between she leaves to the foreign correspondents. The extraordinary thing is that more often than not, in her essays, she pulls it off.

Similarly, just as she wriggles out of the hard issues, she wriggles out of self-revelation. "I am a conceited writer," she tells me languidly, leaning across the couch like a pasha. "I'm ashamed to say that every line of all my books concerns me." Superficially, perhaps, but I think this is a sleight of hand. In fact she conceals herself artfully. The nearest she comes to acknowledging that refusal, or inability, to reveal herself is in her insistence that she finally found her voice, after all these years, in the latter chapters of the slim volume she wrote two years ago called *Trieste and the Meaning of Nowhere*. A melancholy envoi purged of the matronly jollity of its predecessors (she responds to the city by "thinking sad thoughts about age, doubt and disillusion"), this book, she is convinced, is her best—"the most self-revelatory." I am not so sure. Trieste is anonymous; Morris herself calls it "an allegory of limbo." Tucked away in the top right-hand corner of the Adriatic, protruding like a peninsula out of western Europe and into the sea of the Balkans, it lacks the usual characteristics of the motherland to such an extent that in a 1999 poll 70 percent of Italians did not know that it was in Italy at all. In *Trieste and the Meaning of Nowhere* meandering digressions follow Morris's preoccupations—cats, for example—but this hardly constitutes self-revelation. I think it is more a case of self-identification. The city, she suggests, might be Italian by sovereignty, but in temperament it is "more or less alone." So are we all, in the end. As Morris knows.

The flirtatious persona and reliance on humor (she can be a very funny writer, and in person she loves to laugh) contribute to the crafted illusion of openness and at the same time allow her to hide. She is purposefully skittish: later, as we were chatting in the doorway, she reached up to hang languidly from the beams. She goes on rather endlessly about wanting to consummate her passion in the afterlife with one of her biographical subjects, Admiral of the Fleet Jacky Fisher. When we were in her bedroom, she flung open the wardrobe door to reveal a poster of the admittedly drop-dead gorgeous Fisher. (I later learned that she performs this flourish for all visitors. Honestly, you can't help liking her.) Beneath the surface, she isn't very sociable, rarely accepting dinner invitations and virtually never staying with friends. "I am by nature an outsider, by profession an onlooker, by inclination a loner," she wrote recently.

Whereas, as far as the past is concerned, she cleaves to the Trollopian myth of a golden age, she is pessimistic about the future, in particular about the whittling away of local culture and the rudderlessness she now observes in the world. She claims she has written her last book—except for one that will be published posthumously, or perhaps never at all, as she plans to stow it under the stairs. It is addressed to the daughter who died as a baby.

"It's always haunted me that I never got to know her. It's not exactly a novel, but I shall be entirely free to say whatever I want." She'd like to be remembered as Jan "Empire" Morris but suspects that the tabloid headlines will read, SEX CHANGE AUTHOR DIES.

The fanciful demeanor is so remorseless that you end up wondering what melancholy lurks beneath. So perhaps she was right about finding her voice at last in *Trieste*, as it is her most elegiac book. In life, she rarely lets the mask fall. She escorts me to my taxi wielding a huge umbrella given to her on that fearsomely wet day in 1997 when Hong Kong was handed back to the Chinese (she was there, of course). As I climb in, she asks reproachfully, "Shall I say goodbye to Ibsen for you?"

2003

POSTSCRIPT

In 2008, Jan and Elizabeth were legally reunited in a civil partnership.

Shortly after Sybille Bedford died in 2006 at the age of ninety-four, the French Institute in London invited me to participate in a formal evening in her honor: an *hommage*. I felt a fraud at the institute: the French manage to invest their cultural events with funereal solemnity, and everyone present appeared an Intellectual with an uppercase *I* (you can put it in your passport under "Occupation" in France). Everyone, that is, except the charming, clever Nicky Haslam. I was so pleased to spot him sitting near the back.

Sybille Bedford

t is a great pleasure to pay homage to Sybille Bedford as a travel writer. Those of us toiling humbly on the lower slopes owe her a considerable debt; in a field with few role models, she remains a shining star.

Before considering her legacy, I'd like to look briefly at what the travel-writing genre gave to Bedford. She had written three novels that failed to find a publisher and as a writer was stuck at the starting gate. Then, influenced partly by Martha Gellhorn, she started work on *A Visit to Don Otavio*, the story of a Mexican journey. The experience provided, she said later, "the final kick that set my writing free." In her memoir, *Quicksands*, she explains that when she began working on *Don Otavio*, she discovered "the scope of non-fiction fused with telling a story, or inventing one."

What happened, I think, was this. Bedford found in the travel-writing genre a way of anchoring her ideas in landscape. She could smuggle the indefinable into a portrait of walnut trees fructifying under a warm Mediterranean sun. Travel writing provided her with a structural ballast that fiction lacks.

In terms of the practicalities of the job, she was a writer indigenous to the moment. In a thoughtful essay she wrote for *Esquire* in 1961, Bedford identifies a golden age of travel—one she calls "the early middle period of the automobile." Her golden age, in other words. It is amusing to read her comment, in that 1961 essay, about how times have changed. "And now," she writes, "now that we are all so much cannon fodder for the travel industries . . ." In another piece, published in *Venture* magazine in 1965, she starts, "New ground, these days, is rare." Where would she have gone, had she been born a generation later? There's certainly not enough good claret in the Antarctic.

Now to the richer subject of what *she* gave to travel writing. The answer, of course, is almost everything. Stylistically, she is up there with the gods. Where do I start? The power of her images—a hand holding up to the train window a single round white cheese on a leaf. Her classical piled-up clauses: there is a twelve-line sentence that blasts through Mexican history in chapter 2 of *Don Otavio*. Yet in descriptive passages Bedford instinctively mistrusts the subordinate clause. Her analogies are simple: Roofs spread over the landscape "like a fan." Paddle steamers on Lake Lucerne "like tall mock swans." And who can forget the Spanish catalog advertising sewing machines, its paragraphs "rumbling on like a seventeenth-century funeral oration"?

Multitudinous characteristics queue up for recognition: the judicious use of direct speech; the triumphant fondness for the short final line of a section, a kind of verbal left hook; the painterly imagination that conjures the "lush Rousseau growth of August" or the "heavy-shadowed Daumier world of walls and figures." Then there is the small matter of Bedfordian perfect pitch. Don't you love "the fugitive complexity of an older wine"—that appears in a brilliant article, one of my favorites, called "La Vie de Château"—or "the biblical shapes" of Venetian bread and cheese, in "Winter in Venice," a tiny, jewel-like essay that counts as one of the best things ever written about that overwritten city.

Can I look briefly at the first line of *Don Otavio*? It reads, "The upper part of Grand Central Station is large and splendid like the Baths of Caracalla." Note how very Bedfordian that sentence is—plain vocabulary, two solid Latinate adjectives, and an unexpected, semi-humorous analogy finishing it off. She writes beautifully in *Quicksands* about the making of it. I wonder how many times I have thought of the advice she purloined from Hemingway, about the need to begin every day with "one true sentence."

I didn't mention, in that list of Bedford's virtues as a travel writer, the regular appearance of wry humor. "Carlota," she writes in *Don Otavio*, "appears to have been a high strung woman, full of energies, with an immense appetite for glamour which, devastatingly for her, could only be realized through the intermedium of a husband's career, Maximilian proving in that respect as unsatisfactory as Charles Bovary." There is, though, something even more important than all of this.

It is a distinctive, individual voice—the most valuable asset a travel writer can possess (and indeed she must possess it). What is Bedford's voice? At once arch and wistful; funny and mortally serious. Like Mexico, the setting for *Don Otavio*, as a writer she is a paradox—desert and jungle, violence and sentiment, squalor and perfection. But these apparent contradictions reflect the paradox of life itself. In the first chapter of *Don Otavio* she acknowledges "the New York of the splendid contours"—meaning the crenellated vision from the liner. But she has to add that it is not "the New York of the sordid details," as for a proper Bedfordian portrait one has to have both. Not for her the Jan Morris flashing epaulets.

Like most serious writers, in any genre, Bedford has an acute sense of continuity with the past. "In the spaces of the Plaza Mayor," she writes, "walking over the grave of a pyramid, one is assailed by infinity, seized at the throat [one of her favorite phrases] by an awful sense of the past stretching and stretching backwards through tunnels of time . . . Can this be Here, can one be in it? One is in a legend, one is walking in Troy." The thrill of the authentic experience is conveyed to the reader again and again.

There is too an immediacy, an ability to nail the present. Bedford writes in *Jigsaw* of just what it was that enchanted her about France: "The timelessness of land and sea, and the indelible Frenchness of so much else . . . the conjunction of the perennial austere beauty of climate and nature—scouring mistral, the un-fudging sun—with the sweetness and sharpness and quickness, the rippling intelligence, the accommodating tolerance of the French *manière de vivre* . . . as no other place in Europe, no other place in the world, France between the wars made one this present of the illusion of freedom."

Incidentally, the zeitgeist *has* rendered one or two of her stylistic tendencies obsolete. Her expertly judged classical allusion, for example. Take the wonderful line in *Jigsaw* about a mother leaping furiously up and down on the beach as the young Sybille blithely tows her non-swimming daughter out to sea. Bedford writes, *"La bourgeoisie française à sa proie attachée."* How many of the young women struggling to get their travel books published today would recognize an alexandrine, let alone the Racinian Venus joke. Similarly, the wonky English spoken by foreigners represents a literary device that has run its cultural course, and one would no longer dare.

As a role model, though, Bedford is always with one, as she will be to those young women yet to find a voice. One thinks of her when in a hole: I have in mind the unswept room in Pátzcuaro, the one with a rusty shower bath that dripped and someone else's hairpins on the chest, everything damp, the author reduced to "drinking tequila in speechless gloom" and dining off food that "tasted of swamps." When at last she and E. went to bed, "the muslin nets smelled and had holes, insects whirred and our thoughts ran on malaria." When it happens to me, I think of Pátzcuaro, and resolve not to be miserable, but to make something of it, as Bedford did.

In conclusion, in *Don Otavio*, Bedford writes, "Cooking is at once the most and the least localized of the arts." And so, surely, is travel writing. I mean that the two most enduring aspects of travel writing are localized description conjuring a sense of place and flashes of the universal that disengage the material from map and calendar. In Bedford's prose, one finds the two perfectly married. Her influence lives on.

I leave you with a handful of lines she wrote about Split. "A sudden turn, and one's breath is caught: here under a rectangle of intense night-blue sky, empty and dark, stands a colonnade—we are in the peristyle, the inner temple of Diocletian's tomb, the core within the core. A black sphinx crouches; there are two lions; the place gives off an impression of immense stillness, of imperishable being at the end of the tunnel of time . . . one stands, seized at the throat by emotion, the sense of having come near the heart of classical antiquity."

2006

Nikos Kazantzakis

In 1982, reading classics and modern languages at Brasenose, I added Modern Greek to my degree course. I had flightily decided it might be fun to write about contemporary Greek novels, rather than venerable texts encrusted with scholarly apparatus. Unfortunately, most of the novels weren't any good, but that is another story. In order to learn to speak the language, I spent the third year of my degree course in Athens. I had a job with a literary publishing house and a studio flat in Pangrati, behind the old Olympic stadium. On weekends, I explored the islands in the Saronic Gulf or the nearer Cyclades with a Greek boyfriend. I say he was Greek: he was from Rethymnon and thought of himself as Cretan rather than Greek. When I had time off, we went to Crete. I was twenty-one when I started reading Kazantzakis; my first copy of *Ho Christos xanastauronetai*

(*Christ Recrucified*) fell out of my pack when I hiked the Samaria Gorge and was never seen again. He *was* good. The combination of the poetic and the revolutionary that exemplifies Kazantzakis's work was the perfect foil for my youthful hopes and aspirations, and from then on I couldn't get enough of him. I owe him a debt of gratitude. I wouldn't have passed my Modern Greek finals without him.

Kazantzakis was born in 1883 in Ottoman Crete. He studied law in Athens, then moved to Paris. He subsequently lived for long periods elsewhere, in France, in Germany, and in Russia, but he said that the figs of Crete always beckoned him home. When he returned to the white earth and cornflower skies of Varvari, his ancestral village, he looked through the low doorways at girls weaving, and he said his heart pitched. He did not care for Athens. He said he was African, compared with Athenians. He looked the archetypal Cretan: taller than other Greeks, with a high forehead, olive eyes, and a mustache that lost its handlebars to the advancing years.

Greece was at war with Turkey between 1912 and 1913, and after that royalists and republican Venizelists tore the country apart. In 1918, World War I ended for everyone but the Greeks. They were—as they saw it, and in fact—betrayed by the immoderate optimism of Lloyd George and vague French promises. Then, in 1922, Kemal Atatürk swept the Greek armies into the sea, forcing a million and a half refugees from Asia Minor to share the already inadequate food of six million tubercular homelanders. It was a dynamic background for a man who was a maniacally prolific writer, churning out multitudinous volumes of poetry, essays, philosophy, plays, translations (Homer, Dante, Goethe), and of course the novels. And it gave rich scope for political involvement. Kazantzakis was a natural dissenter and socialist, always part revolutionary and part poet, and it was the tension between the parts—action and contemplation—that generated his creative energy. He tried and failed to get an illegal political movement off the ground in Crete, he was deeply involved in the first communist decade in the U.S.S.R., and the 1930s found him—of course—pounding out news stories on a secondhand typewriter at the Spanish front.

Not many people know that until *Zorba*, which appeared when he was sixty-three, Kazantzakis was known at home chiefly as a travel writer. His hero was Odysseus, the eternal wanderer.* He published travel journalism throughout the 1920s and later worked up his diaries into almost a dozen volumes about England, Russia, Italy, and other places, seeking, or so he said, answers to inner questions in the outer world. In *Spain*, he writes of Ávila, "Dry, deserted, stiff-necked is this towering workshop where the Spanish spirit was tempered." But Kazantzakis's overwrought style often gets the better of him. Here he is in the same book: "Toledo lived in my mind just as El Greco had painted it in the storm: towering, ascetic, scourged by sudden flashes of light, with the arrow of her miraculous Gothic cathedral, like the arrow of the human soul piercing God's thunder-laden clouds." It might have worked without the final image. He tends to the unsubtle in both language and observation. Not for him the finely calibrated shift of feeling. He must have been like that as a person. In his unwittingly funny travel book on England, published in 1939, he chats up two girls by asking if they have read Demosthenes.

Despite the shortcomings, I admired Kazantzakis's efforts to adapt the travel-writing genre to his purpose, and to experiment,

---

*He wrote an epic poem called the *Odyssey*, 33,333 seventeen-syllable iambic verses more or less about life, the universe, and everything, and more or less unreadable. It remained a vitally important work to Kazantzakis, and critics refer to it constantly, but to me it is an elephant in the room. Though I like the ending: the hero dies on an iceberg at the South Pole.

and I identified closely with the conflict, so present in his work, between going and staying. Kazantzakis was full of contradictions, like most of us, and in his intellectual position progressed—if that is the verb—from nationalism to communism, socialism, Buddhism, eschatological nihilism, and every permutation thereof. Even as a nationalist he couldn't make up his mind if he was Greek or Cretan. But his love of freedom was a constant. Both travel and travel writing expressed something of what freedom meant to him. He sought relief by getting on trains and waking under a different sky; he was an unquiet spirit. But he could never quite skewer the freeing sensations of travel in words.

Greece, meanwhile, remained a crucible of despair—first the fascist horrors of the Metaxas dictatorship, then German invasion during World War II. Kazantzakis sat it out on the island of Aegina in the Saronic Gulf. More than 350,000 Greeks died of malnutrition during the occupation. On Aegina, children literally starved on the harbor front. Kazantzakis and his wife stayed in bed to conserve energy. He was a hungry man on a beleaguered island, and to keep himself alive, he wrote a novel—his first. Out of suffering and grief he confected an exuberant story bursting with joy, and he called it *The Life and Adventures of Alexis Zorbas* (*Zorba the Greek*, in English). Set in the 1930s, the book is narrated by a serious young intellectual who travels to Crete to reopen a disused lignite mine. Problems bedevil the project from the outset, but the mine foreman, Zorba himself, effectively redeems them all. The character Zorba is freedom made flesh. He is Sancho Panza to the narrator's Quixote, an explosion of élan, an unpolished figure of rough peasant virtues, the vibrant anti-intellectual Kazantzakis would like to have been, for then there would have been nothing to struggle against. I have never felt Michael Cacoyannis's 1964 film does the novel justice, despite Anthony Quinn's performance.

Even after the liberation the Allies and the Germans kept

fighting on Crete. Kazantzakis went back to walk among the ruins and widows.

In Varvari the low lintels of the houses had black crosses painted above them—one for each male of the family executed by the Germans. Many in Kazantzakis's circle did not find the exploits of Xan Fielding, Patrick Leigh Fermor, and their colleagues during this period quite as heroic as the protagonists themselves. They lived through the reprisals.

After *Zorba* in 1946, novels poured out. There was something of the mystic about Kazantzakis, and he said that dreams played an important part in his life and work. He had no institutionalized faith, a problem the Orthodox Church solved by excommunicating him. Here was another contradiction: the atheist unable to leave Christian themes alone. The bishop of Chios called his Cretan saga *Freedom and Death* "treasonable, antireligious, and a slander against Crete." The Orthodox Church in America weighed in, condemning the novel *The Last Temptation of Christ* as "indecent and atheist." The struggle to achieve a balance, or compromise, between art and politics never reached a conclusion, but in old age Kazantzakis seemed reconciled to the tension between the two. Four months before his death at the age of seventy-four he wrote in his diary of his "struggle between Apollo and Buddha . . . I am still toiling for a synthesis: to love the visible world, to realize at the same time that it is a deception, and thus, knowing how ephemeral the world is, to love it with passion and tenderness." I find that handsome. He was a heroic pessimist.

In the 1950s, Kazantzakis achieved international recognition. Pundits tipped him for the Nobel, and in 1957 he lost out to Camus by one vote. He continued to be involved with socialist politics in Greece, serving as minister without portfolio. Then he settled in Antibes and died on a trip to Germany the year he missed the Nobel. The patriarch refused to allow his body to lie in state in Athens cathedral.

The experience of life under occupying forces appears again and again in Kazantzakis's work, and his views and opinions on the subject resonate today (one thinks of Iraq). His novel *Christ Recrucified* is set in a Cretan village in which a Turkish overlord with a freshly dyed mustache sits on velvet cushions on a balcony above the village square, sipping raki as a boy relights his hookah and the Greeks below battle to stage a Passion play. Rereading it now, I find myself unable to defend Kazantzakis as a stylist. But the book still thrills me, as it is his most Greek novel, and it brings back what Greece meant to me when I was twenty. I was finding for myself those same Technicolor characters who crowd Kazantzakis's Lycovrissi and measure distance in cigarettes (how long it takes to smoke them, not laid end to end), as well as the thick, sweet coffee at Kostandis's café and the boiling red dye that colors hens' eggs at Easter. The villagers' cruelty to an influx of refugees reflects the older Kazantzakis's unflinching gaze: expect nothing, fear nothing, accept the world as it is. I first read the scene in which the hero Manolios hides out in a church on a hot, starless night when I was myself sleeping outside in the Cretan countryside, reading by summer moonlight. Under three silver lamps, Manolios, facing death, contemplates an icon of Christ with carefully combed hair. The chapel smells of wax and incense. "He raised his eyes toward the vault of the church," Kazantzakis writes, "and made out in the half-light the face of the Almighty, bending pitilessly over mankind." This is the Pantokrator, the image of God painted at the apex of Greek churches. Manolios's enemies have swarmed into the airless nave, led by a sweating priest in a gold-embroidered stole. With the door bolted behind them, they press in on Manolios. He can feel their breath on his cheeks. "He looked at the crowd about him; it was as if in the darkness he saw the gleam of daggers." I saw them too, looming up from the cliffs of the Samaria Gorge.

2006

POSTSCRIPT

My love affair with Kazantzakis, and with Greece, had not yet run its course. Five years after I graduated, a robust if uneven portfolio of newspaper and magazine articles netted me a book contract, and I went back to Greece to write a travelogue—not about Crete, which had been well covered, but about the second-biggest Greek island, the little-known Evia (Euboea to classicists) off the east coast of the mainland. I tried to paint a portrait of a rural society on the cusp of rebarbative change. The book was a labor of love, and as a result there is too much labor and too much love but not enough art. It got me started, though, and helped me see what kinds of books I wanted to write.

III | PUTTING A FIGURE ON THE LANDSCAPE

Isabella Bird in the Rockies

sabella Bird was always a heroine to me. The tweed-skirted Victorian travel writer cast off the domestic shackles of home and took to the road, fearful only, ever, of journey's end. She went everywhere, riding an elephant through the Perak jungle and watching Hong Kong burn, in each place a transgressor, an outsider, a freak. At the end of her life she said she liked the Front Range of the Rocky Mountains best, especially a blue hollow below Longs Peak, the toothy 14,250-footer that dominates what is now Rocky Mountain National Park. She lived in a log cabin in the shadow of the peak, listening to coyotes scream in the forest. And so did I, because I was on her tail.

Longs Peak is one of the highest mountains in the Front Range, a southern spur of the Rockies and the first barrier the homesteaders encountered when they trundled west across the Great Plains to fulfill their Manifest Destiny. The Continental Divide bisects the Front Range from northwest to southeast, at one point looping sharply, with the result that the Pacific basin is momentarily east of its Atlantic counterpart. The divide effectively operates as a snow fence in Colorado: more snow falls on the western side, but most glaciers are on the east, because the snow blows over.

Bird arrived in the Front Range in 1873, when Colorado was not yet part of the Union. She was forty-two. Four feet ten, with no teeth, she considered a ride of a hundred miles over rough terrain in subzero temperatures an inconsequential matter. At home she was an invalid, too frail to hold her head up without a steel support; in the Wild West she lived among vagrants and met Rocky Mountain Jim, a one-eyed desperado with a beguiling smile. He was an arrow-scarred bandit known across the free territory for bravado, braggadocio, and brawling. ("There is no God west of the Missouri," Bird wrote in her description of him in her masterpiece *A Lady's Life in the Rocky Mountains*.) But in the flickering firelight of an alpine camp he revealed that he had a heart. "You're the first man or woman who's treated me like a human being for many a year," he told her as they sat under the stars. It was he who accompanied Bird when she summited Longs Peak. "Jim dragged me up," she wrote, "like a bale of goods, by sheer force of muscle."

I pursued Bird up and down the backcountry trails she describes—though they weren't trails then. It was she who broke them. Elk of extraordinary heft grazed in glacier-formed meadows where the Indian paintbrush was just coming into bloom, delicate persimmon petals freckling the onion grass. Higher up, montane forest of ponderosa pine and aspen merged into a denser landscape dotted with bighorn sheep. Around 11,400 feet, the trees stopped abruptly, like a lifted curtain. In the distance, I saw the shining eye of a frozen lake. Cornices and sugarloaves almost filled the sky, and clouds moved between them in a continual displacement of light and dark. I did not see five thousand head of Texas cattle on their way to Iowa, already nine months out, as Bird did. But it was still possible to be alone in a wilderness that, once the railroad had joined up the country, wove itself into the national imagination.

In her letters home to her sister, Bird repeatedly used the words "exhilarated," "intoxicating," and "sublime," and she referred to an "elasticity" in the air that made her feel more alive than she had ever felt in her life. Mountain air everywhere tends

to have that effect—ask a skier—but there is a certain translu-
cence to the light in the Front Range that sharpens every shape
and enhances every shade. Longs Peak in particular has something of the mystical about it, not least on account of the turban
of cloud at the top. "In one's imagination it grows to be more
than a mountain," Bird wrote of Longs. The Arapaho, who revered it, kept an eagle trap on top and used the feathers in their
ceremonies. The glittering red granite boulders appear to have
showered down in a cosmic explosion.

Estes Park is the gateway resort to the Colorado Rockies, with
few attractions. Driving out of it the other way, east through Big
Thompson Canyon, I ended up in the backcountry around Masonville, a fractal landscape thrust from eroded volcanic rock ten
million years ago. The buttes blazed red; you could see why the
Spaniards named the region Colorado. The fields smelled of
crushed juniper, and the air was heavy with heat and burned
light. There was nobody, anywhere. Masonville had two shops,
both selling Harley-Davidson leathers and moccasins. I entered,
browsed, and left both without seeing a storekeeper. Later, I looked
out at the Front Range from the ridge of the Dakota Hogback. It
was a view that moved Bird. In those mountains she saw the aspirations of mankind, our hopes, fears, and dreams, rendered
absolute. It made her feel she was not alone. Like Ruskin, she
believed that natural beauty could knock down the wall between
past and present, compressing all of life into one wonderful
timeless moment. It was a kind of transfiguration, an alchemy
that changed her suffering—the world's suffering—into understanding, and then into pure being.

The first settlers of central Colorado came to pan in 1858,
after a veteran of the California gold rush sieved up placer metal
in the South Platte River near Pikes Peak. Hundreds arrived from
the east in the wagons called prairie schooners, the canvas sides
painted with the words "Pike's Peak or Bust." It was bust, more
often than not. By the time Colorado joined the Union in 1876,

silver had overtaken gold, and Bird, on a southern excursion from the Longs Peak cabin, rode into the heart of the Front Range to Colorado's first silver city. A spur line had just linked George-town to the transcontinental Union Pacific at Cheyenne, and the rails brought hoboes, speculators, and tourists, as well as English sparrows, which nested in the boxcars.

With silver long gone and nothing to replace it, the George-town environs are less populous than they were when Bird rode through the high gulches. My companions on the highway, more often than not, were bikers with bandannas and no helmets, and no silencers either. The region has stagnated since the energetic frontiersmen Bird knew shipped tens of thousands of pamphlets to Europe promising that "the mines and fields of the new west will pour forth golden harvests." Georgetown itself, the Silver Queen, has nothing to live off but its history. Squashed into a narrow strip of land between the granite wall of Clear Creek Canyon and Interstate 70, it is a scrappy town with a reveren-tially preserved historic district, unpaved streets, and a modern half struggling to survive, a typical corner of small-town America in the foothills of the twenty-first century. A few retail outlets of the Silver Shoppe variety battled on, but one sensed that the war had been lost. On Saturday, at the time Indians call cow dust, Denver weekenders began arriving, ready to climb Mount Bier-stadt at dawn. The smoke from their campfires rose from the forest in the Guanella Pass like spires.

Reversing Bird's route (she rode up from the other direction), I crossed the Continental Divide at Breckenridge. Buffalo herds roamed the semiarid high plains to the east. It was an attenuated landscape, parsed of color. Bird called it "an uplifted prairie sea." To me it was Clint Eastwood territory, a land where the fabled drifters of the Southwest roam to a Ry Cooder soundtrack.

Pikes Peak in El Paso County is the easternmost fourteener in the country and the most visited American mountain. A cable car hauls up the hordes. It was enshrined as a national emblem in 1893, when the ascent inspired Katharine Lee Bates to write "America the Beautiful." To avoid it, I departed from Bird temporarily to drive from Manitou Springs out onto the Great Plains, so I could look back and see the Rockies as the pioneers did. After so long in the mountains, the plains were like the planet turned onto its side. Only windmill water pumps and the prongs of long-horned cattle pierced the flatness. The roads might have been drawn with a ruler, and the intersections with a set square. The ranches had names like Bald Eagle, Dry Creek, and Jonathan's Cut, posters advertised the forthcoming "19th Annual Machine-Gun Shoot," and at Ellicott a highway marker announced, "No Motorist Services for 95 Miles." The air was so still it was all glare, and the sky covered the plains like a bowl.

At Rush, the Tres Hermanos store sold *chicharrón* and pregnancy-testing kits. The bored young Mexican at the till had come after five years in Chicago. He and his parents and sister lived in a trailer out back. It had pretty window boxes. Rippling cornfields stretched to the horizon, a hot wind blew out of Kansas, and I walked on public land among burrowing things and cacti. In Ordway, a digital thermometer on Main Street announced 92°F. These were poor, agricultural plains communities, not the Fattytowns of the urban corridors. At Ordway's Columbine Saloon, two men sat on home-hewed bar stools equipped with arms, presumably so patrons couldn't fall off. There was a pool table, stalls with buttoned vinyl banquettes, heavy metal music, and a smell of piss.

I returned to the blue hollow, as Bird did. "It is uninteresting down here," she wrote before setting off again for the beloved log cabin under the mountain. "I long for the rushing winds, the piled-up peaks, the great pines, the wild night noises, the poetry and the prose of the free, jolly life of my unrivalled eyrie." Who wouldn't? She kept house for a couple of woodcutters for a month, dusting the cabin with a buffalo's tail and frying venison steaks in home-churned butter. She woke with the sheets frozen to her lips and fine snow hissing through the chinks in the walls. In a letter to her sister, Bird said that in the Rockies she realized how little one really needs. She found the freedom to be herself in the clear Front Range air. Extraordinarily, she managed to nail those feelings in words. *A Lady's Life* made her famous, and Bird became the first female fellow of London's Royal Geographical Society, an unprecedented reflection of genuine admiration on the part of the walrus-whiskered satraps of that deeply conservative institution.

Before the dreaded plane home, I drove the forty-eight-mile Trail Ridge Road, the highest continuously paved highway in the United States. At one end, the eponymous body of deep water at Grand Lake is the headwater of the Colorado River, and it was sacred to the Ute people, who called it Spirit Lake. Pine forest fell sharply to the shore, boardwalks creaked, and a Gloria Gaynor classic drifted from the open window of a fitness center, where a woman was pummeling a punching bag. Off Trail Ridge Road, I hiked along the inundated banks of the Colorado in Kawuneeche Valley, in the lee of the Never Summer range. A ribbon of cloud hung parallel to the ground halfway up the outer edge of the pines on the lateral moraine. A river otter skulked around the collapsed walls of a dude ranch.

Five feet of snow lay banked on the side of Trail Ridge Road. At the highest point, almost thirteen thousand feet, prairie falcon butterflies hovered in the nooks of the Lava Cliffs, whimsical tuff formations created by a volcanic explosion in the Never Summers. A kind of peace came down, like a benediction. Bird would have loved it. But it was inaccessible in the 1870s, even to the hardiest traveler. I thought I had lost her up there. But at a lookout facing Desolation Peaks, the national park people had erected a metal sign quoting her: EVERY VALLEY ENDS IN MYSTERY, it said. It was she who was following me.

2011

Chen Yifei: An Artist in China

A dapper man saunters into a bar in Shanghai, his hometown. Heads swivel. By the time he has ordered a drink, a squad of voluble youths press around for autographs. It is the scene you would expect in Britain if Liam Gallagher nipped into the Dog and Duck. But Chen Yifei is not a rock star. He is a fifty-year-old realist painter and the most successful Chinese artist alive.

A recent Chen retrospective in Beijing attracted in excess of seven thousand visitors a day. More astonishing still, Chen Yifei has vaulted that most forbidding of Asian cultural barriers and established himself in the international art world. Every one of his New York shows over the past twelve years has sold out, and a Chen recently fetched $250,000 at auction. Now this redoubtable figure is poised to conquer Europe: his one-man show at the Marlborough Gallery opened yesterday in London. He is the first Asian painter to sign an exclusive contract with the Marlborough.

Chen's medium—oil on canvas—owes a hefty debt to the West. The tradition of Chinese oil painting is barely as old as the century, but it developed quickly. Many Chinese artists now work in oils. Critics in both China and the West have noted Chen's draftsmanship, as well as his ability to paint on a grand scale: many of the works represented in the retrospective were six and a half feet square.

The Tibetan tablelands inspired the most beguiling canvases in the British show. Several pictures were conceived farther south in Gansu, a province in China's arid heart adjacent to Inner Mongolia and, in the case of Chen's favored region of Xiahe on the northern banks of the Daxia, occupied almost exclusively by Tibetans. It is a wild, remote landscape of scraped steppe, honey-colored mountains, shaggy goats, and curly-horned cattle, its crisp-skinned people shrouded and swaddled and roped at the waist. What artist could fail to be seduced?

The old stone bridges of Suzhou, a watery and more conventionally pretty landscape a ninety-minute car ride from Shanghai, have proved Chen's most enduring subject. He was taken to Suzhou as a child, when it was poor and accessible only by boat, and he has made it so famous that he gets mentioned on the guided tours. The historic town is the most popular domestic destination in the country. Walking with Chen along the narrow towpaths of Zhou village in Suzhou is a hazardous business. Packs of Chinese jostle us perilously close to the Grand Canal, each person clamoring to be photographed next to the master. The eleven-hundred-mile canal was dug in 400 B.C. to link the Yellow River with the Yangtze. Suzhou has developed into a prosperous area replete with marinas and golf courses. But the canals don't change, or the faces of the old men boiling eggs in vats of teak-colored tea. Chen once said, "No matter what else I paint, I will keep this subject close." Individual female figures suffused in a sentimental glow constitute Chen's third recurrent theme, and one represented in the London show by a Chinese beauty in traditional silks gazing at a bird perched in a wicker cage. An American art critic once dubbed the style "photographic realism," but Chen bristles at the suggestion that his paintings are ever photographic. He prefers the term "romantic realism." In any event, Chen's work is light-years away from the abstracts produced by the Chinese avant-garde.

He was born in Ningbo, Zhejiang, a small province on the prosperous eastern seaboard, but his family soon moved to Shanghai. His father was a chemical engineer and his mother, a Catholic nun before her marriage, a teacher. Chen was the first of their three children. He went to art school in Shanghai, and by the time he graduated, Mao's Cultural Revolution had all but consigned the arts to oblivion. Chen was obliged to absorb the dogma of socialist realism imported from the Soviet Union and deploy his prodigious talents for the greater good of the Communist Party, churning out gargantuan portraits of Mao on factory walls and generally whipping up support for the Red Guards. His parents were considered intellectuals—the worst crime—and the strain of forced labor and barbaric sessions of relentless "self-criticism" killed them both.

Chen never stopped painting, although anything beyond the politically orthodox had to be executed in secret. By the early 1970s, he was established as the leading young artist in Mao's China.

With the demise of the Cultural Revolution, and the advent of Deng Xiaoping's Open Door policy, China opened up to Western influence. Chen is a member of the "thinking generation," a term used to describe the Chinese intellectual elite who experienced the Cultural Revolution at a formative stage of their development and entered, afterward, a period of self-examination. Chen's 1979 *Thinking of History from My Space* typifies the self-analysis that characterizes the work of the thinking generation. It shows Chen himself in a contemplative mood, facing a sprawling collage of spectral sepia images drawn from his country's recent past. The painting seems to suggest an artist groping for meaning among the chaos of twentieth-century China.

Chen married in 1972, the year his father died, and twelve months later had a son, Chen Li. In 1980 the family immigrated to the United States. Chen Yifei worked as a picture restorer in New York for a year, signed up with Hammer Galleries, and quickly earned an international following. In 1986 he separated from his wife; she still lives in New York, where their son is a fine-arts student. Chen senior keeps an apartment and separate studio on the Upper East Side, but he now spends more time in Shanghai: he is at home there. The city epitomizes the new China. After stalling in the communist era, it is flourishing in a market-oriented environment, and this year Mayor Xu Kuangdi is predicting double-digit economic growth.

The elegant and affable Chen, chunky for a Chinese man, wears metal-rimmed glasses and well-cut jackets. He travels in a chauffeur-driven green Mercedes and listens to Whitney Houston, intermittently jacking up the volume and singing along. He invites his driver to join him in restaurants and, in the studio, patently enjoys the company of his models, who adore him. Given to frequent volleys of laughter, Chen is urbane, driven, and highly disciplined. He does not drink or smoke. "I never suffer from anxiety," he says. "I am a very happy man. I think life is like water: if you throw anything in, it does cause ripples, but they're soon gone." He embodies Confucian values of refinement, gentleness, order, and decency.

He might be socially adroit, but Chen is also curiously unengaged. He has been sketching in Xiahe for years, observing swathed pilgrims trudging around the walls of the Labrang Monastery, a center of the Gelugpa (Yellow Hat) sect of Tibetan Buddhism. Yet when I ask him what the writing on the creaky prayer wheels means, he says he hasn't a clue. He is the same with everyone: open, friendly, and detached.

Like most successful artists, he is a perfectionist, and he produces an incredible twenty-five pictures a year. An hour and a half before his plane was due to leave for London, he was still in his studio, dabbing at the Marlborough-bound Suzhou canvases, wearing furry mule slippers, a paint-encrusted T-shirt, and antediluvian sweatpants. Even as we eventually rushed out the door (Chen transformed in cashmere suit and silk tie), he spotted a tiny blemish on the cheek of one of his lovely girls, and an assistant hurried to the scene proffering brush and loaded palette.

Financial success has enabled Chen to make films, his other great passion. In 1993 he financed an eighty-minute dialogue-free film set in the 1930s and called *Reverie in Old Shanghai*. It was a psychic journey into his past, stylishly reminiscent of a sequence of music video clips. His second effort, *Evening Liaison*, was a mystery set in the same period. Financed by Hong Kong backers, the film was selected for Cannes in 1995. It is a romantic work, short on dialogue and long on moody suggestion, much like Chen's oil figures. The third, *Escape to Shanghai*, is to be a documentary feature about Jews who fled Nazi Germany and settled in Shanghai in 1938. All three films are set uncontentiously before the communist era.

Talking to Chen about politics makes you wonder what exactly it is that the thinking generation is thinking about. He appears entirely apolitical in his work and opinions. I wondered if he felt compromised by his role in the Cultural Revolution. "Difficult to say," he muses. "At the time, at least we had the chance to practice. Artists often don't know about politics—even now. We just paint nice pictures." It is hard to imagine that someone whose parents died as a result of Mao's struggle to maintain power (what the Cultural Revolution amounted to) is not bitter at the very least. But there is no bitterness visible in either Chen's personality or his work; on the contrary, his female figures contain more saccharine than Splenda, and when I ask him if he feels bitter, he says simply, "I was so young. I didn't think too much about it. I worried constantly about my family, especially my father. But I was able to sketch in secret in the dormitory. I kept working."

Is it the price of survival, this absolute withdrawal from ideology? "All I want to do is express something through my paintings," he concludes. "Art is like religion to me. I want to say to people, 'Love life.' That's my message."

He says there is no longer cultural repression in China, but this year—1997—a filmmaker was refused permission to leave for Cannes, and at the end of last year an avant-garde exhibition scheduled to show at the China National Gallery was pulled by the government even after catalogs had been printed. The economy may have been transformed, but China's political system remains opaque, strong-armed, and, of course, undemocratic. In the cultural sector, specifically the visual arts, the authorities are frightened of anything ambiguous because they can't understand it. Which is why they ignore Chen's sweet figures and benign landscapes.

Early one morning in Xiahe, a time when the turbans of cloud unravel and a fresh sun gilds the mountains, I asked Chen what he thought about the Tibetan situation. He was sketching in charcoal, standing up, and cerise-clad monks hurried around him, bearing copper scuttles of milky tea. "I think it's all right now," he said.

"But so many Tibetans long for independence," I pressed on, "and for the return of the Dalai Lama, their spiritual leader."

"You get independence movements everywhere," countered Chen. "I read about a Texas independence movement in *The New York Times* last week. And the Dalai Lama—he's been away for thirty years. Young people don't know anything about him."

Together we looked out over the waterless scrub. Had I landed on Mars? Later that morning Chen put down his stick of charcoal and told me I should compare today's China with the one he lived in during the Cultural Revolution. "I am an artist," he says repeatedly when the subject of human rights comes up. "I don't know about politics."

It was hard, walking with Chen on the Xiahe steppe, to judge his choice, or even to call it a Faustian pact. When he was a teenager, somewhere in the region of thirty-eight million of his countrymen died of starvation and overwork in the Great Leap Forward and its aftermath. But it was even harder not to think of the armed uprisings involving tens of thousands that had taken place there in Gansu after Mao drastically stepped up food requisitioning in 1958. In one Gansu county where a third of the population died, survivors ate one another.

The Marlborough show will be a sellout. Chen's safe, realistic subject matter and conventional style might be a long way from the happening art scene in China, but he paints from the heart—which is what a lot of collectors want. He certainly doesn't need to sell abroad: the domestic art market is strong. But Chen is committed to the enhancement of his global profile.

"I hope to have a museum show in London one day," he says confidently, "to show all my bigger pieces. Then all you British people will know: this is Chen."

1997

POSTSCRIPT

Chen Yifei continued to paint and sell while branching out into fashion design and even retail housewares, successfully leveraging his fame to set up a business empire that embraced magazines, film production, a modeling agency, and a restaurant in Xintiandi. The Chinese middle classes loved everything he did. In 2005, Chen died of a stomach illness in the middle of shooting another film. He was fifty-nine.

Explorers

Perfect territory. The figures who interest me most are men and women of action and contemplation. Many were misfits, caught between the two. I place myself in this category, albeit a sparrow alongside the birds of paradise on display here.

"For Shackleton," declared a man who knew the great explorer intimately, "the Antarctic didn't exist. It was the inner life that mattered to him." What a curious statement this seems, at face value. Shackleton was among the most redoubtable men of action of the twentieth century—up there with fighter pilots and Hemingway.* Can it be true that he valued the life of the mind as much as its physical counterpart? The division between action and contemplation is porous, and as I have tried to show earlier in this book, some of us need the one—the life of action—as a catalyst to explore the other. My own experience tells me that the life of the mind is a good deal more challenging than the life of action. Anyone can head off into the desert or the snowy waste. It's trickier to sit down and unravel knotty questions about perception and reality. The explorers I have chosen in this section all knew that the glaciers of the mind are the hardest to climb.

GERTRUDE BELL

How could I leave her out? Like so many Victorian women, she flourished abroad, that exotic and open land which afforded freedom undreamed of in the parlors of home. We have already met Mary Kingsley; one might also cite Isabel Burton, née Arundell, the Catholic aristocrat who married the Protestant pauper Richard Burton. Gertrude Bell was among the leading Arabists of the day, and a far more interesting one than that fraud T. E. Lawrence, whom of course she knew. She seems to have admired him rather more than I do. He was able, according to her, "to ignite fires in a cold room." Both worked tirelessly to aid the Arabs in their struggle to establish self-rule.

I went up to Brasenose shortly after they let women in. Almost half a millennium of tradition wasn't going to die in a year or two, but still, my tutors didn't make me sit with my back to them.

---

*I mention Hemingway with misgiving. A man of action, yes; but how keen he was to prove it in words. E. B. White caught his style when he parodied him with the spoof title "Across the Street and into the Grill."

On the Far Edge

Besides reshaping the political map of the Middle East, Gertrude Bell was a noted scholar and a distinguished linguist. Literally and metaphorically, she entered uncharted territory. The last five decades each had its biography of Bell, but the route from the past to the present is always shifting, and there is space on the shelves for Janet Wallach's contribution (*Desert Queen: The Extraordinary Life of Gertrude Bell*). It is not an insightful book, but it tells a hell of a story.

Bell was born into a family of prosperous Northumbrian industrialists in 1868, a time when Britain was engorged with confidence. When she went up to Oxford in 1886, her tutor made her sit with her back to him because she was not a man. But she showed them all: she gained a first in modern history, went on to publish translations of the Persian poet Hafiz, and in later years produced the critical triumph *The Desert and the Sown*.

Like many before her and since, Bell found a new identity away from that place called home. Although she traveled through many lands, she was happiest in the desert, on the far edge of life. After a week on a camel she could straightaway walk for miles (I was a physical wreck for a month when I tried). It was in Iraq that she made her mark on history. The first woman to serve as a military intelligence officer, Bell had a dazzling career in that field. Self-rule, Bell became increasingly convinced, was the way forward in the Arab world. She advised Churchill at the 1921 Cairo Conference, influencing the establishment of the Hashemite kingdom of Transjordan. She was in on the birth of modern Iraq and made sure that Faisal, her confidant and another Hashemite, became its first king. Lawrence, twenty years her junior, dwelled in her shadow until the American writer Lowell Thomas made him a star.

Slender and red haired with green-blue eyes, Bell was a committed smoker. She never married. Dick Doughty-Wylie, soldier-statesman, poet, and Arabist, was the love of her life, but he already had a wife, and although he was passionately involved with Bell for many years, the relationship remained unconsummated. "His letters," writes Wallach, "made everything she did seem worthwhile again." Doughty-Wylie died on the beach at Gallipoli, and Bell's spirit died with him.

From a young age Bell displayed that apparent contradiction of many strong women who forge their own way: she was actively anti-suffrage. It was only herself whom she saw as equal to men. She did it their way: on the job, she even dressed as a man. But she promoted the education of Iraqi women. Not everyone liked her, and some accused her of arrogance. Until the end, she was closest to her adoring father, having lost her mother at the age of three.

There were other failed romances besides Doughty-Wylie. Wallach states that what Bell wanted most in the world was marriage and children. The black dog hounded her throughout the second half of her life, and two days before her fifty-eighth birthday she killed herself. At her memorial service in London her grieving father said, "I think there never were father and daughter who stood in such intimate relations as she and I did to one another."

Wallach, an American, is billed as a Middle East expert, and she marshals her material well (Bell wrote copious letters, which are extant). The book is stronger on content than style. Besides a crop of anachronisms, such as Lawrence appearing as "a graduate student," and Bell "dating" in late-nineteenth-century England, Wallach has a predilection for the leaden metaphor ("scholars sampled a feast of ideas") and gusts of overheated rhetoric. She can bring a scene alive, though, and does so especially well during the doomed 1919 Paris Peace Conference.

Bell emerges anew from these pages, whether ordering furniture to be shipped out to Persia from Maple's on the Tottenham Court Road, scoffing a fig with King Faisal, or writing heartbreaking letters to her sisters about crushed hopes and abandoned dreams. Sitting in her tent during a hailstorm, she read *Hamlet*, then composed a letter to Dick.

"Princes and powers of Arabia," she wrote, "stepped down into their true place, and there rose up above them the human soul, conscious and answerable to itself."

1997

FRIDTJOF NANSEN

Most of the great men of exploration were too flawed to be called great in any meaningful sense. Even the greats, in other words, weren't great. As Alan Moorehead—still an unbeatable commentator—wrote of that dazzling rogue Richard Burton, "He was one of those men in whom nature runs riot: she endows him with not one or two but twenty different talents, all of them far beyond the average, and then withholds the one ingredient that might have brought them to perfection—a sense of balance and direction."

Can it really only be Fridtjof Nansen in whom all the talents come together? We met Nansen earlier on Franz Josef Land, sledging to safety with one companion and chancing upon an English explorer. Here's a squib I wrote about him for *The Guardian*'s My Hero slot.

A Man for All Seasons

Polar exploration tends to attract more testosterone than talent, and in the Arctic department expeditions have all too often concluded with the inadvertent loss of digits while waiting for the rescue team.

One man towers over the other ice-encrusted sledgers: Fridtjof Nansen, colossus of the glaciers. In August 1895, he and the stoker Hjalmar Johansen battled to 86 degrees north on maple-wood skis, just 230 miles short of the pole. Theirs was the biggest single advance in polar travel for four centuries. A long-faced Norseman with a touch of the archetypal brooding Scandinavian (as well as a hint of the Sphinx), Nansen was born near Christiania, the former name of Oslo, in 1861 and in the course of a tumultuous life became an outstanding scientist, diplomat, and humanitarian as well as an explorer. He was a founder of neurology, discovering that nerve fibers, on entering the spinal cord, bifurcate into ascending and descending branches. They are still known as Nansen's fibers. A Nobel Peace Prize was among the laurels bestowed for his work as a League of Nations high commissioner, in the course of which he had originated the Nansen passport for refugees. Following independence in 1905, he became his country's first ambassador to the Court of St. James's and at one point almost rose to the position of Norwegian prime minister. Perhaps that is why he was a better explorer (and writer) than the rest: he did other things, a man for all seasons. Nansen sensed at a profound level the "yearning after light and knowledge" and, almost uniquely, was able to marry that understanding to physical capability and snowcraft. He once said it was better to go skiing and think of God than to go to church and think of sport.*

When I camped myself on the Greenland ice cap (more a case of *Carry On up the Polar Regions* than *Scott of the Antarctic*), I sensed the ghostly presence of Nansen. It was he, along with five companions, who made the first crossing of that huge country. Of all the frozen beards who had been there before me, only Nansen communicated a sense of the true subjugation of the ego

---

*Which reminds me of the story told in an American seminary fifty years ago. When a Franciscan complained to a Jesuit that his superiors had refused him permission to smoke while praying, the Jesuit replied that he had had better luck because he had asked if he could pray while smoking.

that endeavor can bring. Failure, he acknowledged, would mean "only disappointed human hopes, nothing more," and this great poet of northern latitudes concluded, "If we perish, what will it matter in the endless cycle of eternity?"

2009

CAPTAIN SCOTT

At the end of seven months in the Antarctic, I slept on Captain Scott's bunk in his Cape Evans hut. I use the verb "slept" in its broadest sense: it was more a case of lying awake trying to keep breathing in order to avoid hypothermia setting in. From that bunk, and that hut, Scott set off for the pole on October 24, 1911. He never returned and lies somewhere out there still, preserved in the deep Antarctic ice. It was difficult not to grow sentimental as I huddled in my sleeping bag looking up at the bookshelves where Scott had set his pipe and his photographs of home, shifting on the wooden planks on which he too once listened to polar winds battering the hut. I have chosen three pieces on Scott: one about him, one about his wife, and one about daily life in the hut. This last, which appears first here, was commissioned to accompany a volume of silver gelatin reproductions of Herbert Ponting's photographs. Scott appointed Ponting official photographer on his second and last trip to the Antarctic. His pictures depict life going on in and around Scott's Cape Evans base camp.

Lights in the Darkness

"As Arctic huts go, [it] was as palatial as is the Ritz, as hotels go." Apsley Cherry-Garrard, in his description of the Cape Evans hut in *The Worst Journey in the World*, continues, "Whatever the conditions of darkness, cold and wind might be outside, there was comfort and warmth and good cheer within." It was

Ponting's genius to capture the warmth and good cheer of Cape Evans in photographs.

Fifty feet long, twenty-five feet wide, and nine feet to the eaves, the hut had been prefabricated in Poplar, east London, transported south on board *Terra Nova*, and erected on the ice-covered beach at Cape Evans on Ross Island in January 1911. The site had been selected partly for the access it offered to the Ross Ice Shelf, then known as the Great Ice Barrier. (This immense sheet of floating ice, about the size of France, was to provide Scott's route onto the continent itself.) The hut was insulated with seaweed and heated by a bulbous stove that dominated the interior "like a lighthouse." A bulkhead of packing cases divided the officers' quarters at the far end from the galley and the seamen's berths nearer the porch, a sophisticated acetylene lighting system had been installed, and telephones connected the whole building with two science shelters. When the packing was under way on the West India Docks, Scott and his quartermasters neglected neither patriotism nor leisure: portraits of the king and queen smiled benignly down on their subjects (and on Tryggve Gran, the young Norwegian who went south with Scott), while Nellie Melba and Caruso belted out tunes from the gramophone ("ripping!"). There was even a Pianola that operated automatically using rolls of music. When this instrument was sledged over from the ship and installed at Cape Evans, the first tune it played was "Home, Sweet Home." (The Pianola was unreliable. At the regular Sunday morning divine service Scott led, it once burst spontaneously into "Knees Up, Mother Brown," thereby terminating its deployment for religious purposes.)

Most of Ponting's Cape Evans interiors were taken in the austral winter of 1911, after the ship had left and the sixteen officers and scientists and nine seamen who remained in the Antarctic had settled into a routine. The day began at 8:15, when Thomas Clissold, the cook, served up fried seal liver and porridge. As everyone liked porridge, there was never enough to go around.

During the morning people worked at scientific experiments, exercised the dogs and ponies, or fetched supplies from the stores; on one occasion two men were almost killed by a five-hundred-pound case of hams flying through the air in an eighty-mile-per-hour wind. They returned with ice in their beards for a lunch of bread, butter, jam or cheese (on alternate days), and, twice a week, sardines or lambs' tongues. Tea and cocoa were followed by pipes, then, unless a blizzard was on, they went out again, returning for hut work and a spot of Pianola before a seal or penguin dinner—seal liver curry was popular—and mutton on Sundays. They drank diluted lime juice for its antiscorbutic properties, often with a suspicious penguin flavor derived from the ice slopes from which they quarried water. Alcohol was served only on birthdays, and a careful record was kept to ensure that each man only had one birthday a year.

Bathing was not a priority. "We usually wear our underclothing about a month," Petty Officer Thomas Williamson recorded in the second winter. (When they ran out of soap, Williamson noted that now he wore his pants for longer than a month.) The acetylene was turned off at about 10:30 in the evening, whereupon the hut was dark except for the glow of the galley stove and the silhouette of the night watchman preparing his supper by oil lamp. If it was calm outside, only snores, the ticks of the instruments, or the whine of a dog broke the silence. But it is rarely calm in an Antarctic winter. More often, the roars and howls of a blizzard shook the hut and hurled pebbles against the wooden walls.

Although Scott's main aim on this expedition (his second) was to reach the South Pole, his was also a serious scientific mission. Hydrogen-filled balloons floated into the gloom, attached to fine silk thread and carrying temperature and pressure recorders. Edward "Atch" Atkinson, the nimble navy doctor and former boxer, was doubling as a parasitologist and was often to be found enthusiastically delving in the entrails of penguins.

His corner of the hut bristled with culture ovens, test tubes, and microscopes. Scott, who took an interest in every experiment, had an oddly religious attitude to the work. "Science," he wrote in his diary on May 9, 1911, "the rock foundation of all effort!" Over the winter he arranged an evening lecture program, scheduling three talks a week. But when the geologist Frank "Deb" Debenham spoke on volcanoes, several people fell asleep, and after Charles "Silas" Wright, the Canadian physicist, held forth on "the constitution of matter," he recorded in his diary, "Wonder if any of them knew what I was talking about."

Ponies had been used to pull sledges on at least one Arctic expedition, and Shackleton had first taken them south in *Nimrod*. They had not proved reliable polar adjuncts for Shackleton, nor were they to do so for Scott; nonetheless, the ponies, and the dogs, played an important psychological role at Cape Evans. They were companions to the men in the dark months, even friends—a fact that played hard when the men had to eat them. In the winter almost everyone visited the stables regularly to pat a horse on the nose. Built onto the side of the hut and accessible via a passage off the entrance porch, the stables were the fragrant domain of Captain Lawrence "Titus" Oates, a soldier in the Inniskilling Dragoons, and his Russian groom, Anton Omelchenko. Once a jockey in Moscow, Anton was four feet ten and spoke very little English, though he was devoted to the Soldier, as Oates was known. In fact, everyone liked the laconic Oates. In the warren of officers' bunks named the Tenements, most inmates pinned up images of pretty girls ripped from *The Illustrated London News*. Not Oates. The only picture above his bunk was a portrait of Napoleon. In the perpetual barracking that was a feature of life at Cape Evans, Oates and Cherry were the leading upper-deck Conservatives, locked in warfare against the Liberal faction.

Nicknames flourished. Girls' names were popular, with Lieutenant Harry Pennell metamorphosing into "Penelope" and

Edward Nelson, a biologist, into "Mari." The twenty-seven-year-old Henry Bowers was a goblin-like Scot with red hair, limbs tough as teak, and a hooked beak that had conferred the nickname Birdie. As the oldest man, Scott's chief of scientific staff, Edward Wilson, was dubbed Uncle Bill, and Scott was known respectfully as the Owner, the standard naval term for the captain of a warship. Thomas Griffith Taylor, another geologist, was a gaunt, untamed figure who talked so much that the dog handler Cecil Meares dubbed him Ram-Jatsass. The others eventually discovered that this meant "verbally flowing eternally" in a Tibetan dialect. (Meares had traveled extensively in Tibet. He was a spy.)

Scott was forty-two years old at the start of the expedition. He was not a fatherly leader. He was reserved and subject to black moods that lasted for days. Temperamentally, he was complicated, especially in his self-doubt, which tortured him. The younger men found him unapproachable. "I think," Silas wrote many years later, "it was because we had little knowledge as civilians of the naval system. I for one stood in some awe of Scott." The tweed-jacketed Uncle Bill, on the other hand, inspired superlatives from everyone; his presence in the hut bordered on the sacerdotal. "To all his comrades," Raymond Priestley, yet another geologist, remembered, he was "the nearest thing to a perfect man they ever knew or [could] hope to know."

Of the numerous parties, Midwinter's Day was the most extravagantly conceived and eagerly anticipated. Clissold devised a banquet featuring *noisettes d'agneau Darwinian* and *charlotte russe glacée à la Beardmore*, a June version of a Christmas tree was fashioned from ski poles and feathers, and cigars were fetched from the stores along with the champagne and port. After dinner Scott read scurrilous extracts from the freshly printed edition of *The South Polar Times*. The tradition of the expedition newspaper, begun in the Arctic, had been enthusiastically taken up on Scott's previous trip, when Shackleton was appointed the first editor of *The South Polar Times*. Now the June 1911 midwinter number ran to more than fifty pages and included prints by Ponting and watercolors by Wilson. Production standards were extraordinary, given the conditions. Bernard Day, the motor engineer, made a binding from gray sealskin and plywood and carved a monogram on the cover. Much of the material was in praise of sledging:

> *O Blubber Lamp! O Blubber Lamp!*
> *I wish that I could tell*
> *The glamour of thy smoky-gleam,*
> *The savour of thy smell.*

Despite the winter darkness, the moon and the southern lights enabled the men to enjoy the views around Cape Evans, whether of the Transantarctic Mountains glimmering on the other side of McMurdo Sound, the icebergs silvered with soft moonbeams, or the banner of smoke unfurling from the snout of Mount Erebus, the active volcano that reared behind the hut. "I have seen Fuji," Cherry wrote in *The Worst Journey*, "the most dainty and graceful of all mountains; and also Kinchinjunga: only Michael Angelo among men could have conceived such grandeur. But give me Erebus for my friend. Whoever made Erebus knew all the charm of horizontal lines, and the lines of Erebus are for the most part nearer the horizontal than the vertical. And so he is the most restful mountain in the world." The transcendent natural beauty of that place stimulates a sense of wonder in the human spirit. I know: I lived in another hut at Cape Evans, eighty years after Cherry looked up at Erebus.

Once the sun began leaking light, the men played nine-a-side soccer matches on the ice, though twenty minutes each half was enough in those temperatures. Gran, at twenty-two the youngest man at Cape Evans, had represented Norway at the sport, whereas Anton had never seen a soccer ball before and was not sure what side he was on until shortly before the match ended. They had a go at ice hockey too but abandoned it when the puck, which they had made from shellac and paraffin wax, shattered as soon as it was struck. Then it was back indoors for billiards, played on a miniature folding table with wooden balls so rackety that one was no longer recognizably round.

As the Antarctic quivered on the cusp between night and day—springtime in the far south—the men talked of little but the forthcoming 860-mile trek to the pole, and the long table in the hut was permanently piled with rations queuing to be weighed and bagged. The two remaining motor sledges and their unfortunate carers were to be the first to set out on the long-awaited southern journey (the third had crashed through the ice and into the ocean as soon as it was unloaded, taking Williamson and his dirty underpants with it. He, but not it, was fished out). They finally lurched off on October 24.

This first year at Cape Evans was not one long idyll, as later accounts suggested. What expedition ever is? But they rubbed along all right, given the psychological demands of a polar winter. On July 18, Deb, the son of a New South Wales parson, wrote, "Tempers are beginning to get just a little shaky in one or two cases but produce nothing worse than sarcasm and we still keep up the *Terra Nova*'s reputation as a happy ship." When the ship itself actually did come back at the end of the following summer, some of the men left with it. They were the lucky ones who missed the second winter, a season in which life at Cape Evans was a threnody of grief, loss, and anxiety. The five sledgers in the polar party were dead, though nobody yet knew how or where they had perished, and there were grave fears too for Victor Campbell's six-man group stranded out on the other side of McMurdo Sound. "The scenery has lost much of its beauty to us," Deb wrote, "the auroras are cheap and the cold rather colder." Who can wonder? Every day they looked at empty bunks.

Ponting was among those who left on the *Terra Nova*. He

therefore left us no images of the emotional carnage of the second winter. Highly strung by disposition, and, like many photographers, a loner happiest hidden under the hood of his camera, Ponting was a hard worker, and he was dedicated to the role of what he insisted on calling "camera artist." When he wasn't taking pictures, he was developing films in his darkroom at one end of the hut. He even slept in this room, on a foldout bed. The others ragged him because he asked them to pose all the time (it was called "to pont"), and they found it difficult to avoid making fun of him. There was a touch of the ridiculous about Ponting. Before leaving home, he had been told that pepper was a capital thing to keep your feet warm, and he had brought a case of cayenne to put in his boots.

Ponting's vision of the Antarctic was binary. He wanted to record the beauty of a landscape unparalleled on the planet. But he also wanted to record the human warmth and intimacy of Cape Evans—Griffith Taylor bent over his geology notebooks at a table freighted with books, Clissold in a woolly hat rolling pastry for rhubarb pies, Oates and Meares peering through the blue smoke of a blubber stove making a bran mash for a sick pony. Haircutting, sewing, sketching—these are things we do in our own homes, and here these men are, doing exactly the same in the cold depths of a polar winter. Like the best artists, Ponting recognized that the daily detail casts a long light.

Taken together, Ponting's twin visions have left us a potent memorial of life at Cape Evans. "These days are with one for all time," Wilson wrote in his diary before leaving the hut to die on the trail with Scott, "they are never to be forgotten—and they are to be found nowhere else in all the world but at the poles. The peace of God which passeth all understanding reigns here in these days."

2007

Evolution of a Hero

Captain Scott is one of those perennially attractive figures, able to absorb the spirit of successive generations and facilitate continual reinterpretation. In the early hagiographies he emerged as a Galahad of the snows, embodying all that had made his nation great. In the words of Stephen J. Pyne, one of the best contemporary interpreters of the Antarctic and its mythology, "The dying Scott, like Orwell's dying elephant, became a parable for the dying British Empire." But heroes come and go. In 1979 the polar historian Roland Huntford debunked the first myth and set another in its place: Scott as a paradigm of English emotional inadequacy and reckless waste, his story an allegory of arrogance and stupidity. Huntford's Scott fulfilled the needs of a postcolonial age. So what has David Crane, the latest in a long line of writers seeking the real Scott, produced for us? (*Scott of the Antarctic: A Life of Courage and Tragedy.*)

Robert Falcon Scott's antecedents were undistinguished. Born in 1868, he entered the navy at thirteen. As an adult he was shortish and did not excel. But he reached the rank of commander and in 1901 sailed *Discovery* to the ice—his first independent voyage. Antarctica, as Crane puts it, was "the new Africa," and Scott returned home a public figure, staying at Balmoral with the king and crisscrossing the country to address halls overflowing with moon-eyed admirers. But he still traveled in third-class railway carriages to save money. In 1910, a captain at last, he went south again in *Terra Nova*, and from that journey he never returned.

Crane is temperate in his opinions and never quick to judge. He calmly disposes of many of the claims of Scott's detractors, persuasively arguing, for example, against the case that there was a naval cover-up for an early career blunder. When the truth is unknowable, he does not try to wrest it from insufficient evidence: we cannot tell whether Scott's wife, Kathleen, had an affair with Fridtjof Nansen while her husband was slogging up the Beardmore Glacier. As for the final tragedy, I am sure Crane is correct to state categorically that three crucial weeks of unusually low temperatures killed Scott and his four companions—ten to twenty degrees colder than average every day—rather than incompetence or sentiment (the latter, it has been suggested, leading to Scott's unwise decision to take four companions to the pole because he could not bear to leave anyone out—despite the fact that the fuel rations were packed in units of four). Only in his treatment of Amundsen, I think, does Crane fall into some of the old crevasses of prejudice. Was the Norwegian really any more "ruthlessly single-minded" than his English counterparts?

Into the facts of his narrative Crane weaves a sequence of deeply intelligent disquisitions on a range of issues, from the implications of the abstruse signaling culture in the late-Victorian navy to the history of cartographic fantasy. In his breadth of reference he creates a more nuanced protagonist than his predecessors: the cast of characters on whom he calls to tell his story ranges from Sophocles to Lady Thatcher. He is a fine descriptive writer, able to conjure the grating rasp of wind in the rigging, the whiff of pemmican hoosh after a hard day man-hauling over the plateau, and the rigors of golf played on the ice with red balls. He is adept, too, at the judiciously positioned stylistic flourish—William Peel is "Byronically dead by the age of thirty-three"—and strong on both humor and irony. Here he is, describing the plight of a small group of men who became stranded on a geologizing mission. They were obliged to spend the whole winter in a cave, with one book between them. "For sheer, drawn-out, troglodytic misery, compounded by ptomaine poisoning, dysentery, hunger, uncertainty, mental misery, blubbery filth and *David Copperfield*, the following months are unrivalled."

Unlike previous biographers, Crane identifies an evolution in

Scott's character. Between the two expeditions, a *folie de grandeur* coagulates in the hinterland of his personality. During a protracted quarrel with Shackleton in 1906, for the first time Scott's "defects of character feel something more than the failures of the moment." But his marriage revealed, in the shoals of anguished letters it spawned, an inner life tormented by self-doubt, and overall this is a sympathetic portrait.

"If in small things [Scott] was often found wanting," Crane writes, "in big things very seldom." He rightly holds his man in the highest regard as a writer and judges that Scott's greatest gift to posterity is his "profound ability to make real the experience of human nature at the limits of its endurance." That is a wonderful sentence. Scott's gifts in the authorial department, Crane argues, are based on "close and disciplined organisation" and "a commitment to the literal as well as the 'poetic' truth of a landscape." This, he concludes, "is not simply a matter of 'atmosphere'— any travel writer with a pen can manage that." As I am the only travel writer ever to have written an Antarctic travelogue, I suppose he must mean me. Demoralizing news, but he is probably right.

What has David Crane achieved in these six hundred pages? He has moved polar scholarship forward by dint of scrupulous and exhaustive research. He has produced a sympathetic synthesis for our age—a Scott who is neither hero nor villain. Most important, he has freed himself from the tyranny of the card index to let Scott live again as a man who had the "profound ability to make real the experience of human nature at the limits of its endurance." More, surely, than one could expect from an ordinary biographer with a pen.

2005

Worst Dressed

Kathleen Scott, Captain Scott's widow, was an accomplished sculptress who saw life in bright colors. On her gravestone, she wanted the inscription "No happier woman ever lived." You have to envy that.

She was born in 1878, her father a middle-class Victorian clergyman and her mother soon dead. Her childhood was replete with hordes of relatives, most of them barking mad, but empty of most other things, and the "vagabonding," as she called it, soon began. A free spirit, she liked to sleep outdoors and at the first opportunity took off to Paris, where Rodin came for lunch. She also went to Macedonia to take part in relief work, delivered Isadora Duncan's baby, and did not care what she looked like: James Lees-Milne called her the worst-dressed woman he knew. He, however, was not the marrying kind: those who were grew moon-eyed when Kathleen entered the room, and parts of this book (*A Great Task of Happiness: The Life of Kathleen Scott* by Louisa Young) read like a catalog of suitors. "I must try not to be so engrossedly interested in boys," Kathleen wrote. She married Scott after his first trip to the Antarctic, and she went to New Zealand to wave goodbye when he set off on his last. The Norwegian explorer Fridtjof Nansen was famously in love with her: Louisa Young forswears the contention of Kathleen's detractors that she was screwing Nansen as Scott slogged to the last camp. For some years Asquith visited Kathleen almost every day and tramped the streets outside her house if she was not in. She was also very friendly with Shaw, who, because she was not feminine, said his affection for her was "the nearest I have ever come to homosexuality." A lucky escape, one feels, for both parties.

During the war she worked at the Vickers factory in Erith, Kent, and went dancing three times a day. In 1922 she married Hilton Young, a journalist and politician who later ascended to the Upper House as Lord Kennet; Austen Chamberlain gave her away. Hilton had been turned down by Virginia Woolf, and when he enters the story, half of Bloomsbury follows. At the age of forty-four Kathleen had her second son, Wayland, the present Lord Kennet and the author's father. She was a celebrity, and her work sold.

Young is good on the apotheosis of Scott and on the language of patriotic idealism and mystical romanticism all but forgotten two world wars later. For a biographer she is too partisan over the facts of the expedition, announcing that Amundsen's secrecy was "at best underhand," which is nonsense, and stating categorically—one assumes to annoy the revisionist historian Roland Huntford, her father's enemy—that Scott died last in the tent, an assertion whose validity is simply unknowable.

She refers once to Kathleen working "to hold the shadows at bay," and I was gasping to know more about these shadows; Young also tidies religion away by telling us that Kathleen did not need God, an explanation that is too simplistic for Kathleen, and for the rest of us.

The style of *A Great Task of Happiness* is sprightly, which is good, and sometimes skittish, which is all right, but then it veers toward the frivolously colloquial, which is bad. I applaud Young's refusal to disavow her own modern sensibility, but this inevitably often strikes a wrong note in the context of Kathleen's story. A landlady's sexual peccadilloes are "very Anaïs Nin," and Young flings in phrases like "hanky panky," calling Kathleen "a practiced pricktease." Worse, the prose can be clumsy (on sculpture: "She liked it and it liked her"), occasionally careering into the unintelligible: "In the context of the Antarctic, getting a move on what not something a person should hold their breath over."

Biographies by family members are inherently dangerous. But Young has made a virtue of kinship. Kathleen's spirit is here in her likable granddaughter's boisterous tone; I suspect that she put more of herself into this book than we know.

1995

SHACKLETON'S ROSS SEA PARTY

This is one of my favorite polar stories. I first came across it in the archives of the Scott Polar Research Institute in Cambridge; I was researching the life of Apsley Cherry-Garrard and had called up a sheaf of unpublished documents on the Shackleton expeditions in an attempt to locate a sledging camp Cherry mentioned in his diary. The afternoon light slanting onto the parquet floor from Leinster Road died on my hands as I turned the brittle pages of Arnold Spencer-Smith's tiny, leather-bound sledging journal. He was a thirty-one-year-old Episcopalian padre, sick and swollen purple from scurvy, wrapped in a snow sheet, and lashed to a sledge by teammates laying depots for Shackleton, who was approaching from the opposite side of the continent—or so they thought. They did not know *Endurance* had sunk or that Worsley was navigating that extraordinary boat journey to South Georgia. On one page Spencer-Smith had copied a verse from Isaiah: "Where is the place of my rest?" On the night of March 7, 1916, he dedicated his diary entry to his parents and six siblings, thawing his fingers to write in the blue Primus stove flame. "Bitterly cold," he scratched. "Bag frozen stiff and in a bad position." The next page was blank. He had died.

Not for Nothing

Ten men, stranded without supplies in the Antarctic in 1915. They battle starvation, disease, and temperatures in the minus 90s. Some do not change their clothes for two years. Yet somehow they march close to two thousand miles, in relay, to lay vital food and fuel depots for colleagues about to sledge in from the opposite direction. And looming over them all, unseen yet omnipresent, is the figure of Sir Ernest Shackleton, the leader they call the Boss. It is a gripping story embracing both tragedy and triumph, and Kelly Tyler-Lewis tells it well (*The Lost Men: The Harrowing Saga of Shackleton's Ross Sea Party*).

Shackleton set off on his privately funded Imperial Trans-Antarctic Expedition in August 1914. The war drums were beating in Europe. He had been to the Antarctic twice before and was already a hero in Britain. This time he planned to sail to the Weddell Sea and sledge fifteen hundred miles across Antarctica, following a doglegged course via the pole. He knew he would not be able to pull sufficient supplies the whole way, so he dispatched another ship to the Ross Sea on the opposite side of the continent. The men it carried were to lay a 360-mile chain of supply depots, which his team would pick up on the last quarter of their journey.

The Ross Sea party sailed from Tasmania in December 1914 in *Aurora*, a former Newfoundland whaler Shackleton had bought sight unseen. Making their base at Cape Evans on Ross Island, in the hut vacated a year previously by the survivors of Captain Scott's last expedition, they started sledging immediately. Tyler-Lewis's account reveals chronic deficiencies of equipment, confused orders, and a perilous reliance on chance and weather as men dragged heavy sledges through deep snow while most of the twenty-six dogs perished. And through it all they talked of Shackleton, marching gloriously toward them. Or so they believed.

As the light failed, they settled down to their first Antarctic winter. *Aurora*, moored nearby, served as a floating warehouse for fuel and all other necessities. But in May 1915 a blizzard blew the undermanned ship out to sea, and the horrified crew watched the lit windows of the hut recede into whirling snow and darkness. Glued into an ice floe, the ship had no hope of returning to Cape Evans. Ten men were left in the hut with the clothes they stood up in and less than half the sledging done. They were without food, fuel, and, worst of all, tobacco. The disaster falls exactly halfway through *The Lost Men*, and in many respects it provides a climax before the descending fugue of suffering and disaster that forms the second half of the narrative.

Most of the ten had never met Shackleton. But they believed his life, and those of his men, depended on them. What they did not know, of course—there was no communication between the parties, and none with the outside world either—was that the Boss had never started on his journey.

Tyler-Lewis has truffled out a mass of diaries, logs, and letters. "As the chorus of voices swelled," she writes, "a rich tone poem of their experiences and thoughts began to emerge." They were a disparate crew: an explosive blend of scientists, seamen, and chancers. Significantly, the two protagonists, Ernest Joyce and the one-eyed Scot Aeneas Mackintosh, had both sailed with Shackleton before. Mackintosh, who was in charge, was a lieutenant in the Royal Naval Reserve. Joyce, responsible for dogs, stores, and sledging equipment, was a swaggering hard drinker whose grit and raw talent won out. Tyler-Lewis flags up the tension between the pair from the outset, and while she rightly lauds Mackintosh's loyalty, bravery, and determination, she reveals that many of his leadership decisions were flawed. Throughout her book she uses quotations judiciously, wherever possible allowing the men to speak for themselves. Obliged to improvise, they scavenged rations left by previous expeditions (and preserved by the cold), cut trousers out of old tents, smoked sawdust, and lived chiefly off seal, which also provided blubber fuel. They celebrated Communion in Captain Scott's darkroom and for two summers sledged across the Ross Ice Shelf, known to them as the Great Ice Barrier, up to the foot of the Beardmore Glacier, laying depots of food and fuel in the ice every sixty miles. Each man was pulling over two hundred pounds, on starvation rations and in temperatures in the minus 30s, yet they covered almost two thousand miles in total, most of it with only four dogs and sometimes with sick men lashed to the sledges. They fought snow blindness and scurvy; amputated each other's toes; reduced the rations to a half cup of tea and a quarter of a biscuit. "We are still alive this morning," someone wrote, "so must be thankful." The timing was desperately close, and the months unfurled in an agony of runic calculations as Mackintosh worked out how—if—they could do it. They laid the final depot, as agreed, at the foot of the Beardmore Glacier, that mighty cataract of ice twelve miles wide and a hundred miles long. "If there is a hell," Joyce wrote in his log, "this is the place, and the sleeping bags are worse than hell."

Shackleton's apostles often boast that he never lost a man, but it is not true. He might not have lost a man under his direct command. But three of the Ross Sea party died, and they were his men too. The first casualty, Arnold Spencer-Smith, expired on the second summer march. Engaged on the expedition staff in the role of photographer, Spencer-Smith was always willing to submit to the physical labor still required constantly in a polar camp today and had become a popular member of the expedition. But the Padre, as the others called him, had been terribly sick for sixty-seven days, in the end bleeding from his bowels from extensive internal hemorrhaging. In camp at night, he sank a foot into the ice, unable to change his position. He never complained. On the march, when the wind dropped, the others heard his voice, half smothered by the flap of the sleeping bag, reciting prayers, sometimes in Latin and sometimes in English. His four teammates buried him on the Ross Ice Shelf, too weak to lift the body in the shallow depression. "Simply let it fall into the grave," wrote Joyce.

Later that season, a group holed up at Scott's old *Discovery* hut waiting for the sea ice to freeze before trekking thirteen miles back to their base at Cape Evans. Mackintosh and a colleague decided to make a break for it on May 7, a date the others knew to be far too early, as the ice was not yet fast. But disease and privation had impaired the two men's judgment; tottering bags of bones, they had become crazed in the second, much harder winter. They were never seen again. And the ones who lived stared at the white horizon, searching for men who never came. The Australian physicist Dick Richards emerges most distinctly because, crucially, he lived long enough for a previous biographer, Lennard Bickel (*Shackleton's Forgotten Men: The Untold Tragedy of the* Endurance *Epic*), to interview him in his dotage, and that primary material lives on in these pages. Of the two other protagonists, Mackintosh took his diary with him when he died under the lid of the Southern Ocean. Joyce, who, imperceptibly at first, took over the reins of leadership from Mackintosh, produced his own egregiously self-serving book, *The South Polar Trail*, in 1929, the only published account by a survivor and long out of print.

Meanwhile, *Aurora*, which had drifted for ten months, returned to rescue the depleted Ross Sea party—with the Boss on board. Against all odds, Shackleton had got his own shipwrecked party back to South America alive and then hurried across the world to rescue the depot layers. He was less than honest in his account of this part of the expedition. The Great Showman wrote in his own book *South* that during the troglodytic tenure of five of the Ross Sea men at Hut Point during the second winter, there was "plenty of fresh food and dried vegetables available." This was not true, as Richards testified to Bickel. Shackleton was covering up. In 1928 the polar historian Hugh Mill wrote that "the full tale had better remain unpublished for some time to come." A number of those involved criticized Shackleton for his poor organization in respect of the Ross Sea party. In our own age, bad planning and suffering sit uneasily with the cult of personality that has enveloped Shackleton. But he was ultimately responsible for one of the greatest triumphs in the history of human endeavor in the Antarctic—perhaps the greatest. By this I mean the depot laying. The closing chapters of the story have the plangent twang of a Greek tragedy. Was this small group's journey the most harrowing ever made? I think it might be. But it is more than a tale of survival. Like all the best stories, it is about the triumph of the human spirit and the dignity of what remains when the flesh disintegrates with frostbite and scurvy. At the age of ninety Dick Richards, who said that he had never fully recovered from those months on the Great Ice Barrier, said this: "That the effort was unnecessary, that the sacrifice was made to no purpose, in the end, was irrelevant. To me no undertaking carried through to conclusion is for nothing. And so I don't think of our struggle as futile. It was something that the human spirit accomplished."

2006

POSTSCRIPT

At the time the drama reached its conclusion—1916—it was overshadowed by Shackleton's open-boat journey over a thousand miles away; by the harvest of death being reaped in Europe; and by the absence of a Hurley or Ponting to cement the story on film. The Ross Sea party remained little known outside a small circle of polar aficionados. Why has it not now risen to the surface, when icy adventure tales are modish? While publishers and producers wheel out familiar stories again and again, some of the best persist in obscurity. Take the adventures of the British-born Australian geologist Douglas Mawson. He staggered back to safety in the Antarctic in 1913 after his two companions perished (Belgrave Ninnis fell down a crevasse, taking most of the food with him, and Xavier Mertz went raving mad, biting off his own fingers before expiring in the tent). Mawson ate the dogs—the eyes tasted good—and made it back to base with his body literally rotting: he lost the skin from his legs and genitals. As he crested the last ice ridge, he saw the ship sailing away.

HENRY STANLEY

But first, a word about Livingstone, Laurel to Stanley's Hardy. Or was it the other way around, and was Stanley Stan?

Livingstone was an archetypal Victorian hybrid: explorer, missionary, and scientist. In today's climate he would have been written off before his final expedition, as he was already in his fifties. But in 1865 he set out to find the source of the Nile. Generations of schoolboys have thrilled to the story of Stanley greeting Livingstone in the fetid lanes of Ujiji. I thrilled to it myself at Westbury Park Primary, reading my way through the modest school library by candlelight at home when power cuts shut down public services and ice cream vans with generators lit the hospitals. *Reader's Digest* transported me from West Country gloom to a world filled with the gaudy colors of flame trees, the taste of quinine and *mbembu* fruit, and the dense fume of rotting foliage. In temperatures of 128 degrees, Livingstone's teeth fell out, and he and Stanley suffered by turns subcutaneous maggots, dysentery, pneumonia, and bacterial foot infections that caused tropical ulcers. Supplies sent ahead were stolen, and cannibals lurked in the undergrowth. The ones at Manyuema preferred human flesh raw: to tenderize it, they soaked it for several days in running water.

It turned out that Livingstone had a symbiotic relationship with the very Arab slavers he had so publicly denounced at home. His was not a straightforward story, but whose is? He died in Africa shortly after Stanley departed. He was sixty. His few loyal servants buried his heart under a *mpundu* tree and mummified his body so it could be shipped to Westminster Abbey, where it remains.

He Dead

Henry Stanley provides a fine example of the endless process that is biography. A household name in his lifetime, chiefly for his "discovery" of Dr. Livingstone, Stanley has been relentlessly reinterpreted by a succession of biographers, each influenced by his own prejudices; by his own access to material; and, perhaps most significantly, by the demands of the zeitgeist. The lives already published present a stack of different Stanleys, all layered one on top of the other, like a palimpsest. And here comes Tim Jeal to add the inaugural twenty-first-century layer (*Stanley: The Impossible Life of Africa's Greatest Explorer*).

Stanley was born John Rowlands in 1841. An illegitimate Welsh workhouse boy, he fled to America at age eighteen. He maintained later that a kindly cotton broker called Stanley adopted him there, but Jeal all but disproves the story, the first evidence of his man's remorseless self-mythologizing. Stanley fought on both sides in the Civil War, became a journalist, and bluffed his way onto the *New York Herald*, where the proprietor, the rich and vulgar James Gordon Bennett Jr., dispatched him with unlimited expenses to find the lost missionary-explorer David Livingstone, surely the greatest assignment ever dreamed up on a slow day in the newsroom. (New York society finally ostracized Bennett when he urinated into his fiancée's fireplace at a New Year's Eve party.) In 1871, after a grueling trek in which all his white companions died, Stanley found the destitute Livingstone in Ujiji. He returned to fame and fortune and decided he was an explorer at heart. Like all legendary men of action, he was short.

Although it was his meeting with Livingstone that immortalized him, the next expedition constituted Stanley's finest achievement ("perhaps the greatest journey of all time," according to Jeal). He followed the Congo for eighteen hundred miles and circumnavigated two of Africa's great lakes—in each case the first man to do so. He subsequently took the shilling of the monstrous Belgian king Leopold II, setting up trading stations in all the best spots and paving the way for Leopold to found the colony for which he had longed. During the Berlin Conference in

1885, Stanley began to lose faith in the king's philanthropy, and anyway Leopold betrayed him with his promises. All told, Stanley spent sixteen years in Africa. On his 1887 expedition through the Ituri rain forest to rescue Emin Pasha, he had 389 men with him. One of his subordinate officers, a Jameson whiskey heir, went bonkers, whipping and shooting countless Africans before expiring himself. Many of Stanley's men took concubines. "When you kiss your cannibal," one reflected, "she may have blood on her lips." What a biopic it would make!

He seems to have remained unfulfilled in the emotional department.

"During my long bachelorhood," Stanley wrote, "I have often wished that I had but one tiny child to love." After a series of failed relationships he married Dorothy Tennant in Westminster Abbey, but the longed-for child never arrived, so they adopted a son and settled in Surrey. Jeal is not keen on Dorothy. He thinks she was in love with fame, not with Stanley ("she resembled a great actress, acting out a theatrical role in real life"). Stanley became a reluctant Liberal Unionist MP—Dorothy put him up to it, Jeal reckons, to stop him returning to Africa, and who could blame her if she did?—and died in 1904.

What are the sources? Stanley wrote ten books, though as Jeal painstakingly reveals, they bulged with lies. If Stanley was pursued by eight canoe-paddling, armed Africans intent on plunder, you can be sure their number rose to eighty in the published account. But crucially, Jeal had access to a voluminous archive of letters and diaries closed to previous biographers. Of the secondary sources, the most influential of previous biographies, and in many ways the best, is Frank McLynn's double-decker published in 1989 and 1991. McLynn's portrayal of a thuggish repressed homosexual keen to implement Leopold's murderous policies rather did in Stanley's image. More generally, no subsequent volume has yet challenged Alan Moorehead's *White Nile*.

Jeal states candidly that his aim was rehabilitation. He has previously written a biography of Livingstone in which the process of reassessment was reversed: rather than the saintly figure of legend, selflessly saving black souls (a myth created, ironically, to some degree by Stanley), Livingstone emerges as a distinctly unimpressive character. In this new book Jeal constantly leaps to Stanley's defense, whether on the Leopold issue ("nor in 1878 did Henry have any means of knowing what the king's real intentions were") or on the matter of Stanley's partnership with the Zanzibar slaver Tippu Tip. "Exceptional men," he avers when Stanley criticizes his subordinates harshly, "are often intolerant of those without their drive, discipline and gift for leadership." That is no excuse at all, but I am bound to say that in the end I found Jeal's portrait convincing. McLynn, though, is more intuitively in touch with the spirit of the age, and his biography has an intellectual dimension that Jeal's lacks. As for style—Jeal is also a novelist, and he has a novelist's eye, ably conjuring a twisting caravan of porters preceded by the diminutive Stanley atop a stallion, wearing his trademark flat-topped hat that looked like a lampshade and blasting on his kudu horn.

Modern biographers, in my view, overplay their hand when it comes to the influence of a parentless, loveless childhood. The effect of such a thing must be dramatic, but in what way is unknowable. According to Jeal, Stanley's "old insecurity about his background" was responsible for everything he did. Can it really be so simple? Jeal writes of two opposing poles in Stanley's nature, one craving love and security, the other adventure. But isn't that all of us?

Although he achieved fame—a knighthood, and dinners at Windsor Castle—Stanley was never accepted by the establishment. His moral reputation was questioned, partly because of the Leopold connection and partly because of reports of brutality, and his expeditions were often pursued by controversy (he has often been cited as a prototype for Conrad's Kurtz, which he was not). Postcolonial guilt has probably played a role in modern portrayals; Jeal certainly thinks it has. But, however interpreted, it is a wonderful story, almost epic in scope. Stanley is a figure who invites strong opinions and, therefore, reassessment.

One wonders what his next biographer will make of him.

2007

POSTSCRIPT

What of the Congo today?

In the 1890s the country deteriorated into the very heart of darkness, and so it is again. Livingstone's last written words were a prayer "to heal this open sore of the world." For that miracle, we must carry on praying.

WILFRED THESIGER

Two years before he died, I met Wilfred Thesiger at his old people's home in Surrey. We took lunch together, the dining room overlooking a golf links on which stockbrokers sliced and lofted while we made our way through tomato soup, incinerated roast beef, and rhubarb crumble. Thesiger was ninety-one, subdued, and somewhat beaten in spirit, but physically upright, his hawk-like profile as noble and proud as ever. We talked a little of the old days, but his heart wasn't in it. A fire had gone cold. That night I reread *Arabian Sands*, in my opinion his best book. In its pages the fire burned as brightly as ever.

A Life of Savagery and Color

Wilfred Thesiger, writes Alexander Maitland in his long-awaited authorized biography (*Wilfred Thesiger: The Life of the Great Explorer*), was "the patriarch of modern exploration and travel." For six decades Thesiger roamed the loneliest places on the planet, returning intermittently from tents and smoke-filled hovels to the lordly glamour of the Travellers Club in Pall Mall, where he arrived for lunch in a bowler hat and pin-striped suit. He thought of himself as the last in a noble line of overland travelers, a refugee from an Augustan age, and in a way he was— except that Thesiger was not motivated by geographical prizes. His aims were mostly private. And that, of course, is more complicated.

Born in 1910 in the British legation in Addis Ababa, he spent an idyllic early childhood among flashing swords, prowling beasts, and Galla horsemen wearing leopard skins and velvet. He liked to say it prepared him for "a life of savagery and colour." When he was nine, the family returned to England, and the young Wilfred was dispatched to prep school in Rottingdean, where he was thrashed till he bled; to Eton, where he met Haile Selassie; and to Magdalen College, Oxford, where he boxed for the university. In 1933 he returned to Addis to follow the Awash to its source. After that, he was off—to the Sudan, Syria, Palestine, Morocco, India, Jordan, Kenya, Tanzania, Ladakh, Iran (which he insisted on calling Persia until the end of his life), and southern Iraq, where he made his name and wrote his best books.

He always traveled on foot with tribal companions and baggage animals, rarely accompanied by other Europeans. He spoke Arabic well. A keen ornithologist, he collected thousands of specimens for the British Museum and, at least until the latter years, was a passionate hunter: he had the collarbones of his seventieth lion mounted in gold by Asprey, a top London firm with a royal warrant dating back to the nineteenth century. In World War II he served under Orde Wingate in Abyssinia, collecting a DSO, then in Syria and North Africa with various elite units of the British military. Although most of his travels were undertaken for their own sake, Thesiger achieved a number of geographical firsts, notably two crossings of the Rub' al-Khali, southern Arabia's Empty Quarter, the largest sand desert in the world. In the late 1970s he settled in Maralal in Kenya with an entourage of young Samburu men he called his "sons." The queen knighted him in 1995, and he won every geographical medal going, ending his life in England in 2003 at the age of ninety-three.

Maitland was Thesiger's close friend as well as his literary executor. He is a diligent researcher and in clear, steady prose movingly evokes emotional climaxes such as the death of Thesiger's mother and the humiliating fleecing he endured at the hands of the Kenyan "sons": between 1978 and 1994, Thesiger spent in excess of half a million pounds on them.

What does this book add to Thesiger's 1987 autobiography, *The Life of My Choice*, or to Michael Asher's *Thesiger* (1994)? Maitland's principal advantage is his exclusive access to an archive of letters, diaries, and manuscripts, and with it he is able to clear up the many inconsistencies Thesiger introduced into accounts of his travels through exaggeration and embellishment. The detailed information here is unrivaled, and Maitland has certainly produced the most authoritative account we have. He ably conjures the smell of fresh milk in a smoke-cleansed gourd, the crackle of camel hooves on salt flats, and a huddle of men crouched around a fire under a spray of desert stars. In the psychological landscape he is less sure-footed. One does not close the book with a sense of the inner man.

Throughout his life, Thesiger surrounded himself with teenage boys. In Kenya he shared his bedroom with a sixteen-year-old he referred to as his "bodyguard." "Sex doesn't come into it," he said. He implied a lifetime of celibacy, and Maitland takes him at his word, referring vaguely to "furtive embraces and voyeuristic encounters." While prurient speculation has no place in a serious biography, I can't help thinking that more analysis is required here.

Our hero does not emerge as a sympathetic figure. Even by the standards of the time he could be priggish; he had no sense of humor; his self-belief was impregnable; of independent means himself, he scorned those obliged to work for a living. ("She is writing articles for *Vogue*, which is about her level," he wrote of

Lesley Blanch when he met her at a party in Tehran.) But who cares what he was like when he wrote so well? Both *Arabian Sands* and *The Marsh Arabs* are enduring poetic masterpieces— more than one can say about the tomes of the tin-pot heroes who crowd the front pages today.

Tall and austere, with craggy good looks, Thesiger is often called a Romantic. He was not so in a Wordsworthian sense: he did not see the sublime in nature. Only people gave the wild places meaning for him. But he was a Blakean Romantic, recognizing the perils of industrialization and dreading the transformation of technological progress. His life, like his work, is a lament for what we have lost: for the traditional life as it was lived for a thousand years, before the transistor radio replaced the bard. "Now that the main road is built," Thesiger wrote of the route from Kabul to Mazar-i-Sharif, "the lorries thunder by; the camel caravans are gone, their bells stilled for ever."

2006

Climbers

was sitting on my bunk—one of six in the windowless cabin of a cargo ship threading through the channels off the coast of southern Chile on the three-day voyage from Puerto Eden to Puerto Montt. It was 1993, and a thin, boyish man in the bunk below was reading *1984*. I offered him a swig from a bottle of pisco, and we got talking. He had been climbing in Torres del Paine and was on his way to Bariloche in Argentina to sell his mountaineering equipment to raise cash for a plane ticket home to Wales. He told me that on the way up, dangling from the rock faces, he sucked *dulce de leche* (sweetened condensed milk) from a tube he had rigged up attached to a pouch in his pocket. I like neat *dulce de leche* too, but I spoon it direct from the jar into my mouth while standing barefoot in the kitchen.

This climber—Paul Pritchard—spoke quietly of an uncompromising passion for the mountains and the life-affirming satisfaction he found when the oxygen got thin. The encounter ignited an interest that still burns, not in climbing, as I am no mountaineer, but in the literature: how climbers express the urge to risk everything for the sublimation of the summit. After our Chilean encounter, Pritchard went on, higher and higher. In 1998 he tackled the Totem Pole, a monolithic sea stack off the Tasmanian coast. On that climb, a boulder the size of a television fell on his head. He survived appalling brain injuries, became a motivational speaker, and wrote three rather good mountain books himself.

Orienteering literature, like every other kind, conjures its period. Recounting his slog up the 25,645-foot Nanda Devi in 1936, Bill Tilman concluded with a description of his summit dash with Noel Odell. The cold air was still, and the sun glittered off distant Himalayan peaks. The pair had climbed higher than any man before them. "I believe," wrote Tilman, "that we so far forgot ourselves as to shake hands on it." The true books are about more than peaks and crampons—Gaston Rébuffat's *Starlight and Storm*, Heinrich Harrer's *White Spider*, and let's not forget *The Ascent of Rum Doodle* by W. E. Bowman. The best contemporary climbers can offer is Joe Simpson. But that is quite good enough.

Simpson is not a crampon and testosterone man. He likes to nose up against the psychological barriers. Having opened up his "baggage of fears and dark terrors" in *The Beckoning Silence*, the fifth in his mountaineering cycle, he tries, as he has before, to answer the ineffable question, Why climb? Simpson has more self-knowledge than most, but in the end I don't think any of us has much of a clue about why we do anything.

When reading Simpson, I skim past the technical data (the failure of a prototype lightweight camming Jumar, or how a waterfall ice grade 6 differs from a grade 7). His success has always been predicated on the allegorical potential of the mountains, and it is this that has won him a large and devoted readership far beyond the climbing fraternity. In *The Beckoning Silence* he returns to the theme of climbing as a metaphor for living, meditating ruefully on "the half-lost, half-won game of life that we could never quite finish."

Simpson nearly died in 1985 when he tumbled off the unclimbed west face of the twenty-one-thousand-foot Siula Grande in Peru. He told the story of his survival in *Touching the Void* (1988). He and his climbing partner Simon Yates had reached the summit, but Simpson broke his leg on the descent. Yates lowered his friend down the mountain until he inadvertently suspended him from the edge of an overhanging ice cliff. In imminent danger of being hauled off the mountain and unable to pull Simpson back up, Yates was forced to cut the rope. Simpson fell into a crevasse, and Yates, finding no sign of him and sure he was dead, descended to base camp. But Simpson managed to crawl to safety, and *Touching the Void* tells the story of those four days of agony during which he teetered on the brink of life.

Joe and I were both young authors at Jonathan Cape, and we met in the office of our editor, the much loved, much missed Tony Colwell.* Joe hated coming down to London from Sheffield. He was living on the dole there when he wrote *Touching the Void*, finding the whole process agony. In 1987, Tony had been allowed to pay Joe an advance of £2,000 (under the sufferance of Tom Maschler, his boss at Cape, who thought the book a rubbish

---

*Between delivery of the typescript and production, I would regularly trek down to Vauxhall Bridge Road for an editorial drubbing. "Too bored to read on here," Tony wrote in red pen in the margin of an early draft of *Terra Incognita*.

idea). Tony told me that at one point Joe rang to say he simply couldn't go on; *Touching the Void* would never see the light of day; he was going to pay back the advance.

Tony coaxed him out of it, and you know the rest: in excess of a million copies sold worldwide, and a big-screen documentary. Joe went on climbing. Since writing *Touching the Void*, he has spent eighteen months on crutches, developed osteoarthritis, endured nine operations, and amassed a world-class collection of pins, plates, wires, and nails. "Maybe it's just me," Simpson argues with himself when a colleague reckons the seracs towering above them look safe. "I'm getting too cautious for this game." And yet, and yet: the crunch of ice in thin, heady air, the feel of the screws gaining purchase, and the whiff of a brew in a high bivvy after a hard day on the rock face—Simpson evokes the thrill of altitude better than anyone.

Funerals crop up a lot. Joe once told me that he loses a friend a year to the mountains. In *Dark Shadows Falling* (1997) he launches a polemic against the competitive spirit of the contemporary climbing community. "The attrition of friends over the years had begun to eat away at my confidence," Simpson gloomily concludes elsewhere. And who can wonder? In *The Beckoning Silence* the doubt that has been gathering like a thundercloud breaks out into a storm. On a perilous ice climb in the Alps the forty-one-year-old Simpson allows himself to be persuaded to continue by a colleague's poor call. "In the past I might have felt that this was what it was all about," he writes. "This was where you defined yourself, balanced tenuously between life and death." Now his misgivings consume him. Shortly afterward, stranded in the freezing shadow of an avalanche high in the Bolivian Andes, he confesses, "I began to realize that I no longer loved the mountains."

Redemption, however, was near to hand. Simpson went on to tackle the formidable north face of the Eiger, a caper that involved crawling almost two miles uphill on his hands and knees. During an especially brutal storm two young Englishmen who had been climbing just above Simpson and his partner hurtle past them to their deaths. Simpson retreats "calmly and in good order," though you and I might not have described what he was doing as calm, as rocks the size of footballs, dislodged by the storm, were continuously whizzing past his head. But he fell back in love with the Alps.

2002

Going Strong for the Top

It is one of the most exuberant moments of modern British history: a climber on the summit of Everest holding aloft an ice ax strung with a dancing Union Jack. Back at home, news of the ascent breaks on the morning a beautiful young queen is crowned, evidence that a new Elizabethan age was surely dawning after the horror and grief of war and the grinding austerity that trailed in its wake.

Just fifty years on, Everest is a holiday camp for the super-rich. In his bestselling account of the 1996 season, *Into Thin Air*, the climber Jon Krakauer describes a New York socialite holding a rope and being towed up the mountain by a Sherpa. Three years before that, forty people summited on the same day. Photographs of base camp invariably reveal an untidy carpet of spent oxygen cylinders. As for the wonders of satellite communications: they reached a grisly climax on Everest when the New Zealand guide Rob Hall was patched through to his pregnant wife at home as he sat dying in a snow hollow on the South Summit next to a dead client. His wife never saw him again.

Contemporary climbers and adventurers are compromised, compared with the innocent Edmund Hillary and his colleagues. The field is so much more crowded, the race for sponsorship so much more intense. Perhaps as a result, the role of the ego, always critical, has overreached itself. It is impossible to imagine leading adventurers of today remarking of themselves, as Hillary did recently, "I have always recognized myself as a person of modest abilities."

Before the triumph of 1953, the unclimbed Everest had cast a spell over the Western climbing fraternity for several generations. The later Victorians and Edwardians were peculiarly keen on rushing up mountains in tweed jackets, and many had a crack at the big one. Most famously, George Mallory and his golden-haired companion Sandy Irvine entered British mythology when they vanished into the mists of the 29,035-foot peak in 1924, "going strong for the top."

Twenty-nine years later, Hillary and Tenzing Norgay were led onto Everest by John Hunt, a Sandhurst-trained colonel in the Rifle Brigade. When the Royal Geographical Society selected him for the role, Hunt was serving in Germany with the British army of occupation. His final team consisted of twelve climbers and thirty-six high-altitude Sherpas. They attacked the mountain siege-style from the south side, with various pairings battling up and down the slopes, establishing camps, carrying loads, and gradually pushing upward. Hunt's route followed the rugged, icy slopes of the western cwm. At 21,200 feet the men established advance base, and then, at the head of the cwm, faced the Lhotse glacier. They had no long-distance radio, just a heavy metal box that the climber could sling around his neck in order to speak through a rubber mouthpiece to base camp. This was before the plastic age, so even the simplest items were heavy. In addition, much of the gear was unsuitable for low temperatures. Even with today's high-tech equipment, everything takes longer once the mercury drops. I know from my own experience in the Antarctic that fiddling with the frozen fuel pipe of a Primus stove can take hours and that one recalcitrant crampon strap can wreck a day. Imagine what life was like for Hunt and his men:

two to three hours of struggle after waking just to make tea, strike camp, and prepare for the next haul.

After negotiating the Lhotse, Wilf Noyce and Sherpa Anullu pioneered a route to the 26,210-foot South Col. Hunt then sent out the physicist Tom Bourdillon and the brain surgeon Charles Evans. These two were trying out a bulky closed oxygen system that used soda lime to absorb carbon dioxide (it weighed fifty pounds and didn't really work).

They passed the point reached by a Swiss expedition the previous year, then pushed onto the crest of the South Summit, higher than anyone had been before but not the top of the mountain. Hunt had not designated a particular pair of climbers for the summit: it was to depend on circumstances and performance. Bourdillon and Evans had always been likely candidates. Now Evans, whom Hunt had put in charge, had a tough decision. Bourdillon was desperate to keep going, but they were already low on oxygen and shattered. After an argument, insofar as one can have an argument wearing a balaclava, they came down.

Back in the saddle of the South Col, Hillary and Tenzing were waiting.

The long-faced Hillary was one of two New Zealand climbers on Hunt's expedition. A large, easygoing beekeeper, he had started climbing late, at twenty-six, but over the next eight years had quickly built up an impressive range of experience. His partner, Tenzing Norgay, had a dazzling reputation: a year earlier it was he who had got to within 750 feet of the summit of Everest with the Swiss mountaineer Raymond Lambert. Because of his experience, Hunt had made Tenzing a full team member, as well as sirdar, or foreman, of the Sherpas.

Hillary and Tenzing had both performed strongly so far. Yet as he watched their tiny figures inching up the white slopes, Hunt, who had himself humped gear up to 27,350 feet, was anxious. Six serious attempts had failed that year on Everest. Furthermore, a French team already had permission to mount a big expedition in 1954, and the Swiss were booked in for 1955. It seemed certain that this was the last chance for imperial Britain.

On May 28, Tenzing and Hillary pitched their tent (still canvas then) on a perilously narrow ledge and enjoyed a supper of chicken noodle soup, sardines on crackers, a tin of apricots, biscuits, and jam accompanied by hot sweet lemon water and coffee. Amazingly, they managed to sleep. On May 29 they set out at 6:30 in the morning. The temperature was minus 80°F, and Hillary had been obliged to thaw his frozen boots over the Primus flame. Breathing oxygen at less than one gallon a minute, they reached the South Summit at nine o'clock and looked over a vista of the soaring Makalu rock ridges and, farther back, the peak of Kangchenjunga. Before them, a thin skin of ice covered deep, soft snow. The Gothic ice walls rearing above were being squeezed by hundreds of tons of glacier ice, and the men knew that they were working under the constant threat of avalanche.

On the final haul to the main summit, Hillary noticed an ice cornice hanging over the mighty Kangshung Face and wondered if it might collapse as he climbed. "We seemed to go on for ever," he wrote of the final slope. He was cutting steps in the ice as he nosed upward, roped to Tenzing behind, "tired now and moving rather slowly." They were breathing heavily through the frosty valves of their oxygen tanks.

At 11:30 they moved onto a flattish exposed area of snow with nothing but space in every direction. This was it. Hillary revealed his Anglo-Saxon antecedents by stretching out his glove for a handshake, but Tenzing threw his arms around him. They had done it.

Does the use of bottled oxygen diminish their achievement? Were the Italian-Austrian pair Reinhold Messner and Peter Habeler the first to climb Everest properly when they surged to the top without supplementary oxygen in 1978? It depends on your point of view. Personally, I think that each generation stands on the shoulders of the one that went before and that neither achievement ranks "higher" or "lower" than the other. I doubt if Messner and Habeler would have made it unaided back in 1953, when Everest was unclimbed.

The first ascent captured the public imagination in a way that amazed its protagonists. Hillary was halfway back to Kathmandu on foot (the expedition had no vehicles) when a letter arrived in the hands of a Nepali runner announcing that the climber had been knighted. Hillary thought it was a joke at first ("I did not regard myself as suitable knightly material," he said). Tenzing got the George Medal: as a non-Commonwealth national, he could not be knighted. In Kathmandu, and everywhere they went afterward, Hillary and Tenzing were mobbed. Both are still household names today, half a century on. Perhaps inevitably, a current of conflict ran even between this noble pair. In his book *Man of Everest*, Tenzing recorded that Hillary's account of the climb was inaccurate and that his, Tenzing's, role had been diminished. The Nepalese king irritated Hillary by telling him that Tenzing said it was he, the Nepali, who was first to the top. But there was to be no debunking of Everest '53. On Coronation Day one newspaper headline in London ran, ALL THIS AND EVEREST TOO. The triumph on the snows revealed, or so people thought, that being British still meant something, even as the empire tottered toward extinction.

Inaccessibility and primitive media contact meant that romance still clung to mountain men in 1953, just as it had in 1924, when a British team lugged bow ties and sixty tins of quail in foie gras to Everest. The men themselves were different too. Mallory's fellow climbers were almost all classically educated, and they regularly knocked off a few iambic pentameters around the campfire.* Hunt's epic expedition has come to symbolize the last

---

*Throughout the twentieth century, critics have associated the demise of classics with general intellectual deterioration. When I sat the entrance

gasp of that tradition (the climber Wilf Noyce was a poet and schoolteacher, like many of his predecessors). Hillary himself remains the quintessential hero—long limbed, indomitable, forever young.

The professionalization of sport, reduced risks, incomparably faster communications: one way or another, the thrill of peak bagging has disappeared with leather crampons. In 1995 thirty-three-year-old Alison Hargreaves became the first woman to summit Everest without oxygen. A month later she was dead. She disappeared on the steeper, colder slopes of K2, the world's second-highest mountain. Her death unleashed an orgy of re-criminations. She left two small children, to the fury of the press, which ranted about her reckless irresponsibility. The moral climate has altered in the half century since Hillary's triumph. Now that most geographical goals have been attained, we are asking, increasingly, what is the point?

Perhaps Ellen MacArthur stands out as a heroine for our time. But I wonder if her triumphs will be vividly remembered in fifty years. Only the image of Neil Armstrong wobbling about on the moon has captured the public imagination quite as dramatically as those two muffled climbers on the summit of Everest. Anyway, the unlikely heroes are always the most beguiling, and few are as unlikely as the affable Hillary. The first person he met on his way back down the mountain was his colleague and friend George Lowe. "Well, George," said Hillary, "we knocked the bastard off."

1998

---

examinations to Oxford in 1979, I was required to translate "The quality of mercy is not strain'd" and the rest of Portia's speech into Greek prose. At the subsequent interview, a don told me candidly that my effort had been poor. "And of course," he said, "forty years ago we could ask candidates to translate the same passage into iambic pentameters."

How does one write about people? You can't know someone else, even if you live in the same house. Unknowability fascinated me. I had read Edmund Morris's 1979 biography of Teddy Roosevelt and admired it deeply. Morris had since been commissioned to write the official life of Ronald Reagan. The Great Communicator was still in office, so for a decade Morris shadowed him: on Air Force One, at Reykjavík, into the bathroom (see below). When Reagan faded away and Morris began to write his book, I heard through the grapevine that grappling with the intractability of someone else's inner life had tormented Morris to the extent that he had decided to write the biography with an invented-narrator device. "My aim," he was quoted as saying, "was to give physical flesh to the biographer's mind. It was there already. I just gave it flesh." Morris did not in any sense intend to fictionalize, nor did he. By making the writer a contemporary character in the story, he was able to extend the closeness of observation. This fascinated me even more, and I persuaded *The Telegraph* to send me to Washington to interview Morris about his tactics.

Writing Ronald Reagan

t all happened to Edmund Morris when he wrote *Dutch*, the biography of Ronald Reagan to be published simultaneously on both sides of the Atlantic this coming week. Already the award-winning biographer of a long-dead American president, in 1985 Morris became Reagan's official biographer and for a dozen years followed him everywhere except the lavatory.

Morris's first book, published in 1979, was called *The Rise of Theodore Roosevelt*, and as debuts go, it wasn't bad: it won Morris a Pulitzer. It also hooked him the Reagan commission, as Ronnie admired *Rise* so much that he invited Morris to the White House. The president had read the book during his first few weeks in office, in bed, with Nancy beside him reading a biography of Edith Kermit Roosevelt by Morris's wife, Sylvia. "I began to hear from friends," says the affable Morris, "that the administration thought it would be a good idea for a historian to hang around the White House, and that if I wanted to pitch for the job, I'd get it."

He backed off, because he didn't think Reagan was interesting. But as the presidency developed and "got more and more dramatic," Reagan began to intrigue him. In the spring of 1985, Morris asked if he could write the book after all. The president's team said yes, and Random House signed Morris for $3 million. Neither Reagan, nor Nancy, nor the White House ever raised the subject of text approval.

In terms of biographical style, *Dutch* (an early Reagan nickname) is a different beast from the solid, straightforward *Rise*. Morris had a debilitating false start: he spent several years writing Reagan's biography in the orthodox style. "By writing about him 'from the outside,'" he says, standing against the library window of his immaculate house on Washington's Capitol Hill, "I completely failed to penetrate the man.

"Then, one day in October, I was walking through the oak trees in the Capitol grounds here. I stepped on an acorn and had what you call an epiphany. I was thinking about Reagan walking over the acorns in the grounds of Eureka College, Illinois, in the fall of 1928. I was overcome with longing to see him as close up as I was seeing him in the White House. As I stepped on the acorn, I said to myself, I wish I could have been there. And a voice in my head said, *But you were there*, in a sense." Morris decided to create a backward extension of himself to tell the first part of Reagan's story. The narrator, called E., mutates into Morris himself in the year 1964. E. and Morris function as Reagan's doppelgänger.

"Biographers are doppelgängers of their subjects, to a certain extent. In a creepy sort of way they begin to accompany their subjects through life. When I was reading Roosevelt's private diaries about the girlfriend he had at college, I felt I was voyeuristically looking through the bushes when they were spooning in the wood."

Morris constructed a life for the narrator that was loosely parallel to Reagan's life, with the result that the first part of the story is told from a close but disconnected point of view. Then Edmund Morris himself takes over, so two people tell this long story: one is made up and one is real. And not only that. Morris went on to deploy a range of unconventional forms in order to purvey his material. One chapter is written in the form of four film shorts and includes this piece of advice: "Any director wishing to shoot the following material should apply to Reagan's lawyers for permission, since these are his memories, not mine."

Morris says that this is just another way of presenting his material. Well, yes. But it represents an imaginative approach to the biographical genre surprising in an official presidential life. Does it work? I think it does. Morris has written a magnificent authorized presidential biography in a wildly unconventional and idiosyncratic form. *Dutch* is enthralling. (And this reader despises Reagan.) In addition, unlike Reagan himself, the book is funny. "I drove through drifting drizzle to the new Canadian embassy at the foot of Capitol Hill," reports Morris at one point, "where Allan and Sondra Gotlieb were bidding good-bye to half a thousand close friends."

I have often wondered if biographers come to resemble their subjects, like dog owners and their dogs. It seems not: whereas Reagan wasn't interested in anyone except himself, Morris asked many questions about my own inconsequential work. He is thoughtful, genial, and measured, and I can see him on every page of *Dutch*. Most of the literary references and allusions in his prose would have been completely lost on the Great Communicator himself. He evokes *la peste* (the plague) in Camus's novel as a metaphor for the fall of France in 1940; Philip Larkin's images of snow falling; "a more mystical sense of universal harmony, which is the legacy of German Romanticism." You end up more interested in Edmund Morris than in Ronald Reagan. Perhaps all biography is covert autobiography. Perhaps all writing is.

America is Morris's adopted country. His parents are South Africans of English descent and raised three children in Kenya. Edmund, the eldest, dropped out of university in South Africa and in 1964 moved to London to work as an advertising copywriter. Four years later, he shifted to the United States, and now, a youthful fifty-eight, he says he feels "completely American." He certainly doesn't sound it. If you heard him on the radio, you'd think he'd never left the home counties.

He and his English wife, Sylvia Jukes Morris, shift between the Washington house and a New York apartment. Capitol Hill might be the political hub of the nation, but its wide, clean streets are pervaded with an Orwellian quietude. Morris says it is so silent in the evenings that he can hear his heart beating and that he much prefers his noisier New York abode. Nonetheless, he chose to live on the Hill rather than in the livelier Georgetown, perhaps to feel closer to his enigmatic subject. Enigmatic, yes. But how many forests have been sacrificed to fill Reagan's archives! Morris notes in the book that archivists at the Reagan Presidential Library "meticulously" store "every last lunch voucher of the White House Interagency Low Income Opportunity Advisory Board."

"Virtually none of the material was worth looking at," Morris says, "because Reagan kept all of himself to himself. All I cared about in those documents were the little squiggles he wrote in the margin. I am interested only in character and the narrative of character."

Even the few things Reagan did reveal had to be reinterpreted. Morris talks about a special symbol he used in his notebook when taking down what Reagan said. The symbol meant "He feels the opposite of what he says." Inevitably, Reagan's autobiography, ghosted by Robert Lindsey and published in 1990, stands like a wraith next to the corporeal *Dutch*. "He wasn't a liar," says Morris, always quick to spring to Reagan's defense.

"He was a man who glossed his past. He obliterated things he didn't want to remember. By dint of being by nature an actor, and moving from production to production, his memory was short.

"When I confronted him about his desire to join the Communist Party, I knew he was going to deny it, so I put my face up close to his and looked into his eyes. I wanted to see the flicker in his pupils. There was absolutely no flicker. 'Oh, no, no,' he said." The four volumes of Reagan's diaries, reverentially bound in the president's private papers, are hardly guides to the man's inner life. Morris notes that one of the only idiosyncrasies in them is "an extreme conscientiousness in tabulating the number of times his speeches were interrupted by applause." A touch of the Evil Empire.

Because he was so opaque, Reagan was a particularly challenging biographical proposition. Yet I wonder if one can ever glimpse the inner life of another, except perhaps through great poetry. Morris thinks you can catch vestiges of it. "One sees the inner life in the merest conversational exchange, if one is acute."

He handles the onset and advance of cognitive frailty with great sensitivity, crystallizing it into moments, such as the one in a Tampico diner when Reagan spools out the same old Hollywood stories, but this time leaves out great chunks, "while Nancy picked at her salad, her face a mask"; or Reagan's homage to Baroness Thatcher at his own eighty-second birthday party, at which he toasts her twice, at length, and in exactly the same words.

Then Morris visits him at his imposing suite of offices on top of the highest glass tower on Avenue of the Stars in L.A. and finds him alone behind his huge desk, bent over comic strips neatly cut out for him from the *Los Angeles Times*. Morris puts it like this in his book: "He had long since stopped recognizing me; now I no longer recognized him. For all the intimate familiarity of that face and body, and the soft husk of his voice, I did not feel his presence beside me, only his absence."

Many biographers writing about living people have had the uncomfortable experience of knowing more about their subject's youth than the subjects can remember. But in Morris's case the disparity was attenuated toward the end by Reagan's Alzheimer's. "An odd, Dantesque reversal of roles had occurred," he writes, "as if I were now the leader rather than the led." The metaphor becomes reality in a scene in which Morris takes Reagan back to the house in which he was born—a place the president had not visited since he was a tot. "Neither of us could have foreseen how shocking that moment was," Morris comments. "I had led him to the very point of his origins."

In the end he stopped interviewing Reagan, because he was afraid he might lose his objectivity. Yet *Dutch* cannot be called an objective book (what biography can?), in that Morris is frequently overt about his feelings. Most notably, he describes his reaction to Reagan's "sunset of my life" letter, in which the former president announced to the American people that he had Alzheimer's. Morris read the letter in the papers, walking home from a newsstand in Washington with his wife. He writes that at that moment he felt love for Reagan. I wondered what academic critics might make of that kind of authorial intervention in a scholarly work (the first draft of the typescript included more than three hundred pages of notes).

"From the moment I stepped on the acorn, I knew this book was going to be hugely controversial," Morris says, getting up to switch a pair of books that have been misfiled in the alphabetically arranged bookshelves. "I can only write what I feel. If one stops to think about the effect one has on academic critics, one would never write anything worth a damn."

Morris has observed power in action more closely than anyone who wasn't actually employed by the administration—and more intimately than the majority of those who were. Even after twelve years, this urbane man is awed. But like many who come into contact with great figures, he was struck by Ronald Reagan's ordinariness. "I stood in Reagan's bathroom at the ranch watching him put cream on his nose and seeing the toilet cover on his loo, and the utter ordinariness of this little room and me and him, and I thought, this is the leader of the free world." So he did follow him into the lavatory after all.

At one point he writes that he didn't think it was his business to ask the names of the women Reagan slept with between Jane Wyman and Nancy, though he does say there were a lot of them. Most biographers would feel that that was their business. "I feel literature should respect privacy," says Morris. "If a man chooses to make his sex life a public issue, like Oscar Wilde did, it's public property. But otherwise, I don't think it's the business of literature to pursue it. Naturally, I'm curious. There are a few things I've found out about Reagan's sex life which I've just not put in the book."

Biography is a mucky job. No wonder it has a poor public image. George Eliot said biographers are generally a disease of English literature, and Larkin memorably satirized one of their tribe as Jake Balokowsky in his air-conditioned research cell, all sneakers and university grants. "Larkin is right to feel wary," says Morris quickly. "There is something intrusive about what we do—and something I don't quite like." And yet there is also something endlessly fascinating about swimming around in someone else's life. In the last paragraph of his prologue, Morris muses,

"Memory. Desire. What is this mysterious yearning of biographer for subject, so akin to a *coup de foudre* in its insistence?"

Not only is Morris always walking in another man's shadow. His wife is writing a second volume on the writer and diplomat Clare Boothe Luce (the first came out in 1997). The couple share an editor at Random House in New York. Clare Luce appears in *Dutch*, and Morris writes that he was "almost as involved in her biography as Reagan's."

He voted for Reagan, though he thinks that isn't relevant. There is a degree of ambiguity in Morris's attitude: at one point during our conversation, he refers to Reagan as an idiot savant, an opinion latent in the line he recently dreamed up when asked to sum up his subject, namely, "He was America, but he wasn't much else." Overall, Morris clearly admires him very much: the Reagan who walks off the pages of *Dutch* is a latter-day Caesar, bestriding the world of smaller men (Morris often emphasizes his physical stature). So was he relieved when he realized Reagan would never read the book?

"No. He never cared what anyone said about him. Those around him care very much about what people write. But he was so massively self-assured and incurious about himself he didn't care what other people thought."

That's an inhuman characteristic, isn't it? Morris pauses. "Superhuman."

"You mean, a sort of *Übermensch*?"

"Oh yes," he says. "He was an *Übermensch* if ever there was one. Totally unaffected by ordinary human vanities and passions."

I liked Edmund Morris very much, but I was uncomfortable with the way he turned so many Reagan characteristics, especially in the later years, into noble things. I longed for a little more mockery—though *Dutch* does include a corker about a speech in which Reagan pronounced the surname of Albert Camus to rhyme with "famous." Morris indulges in a kind of Reagan nostalgia created by what he calls "Clinton's squalid example." It has been said that Reagan was so respectful of the Oval Office that he never removed his jacket when he was in there. What would he have thought of what Clinton did in it?

Morris smiles. "At a press conference a few years ago a reporter asked Clinton what kind of underwear he wore. Clinton said, 'Briefs.' If Reagan had been asked that, he simply would not have understood the question. He would have been completely bewildered. But in fact he would never have been asked, because there was something about him that commanded respect. Whatever you thought about him politically, Reagan exemplified the dignity of the state."

All literary genres evolve, and hybrid forms of conventional nonfiction have become an increasingly prominent feature of publishers' lists. *Dutch* is the first major biography of our time to be written in such a very unorthodox form. Morris was not apprehensive about its reception. He is not an anxious man. "I think I have expanded biographical technique, maybe to a dangerous degree," he says calmly. *Dutch* will undoubtedly be influential. Other biographers will come along, stand on Morris's shoulders, and treat the genre in a more elastic way still. After all, says Ronald Reagan's biographer, "even the most serious, orthodox work of nonfiction is a refined form of fiction, isn't it? All we really write about is perception."

1999

POSTSCRIPT

The sharp-eyed reader will note that I took to Mr. Morris. We became friends, meeting often over the years in London and New York, where Morris moved post-*Dutch*. He has written two further magisterial volumes on TR (as we have come to know him, the installments identified like models of a car—TR2, TR3). As for my prediction that *Dutch* would be influential: it wasn't.

Academic critics mauled it with the viciousness only academia knows, and the rest of the critics obediently followed suit. I think the book was ahead of its time. V. S. Naipaul once said that good books make their way in the end, no matter what happens in the short run. I believe *Dutch* will be valued, one day, as the masterpiece it is.

You can see where this was leading. Life writing is a form that interests me deeply, and in about 1998 I sensed the moment had come to move on from the kinds of essays reproduced here and masquerade as a full-length biographer. One was simply adding a person to the landscapes one had depicted as a travel writer. The landscape remained, but an individual human drama set it in perspective. I knew I could only write about travelers, and I knew I could only write about minor figures: I lack the confidence to tackle an Eliot (George, or Thomas Stearns). As the second part of this next short essay reveals, this was to mean working with a serious lack of material.

And So the Years Passed

As a rookie biographer, I struggle hardest with problems created by the frailties of evidence, putting style aside (if only one could). The issue first revealed itself when I was writing the life of Apsley Cherry-Garrard, one of Captain Scott's men and the author of the 1922 polar classic *The Worst Journey in the World*. For Cherry's last restless decades I relied on the testimony of his widow, Angela, a woman in her eighties who, like most of us, could not reliably recall what happened half a

century ago (though she thought she could: she saw it so clearly).
During World War II she and Cherry lived near Baker Street in
London in a sixth-floor flat underneath Bertrand Russell, his
third wife, Patricia Spence, known as "Peter," and their school-
boy son, Conrad. Angela told me how Cherry, lost in the fug of a
black depression, had become so enraged by the sound of the
Russells playing the piano that he dispatched his wife upstairs to
ask them to desist. This was an intimidating task: a young woman
from the provinces issuing orders to one of the towering intel-
lects of the Western world. When she havered, Cherry persisted,
"I'd do it for you," as if that situation would have been remotely
comparable—he was a famous landed gent of sixty. Anyway, I
wrote to Conrad, by then the fifth Earl, at the House of Lords, to
ask if he remembered his grumpy neighbor. He did, and offered
perceptive comments from a mature perspective. "But," he concluded the letter, "we never owned a piano."

In the absence of a primary source (a delivery note from the
piano company), what is one to do? Had Conrad Russell not replied to my inquiry, the temptation to deploy unreliable memory
as if it were fact would have been irresistible.

Even when there is a primary source, it has the habit of conflicting with another primary source. What do you do when you
reach an unbridgeable abyss of ignorance between two contradictory bits of evidence? I was piecing together the life of Edith, the
youngest of Cherry's five sisters. Born in 1896, Edith was always
a shadowy figure in the family saga. A physically weak child, she
was designated an invalid and confined to a wicker spinal chair.
She features in photographs parked under far-off chestnut trees
with her nurse while siblings rampage in the foreground. Nothing further is heard of Edith until 1923, when she appears in a
magazine standing on top of the Matterhorn in boots and a good
tweed skirt. I had material about the beginning of her life and
material about the end: yet the one was so different from the
other that it seemed impossible to trace a route between the two.

A third serious problem was queuing up for attention. It emerged that the information I did have was disastrously unevenly spaced. Most biographers are familiar with the agony of the declining decades—that yawning phase about which one longs to write, "And so the years passed." In my case the problem was acute, as Cherry's Antarctic expedition—the emotional focus of his life—reached its dismal conclusion when he was twenty-six. I still had forty-seven years to go, years in which not much happened, barring a couple of world wars. Never again. My next and current subject, Denys Finch Hatton, died at the age of forty-four. Onward to Keats and Chatterton? In the Finch Hatton case there is almost no primary material: he did not keep diaries, fewer than a dozen of his letters survive, and as he pranged his plane into the Ngong Hills in 1931, hardly anyone alive remembers him. This was my fourth problem, and I'm finding it the most challenging. My only comfort is the knowledge that an absence of sources is not necessarily a handicap. Hilary Spurling wrote her brilliant second volume on Ivy Compton-Burnett out of fifty years of postcards saying please come to tea.

How is one to fill the gaps? You can't make it up; you can't invite the reader to take his choice; you can't do nothing. I battle daily not to gratify the biographer's need to impose coherence, seeing so clearly that in my own life there is none. All I have learned so far is that one must work out a way of conjuring the past without resorting to fiction. In other words, although biography cannot invent, it can find other ways of bringing a subject alive in the hearts and minds of the reader. I recently spent many weeks in the basement archives of the McMillan Memorial Library in Nairobi, reading local newspapers from the 1920s. I found the small ads riveting. A detail can cast a long light, and this is especially true where there is an absence of material. Just as the seconds in one's own life often count for more than the hours—even the years—the solitary detail can work hard. Everywhere one looks in high art this is the case: in Auden's poem "Musée des Beaux Arts" suffering takes place while someone else is eating, or opening a window, or just walking dully away.

There's another thing about material, though, more important than all the above. It's to do with the *quality* of the material. Biographies are not, as John Updike contended, "just novels with indexes." The best ones combine scholarship with imaginative storytelling (Michael Holroyd's *Augustus John*, David Cecil's *Lord M.*, about Melbourne). It might be a truism to say that the reader doesn't need all the facts, he needs the fertile ones, but if so it is a truism with which many writers of biographies appear to disagree. As Thomas North, the sixteenth-century translator of *Plutarch's Lives*, put it, "What signifies it to us, how many battles Alexander the Great fought; it were more to the purpose to say how often he was drunk." The subject's inner life is the life we care about. Now I come to think of it, a gap in the material is a useful metaphor for the inner life.

I'm sorry to go on about metaphors, but it seems to me that the elusive, unreliable, and flame-like nature of primary material is not unlike the human spirit—capricious, contradictory, and inconclusive. The gaps represent the fundamental, immutable isolation of one human being from another. Whom do we really know? But seeing through a glass darkly is still seeing. Or is it?

2003

Denys Finch Hatton, the subject of my book *Too Close to the Sun*, was an English aristocrat who went to British East Africa—now Kenya—in 1911 after a brilliantly unconventional progression through Eton and Oxford. A buccaneering adventurer of the old school, he dabbled in trade, in mining, and in farming, fought in the British East Africa Campaign—the last untold story of World War I—and finally became a white hunter. He took the Prince of Wales on monthlong safaris twice at the end of the 1920s. That was the POW who became Edward VIII. The safaris were a nightmare for Finch Hatton. All HRH wanted to do was shag the young wives of the district commissioners. Which he did. Finch Hatton was the open road made flesh. His lover Karen Blixen immortalized him in the poetic memoir *Out of Africa*. That was where I had first noticed him: his mysterious otherness caught my attention. He appeared as the eternal wanderer.

In terms of a career—positions held, books published, the shibboleths of success listed in *Who's Who*—there was nothing. Our hero would long ago have descended into obscurity were it not for Sydney Pollack. Observant readers may have noted, in recent years, a vogue for books with subtitles such as "The Story of the Man Who Invented Maps" or "The Life of the Fellow Who Discovered Oxygen." The subtitle of *Too Close to the Sun*, on the other hand, might have been "The Story of the Man Who Never Did Anything At All"—though this would not have impressed the marketing department at Jonathan Cape.

So why, as people so frequently ask, did I want to write about him? Well, I like people who paddle outside the mainstream. As a writer I don't fall into a category, and I like subjects who don't either. Finch Hatton was nothing if not a bundle of contradictions, and that was a model truer to my own experience of life than a rational, coherent, and stable personality would have been. More important, Finch Hatton's life illustrates many themes I find attractive—that of unfulfilled promise, for one, and the vagrancy of the heart, for another. In poetry or novels it is accepted that the human heart is the place where the real dramas are acted out. So it must be with biography. If you took this argument to its logical conclusion, you might end up writing about a wholly unknown figure. After all, one admires novelists who re-create the lives of ordinary people in all their minute detail—I'm thinking of Arnold Bennett or Balzac. The specific bigness of a great beast of a subject can all too easily squeeze out the universal themes.

What I wanted to know most of all was why Finch Hatton did things. But what is motivation? It is a deep-sea fish, swimming around in the feculent depths of the subconscious. Which of us can say that we understand the tangled skeins of fears and desires that control our own behavior, let alone those of a long-dead stranger? In his novel *Chloe Marr*, A. A. Milne writes of one character, "If in the end [he] still remains something of a mystery, [we] should not be surprised: for every human being is a mystery, and nobody knows the truth about anybody else." The truth is more complicated than it seems in any biography. So there I sat, year after year, with only the dead for company. I searched for clues among the unending clutter of hours and years. Sifting through the versions, discarding the unreliable and the unprovable, I asked myself what we can know of a man. Increasingly, as I indicated at the conclusion of the last essay, I came to see the lack of material not as a biographical handicap but as a cipher for the unknowability of anyone else's inner life (or of one's own, for that matter). The absence of data itself stood for that lurch toward certainties which so often stalls before arriving at a conclusion. This sustained me when I heard little but the sound of trees crashing across my path.

0 Miles _____1_____2
0 Kilometers _____2

Learning to Belly Dance

When I learned to samba in Patagonia, my teacher told me to pretend I had a stick of chalk up my bum and draw a figure eight. I was prepared for anything when I turned up at my first belly-dancing lesson. It took place in a high-ceilinged gym around the corner from my flat in Camden Town. A flunky marched in to wash the walls while the class was in progress, fumes of Jeyes cleaning fluid standing in for the whiff of the souk and the grating of mop against pail for the swish of silken robes.

I had recently returned from seven months languishing in the wastes of Antarctica, and anything associated with heat or hot places calls to me like a siren. When, therefore, I spotted an advertisement for belly-dancing classes in the *Camden New Journal*, images of sultry nights and warm, exposed flesh crowded into my frosted brain. I signed up immediately. The course involved classes at 6:30 on four consecutive Thursdays, at £3 each.

No sooner had I enrolled than I discovered belly dancing is enjoying a renaissance. Classes are breaking out all over the place. This, I concluded, must be another symptom of the benign 1990s: written off by feminists as one more hideous symbol of patriarchy and the ritual humiliation of women, belly wiggling has been rehabilitated because, don't you know, we're doing it for *us*. We have reclaimed our bodies and loosened our cultural moorings while we were about it.

A woman signing up at the same time confided that she found the idea of learning to belly dance liberating. "I mean, it's empowering yourself. And belly dancing kind of says that it's all right not being the shape of a supermodel." I always knew there was a reason why I do not make the effort to be more like a supermodel. It's so that I can belly dance!

Eight women turned up for the first lesson. We cowered at the back of the gym trying to make ourselves invisible while the teacher flapped around a Jurassic cassette player. One of the eight was a retired history teacher of sixty-one, another an unemployed young woman called Sharon with two rings in her nose, a third a senior civil servant. Our teacher was a diminutive Moroccan called Leila who launched her introductory talk by assuring us that belly dancing constitutes such good exercise, both internal and external (whatever that means), that doctors recommend it for pregnant women. After four lessons, she declared, we might consider turning professional. I thought this unlikely in my case, but you never know: the bottom might fall out of the travel-writing market, and it's wise to have another string to your bow.

Leila distributed scarves for us to knot on our hips ("it accentuates the figure"). Mr. Leila, a sphinxlike Egyptian, turned on the cassette player, and Leila set about demonstrating the basic movements of the dance, a combination of steps, swings, thrusts, neck slides, and shimmies, the latter a kind of wobbly shoulder rippling. We copied woodenly. Then Leila showed us how to thread the components together and make a sequence; it was all about hips rather than belly, and there was not a navel in sight. Fluidity of movement is everything, and it was this that we found the hardest. "Translate the music with your bodies!" cried Leila.

Everyone except the history teacher was very bad. The Egyptian began sniggering uncontrollably. Leila kept looking at her watch. What she liked was not teaching but dancing, and boy, could she dance. Shoulders thrust back, overflowing bosoms flung forward, and eyes blazing, she was a study in concentrated provocation.

At the end of the class we were dispatched with instructions to practice a series of exercises that included shutting an imaginary door sharply with our bottoms and holding a pretend stick at waist height with both hands, swinging the hips around to hit each end in turn. "Try it at the bus stop," suggested Leila.

Everyone came back for more. During the second session we learned "traveling," the technical term for moving backward and forward or from side to side with little tippy-toe steps and accompanying hip swings and arm gestures. Halfway through the class we moved on to a bit of North African technique; what we had been learning hitherto was apparently Egyptian (for indeed the forms of the dance are numerous), and Leila was anxious that we shouldn't get bored. Moroccans, it turned out, place even more emphasis on hips and shoulders. We were equally lamentable at this new style, though by this time we had dispensed with our inhibitions and were swinging our hips around wildly at the slightest provocation.

My third lesson took place after an afternoon in the Marquis of Granby pub with my friends Jeremy Lewis and Dennis Enright, none of us able to face our treacherous typescripts. By the time I got to the gym, I was in fine spirits, and the effects lasted right through the class, with the result that I broke the rule I had imposed on myself at the start of the lessons. Outside the gym I was never, ever going to let anyone see me belly dancing.

Tripping lightly back to my flat, a Moroccan tune on my lips and a shimmy quivering on my shoulders, I was apprehended by my downstairs neighbor, the drop-dead gorgeous Ahmer, a physics undergraduate at University College. "Hello!" said he. "Fancy a cup of tea?" One thing led to another in his basement flat, and the next thing I knew I was demonstrating my newly acquired skills in front of the television set.

The dancing got off to a poor start when I trod on Ahmer's last slice of pizza, but I felt the situation was retrievable until I noticed that he was rolling on the sofa convulsed with laughter and calling out to his multitudinous Byronic roommates, who appeared out of every orifice of the building to watch the freak show.

After a week, I was able to consign this humiliating episode (what I could remember of it) to the basements of memory and pitch up for the last session. This began with the whole-body shimmy. "Imagine an electric shock all over," said Leila. "But you'd be dead then," said Sharon. This was certainly a case of more jelly than belly. Other exciting new movements included the shoulder shimmy combined with wrist flexing, which was like simultaneously rubbing your tummy and patting your head, and the tease, which involved moving provocatively forward making beckoning gestures and then retreating swiftly, presumably the quarry having been ensnared. At the end of the class we shimmied in unison across the gym and into the pub, where Leila asked if anyone was considering going professional. I said I was sticking to the day job.

1994

Learning to Striptease

I recently published a biography of a man who died many decades before I was born (*Too Close to the Sun: The Audacious Life and Times of Denys Finch Hatton*). Emerging from that tunnel, I found myself casting around for a new interest that would bring me into contact with live human beings. I had spent too long bent over a desk in provincial archives, fingering friable sheets of paper that spoke of forgotten loves and hates (or, all too often, visits to the dentist). I had lost my appetite for flesh and blood: how treacherously easy it had been to lead someone else's life instead of my own!

Action was required. The acquisition of a new skill, perhaps, at one of the night school courses on offer in the capital. I wanted to get away from books, so languages were out. As I stagger toward middle age, any vestigial interest in matters domestic has vanished with the last black hairs among the mass of pewter. Cake decorating and Vietnamese cookery were therefore also embargoed. I toyed with origami, yoga, Irish dancing for beginners, and car maintenance before hitting on the ideal hobby for the jaded biographer.

I enrolled at the London School of Striptease.

This little-known institution offers a range of workshops and courses with names like Grin and Bare It. After a series of helpful conversations with the owner and sole instructor, Joan, I opted for a two-hour one-on-one starter session. The school does not have a permanent home, but rents space in various halls, so I met Joan on a rainy Monday night in an exciting cloak-and-dagger operation involving coordinated mobile phone calls and a café in Kilburn.

Joan drove me to the hall in her Mini. She was a voluptuous, salt-of-the-earth character in her early forties, and she had pale English skin and Pre-Raphaelite hair the color of butter. She had been stripping for more than twenty years, returning to the profession after a spell abroad when she had to raise cash to get her cat out of quarantine. The small late-Victorian brick hall she had rented for the night had a blocked-up fireplace and, around the sides, Formica tables strewn with sheets of paper recording the minutes of a neighborhood-watch committee meeting. Mysteriously, a tin of Pedigree Chum stood on the mantelpiece.

Joan studied my attire and picked an outfit for herself from a portable wardrobe of lace, net, nylon, and feathers. Before the off (so to speak), we perched on a couch under the arctic light of a fluorescent tube while Joan zipped through the ground rules. Cut labels out of underwear, as they tend to stick out; always wear stockings and high heels; never wear a dress or a top that goes over the head. "And remember," she added as she stood up to insert a *Best of the Eagles* cassette in the tape player she had brought, "to pick off bits of lavatory paper that might be clinging to your woo-woo."

The basics were obvious enough, once you knew them: use all the space available, give the punters a good look at each new bit as it is revealed, throw lascivious glances over your shoulder, and, above all, make eye contact. Actually getting my clothes off with a degree of seductive elegance was trickier than anticipated. ("Think of yourself as a gift, unwrapping yourself slowly with delight at each new part that you reveal.") Joan demonstrated undoing her bra with her back to the audience, swiveling around with her hands crossed over her chest, then lowering both straps simultaneously with her fingers while keeping the bra pinned to the sides of her body with her upper arms while bending forward. To me this was a baffling, Houdini-like maneuver, and it was at this point, catching a glimpse of myself in the mirror as the Eagles worked their relentless way through "Hotel California," that I realized the enormity of my Marks & Spencer panties.

We struggled on, twisting and flicking. Joan explained the dynamics of hip wiggling and advised against lighting the venue with candles on health and safety grounds. There was a lot of bending involved; the mantelpiece turned out to be an essential prop for what Joan called "bottom work." I found myself reading the Pedigree Chum label.

In the church next door, a team of bell ringers began practicing. Above the peals I heard Joan say that it was important to fling all garments well clear as they were discarded, otherwise the floor swiftly resembled an obstacle course. Also, it was vital to bring the legs together before embarking on the removal of lower garments. I failed to grasp the mechanics of this operation and fell over while grappling with my knickers.

Joan was a born teacher. Articulate and methodical, she thought carefully about the best way of explaining each move and took trouble to offer praise and encouragement even when it was clear that none was due. She was the real thing, an old pro and a showgirl of the Shirley Bassey school of entertainment. I liked her enormously, and when I had completed my first full solo routine and stood flushed before her wearing only my stockings as the Eagles droned tinnily to a halt, she clapped her hands and gave me a big bare-bosomed hug.

While we were dressing, she talked about her business plan. Having run the business for two years with no advertising and proved that demand for her services exists, she intends to market the school more aggressively. Although she is happy to offer advice about job opportunities, her core market does not consist of putative professionals. "Only about five percent of my clients are looking for work. The rest want to strip for fun—many of them not even for a specific man." Her oldest student so far has been fifty-six. "I'm longing to teach an eighty-year-old," she said. "Seduction is in the mind."

Despite her optimistic prognosis for the school, it turns out that stripping, like everything else, has changed for the worse. "In the old days a girl had twenty-five minutes," she opined, her eyes shining as she recalled a utopian epoch of clubs cloudy with the smoke of unfiltered Player's. "We used elaborate props—I had a friend who took half a Morris Marina down to Soho twice a week. Now you get three minutes if you're lucky." The bell ringers reached a climax. Joan pushed her buttery hair behind her ears and smiled wanly, the Freddie Trueman, now, of the feather boa. "It's all about money these days."

Despite my gargantuan underwear and outsized lack of ability, Joan had made me feel that enjoying myself was all that mattered. I have not performed since (I rushed home after the class to demonstrate my new skills to my partner, but he had fallen asleep listening to *Gardeners' Question Time*). Nor have I yet informed the Society of Authors so that other spent biographers can refresh their appetites. But I often think about stripping, and now, returned to the provincial archives, I catch myself spinning fantasies of undressed victory over the cold and closely buttoned dead.

2002

POSTSCRIPT

Richard Ingrams commissioned both of the above pieces for *The Oldie*. They were to give me something to do between books. For the first, Ingrams got Willie Rushton to paint me on the job. He put in a row of inscrutable Oriental spectators, each wearing a fez. I, of course, looked ridiculous, even though Rushton was kind to my quivering belly, but I loved the picture—we all did. I had no money whatever at the time, and buying the original was out of the question. I so wish I could have. I bet it went in the bin. The last time I was between books, Richard again commissioned me to learn a new skill. "I think," he said firmly, "the days of dancing and stripping are behind you." And he sent me on a home-plumbing course. I have not reproduced the piece here. Too demoralizing.

Here's another article, however, in which I made a fool of myself, this time for *The Telegraph*.

Wing Walking: Oh, the Terror

I lurched on the upper wing of the 1941 biplane as it looped over the friendly Cotswolds. Of course, I was strapped to a frame. But still. A winterish southwesterly flattened my cheeks while the invisible pilot below curved us over a herd of Friesians at a hundred miles an hour. I tried to think about the first wing walkers, those pioneering aviatrixes from the heady era of bug-eyed goggles, tight flying suits, and elegant curls of contrail. But I had to concentrate on wiping off the snot the wind had hoovered from my nostrils.

To learn about the revival of wing walking, I had traveled to an airstrip in Gloucestershire to meet the aerobabes of the only professional team in Europe. At AeroSuperBatics company HQ—a reconditioned engineering shed on one side of the strip—I was greeted by twenty-year-old Lucy Foster, a glamour-puss from central casting with waist-length blond hair and a baby-pink Mazda parked outside. Later in the morning, before going up myself, I watched Foster, already in her third year as a wing walker, do her thing in the air. Not only did she adopt a range of balletic positions from the top of the plane while it looped the loop. By swiveling the "rig" (the frame to which wing walkers are attached), she actually performed a handstand during a flyby before climbing down into the open cockpit *while still in the air.* This was synchronized swimming in the sky, an air dance with the showmanship of the circus ring. Small wonder that five million people every year watch the AeroSuperBatics team perform.

As she was defrosting in the shed afterward, I asked Foster what started her off. "My father's an engineer," she explained, simultaneously picking flies from her teeth and chipping blocks of snot from her cheeks, "and I grew up around planes. When I was seventeen, Mum spotted an ad in a newspaper for wing-walking recruits, and I came here for an audition. I loved it from the first time I stood on a wing." Mum surely regrets it, when she sees her baby dangling upside down at a thousand feet? "She never admits it," Foster said with a grin, "but Dad films me when I'm wing walking, and when I watch the footage, all I can hear on the soundtrack is Mum saying, 'Oh . . . my . . . God . . .'" Shortly before my own airborne debut, the éminence grise of the wing-walking renaissance ambled into the shed. Essex-born and public school educated, fifty-nine-year-old Vic Norman is a bluff and affable figure whom it proved impossible to dislike, personalized license plates notwithstanding. His father was a pilot and often went up with young Vic on his knee. When Vic was sixteen, he fell in love with the 1960s model Ann-Margret after meeting her at a Stones concert at Leyton Baths in east London (the promoter had erected a stage over the water). She lived on the King's Road, so Norman ran away from Millfield School and enrolled in the Chelsea College of Aeronautical Engineering on nearby Sydney Street. "I got my pilot's license," he says, "and started mucking about with biplanes. They were cheaper than racing cars then. And I liked them more—flying was three-dimensional." He taught himself aerobatic maneuvers from books and, twenty-six years ago, started working the air shows. Now based in the Cotswolds, he has chalked up in excess of fifteen hundred performances.

Convinced that he could popularize wing walking, Norman founded AeroSuperBatics in 1989. The firm now has four Boeing Stearmans, the two-seater biplanes introduced by the Stearman Aircraft Division of Boeing in Wichita, Kansas, in 1934. The machines have fabric-covered wooden wings, single-leg landing gear, and an overbuilt welded-steel fuselage, and their simple, rugged construction made them ideal trainers for novice pilots. The Stearman became an unexpected success during World War II, and when the fighting stopped, the surviving biplanes were deployed as crop dusters. Now Norman and his team of five pilots (three full-time and two part-time) and two engineers have modified Stearmans for their third incarnation: the entertainment business. "We fit them with bigger engines so we get a better rate of roll," Norman explained as we toured the hangars. "Stearmans are ideal for air-show work, as they fly as low as thirty feet and as high as one thousand." The team is currently sponsored by the French skin-care company Guinot, and its candy-pink livery perfectly suits the image of 1940s starlets.

Until 1991, AeroSuperBatics operated from Gloucestershire's

Staverton airfield. Then, while reading an aviation book, Norman learned about an early Royal Flying Corps base established in the area in 1916. With the help of Ordnance Survey, he located it—by then a harlequin of plowed fields with cows in the engineering shed. With two partners, Norman bought the field and restored it to its former status (one of his co-owners is Pink Floyd's drummer, Nick Mason). He furnished the shed now with aviation ephemera, including information posters produced for the first batches of pilots ever to train for aerial combat. "While downing a Hun," reads a 1919 poster, "your machine may have been seriously damaged without your knowledge. Under these circumstances, any unnecessary stunting is to be avoided." The long photographs depicting rows of beaming, newly qualified boys are almost unbearable, when one considers that the average life expectancy of an Allied pilot on the western front was eleven days.

Despite this murderous rate of attrition, after the armistice many surviving pilots returned to Blighty desperate to keep flying. War-surplus biplanes were cheaply available, and entrepreneurial airmen began touring the country, landing in fields to take members of the public up for joyrides. Hardly anyone had ever been in a plane. The pilots cultivated the image of lovable rogues who raised a storm wherever they went, and as they slept in barns, the expression "barnstorming" came into existence. But as the public got used to them, the pilots had to become more daring, buzzing main streets at low level, dropping parachutists into fields, and, eventually, inveigling engineers and girlfriends into climbing up onto the top wing and prancing about—a routine they called wing walking. The era spawned the first lipsticked aviatrixes—among them the American Ethel Dare, the Flying Witch, a parachutist turned wing walker who performed the first-ever wing-to-wing transfer.

Unsurprisingly, the casualty rate was high (the Flying Witch plunged to her death at an air show in Michigan), and the

U.K. Civil Aviation Authority banned wing walking in 1933. But AeroSuperBatics worked out a way of maintaining safety standards in and on biplanes, eventually, in 1989, becoming the first company to be granted permission for performers to climb out of the cockpit since 1933. Business is flourishing. Last year the team turned out 104 times, working a variety of events from music festivals to air shows and even weddings and traveling from Nice to Dubai. The previous year they went to China, greeted, according to the pilot Martyn Carrington, "like pop stars. We autographed babies and were stampeded when we emerged from the vehicle. Hundreds of millions watched us on television." Wherever the location, the average show lasts twelve minutes and involves either two planes ("ships") or four: if you're thinking of hiring them for your nuptials, a two-ship display will set you back about $2,500, though costs increase as the team moves away from its Gloucester base. The Stearmans cruise at a hundred miles per hour, the fuel tanks so small, and the engines so big, that they can only remain airborne for two hours.

Norman speaks protectively of "the girls" (you're never a woman as a wing walker). "We carry out risk assessment on every aspect of the shows. Walkers are attached to the plane at all times. When they're not strapped into the rig, they are tied to the cockpit with a safety wire and carabiner. We have to plan meticulously, as, while pilots can communicate with one another by radio, girls are reliant on hand signals. If the pilots want the girls' attention, they wiggle the wings. And we change the program according to the weather. Basically, we have three different displays, each tailored to conditions: one for bad weather, one for medium, and one for good."

At the mention of bad weather, the wing walker Sarah Tanner winces.

"When it rains," she told me, "the wings get really sharp on your feet. Your lips bleed, because you have ice pellets zapping into your face at 150 miles per hour. When it's like that, we have to wave at the crowd with only one arm, as we need the other to protect our faces." Twenty-five-year-old Tanner took up the sport after a degree in arts management from the University of Leeds.

"It was something I've always wanted to do," she says. "Like Lucy, I have a dance background, and wing walking is dancing in the sky."

The company is looking to recruit two more full-time walkers. Candidates must be fit and agile and strong enough to climb around an aircraft against 150-mile-per-hour wind pressure. "Oh yes," adds Norman, "and you must be under five feet seven, as if you're taller than that, when you swivel upside down in the rig, you smash your head into the wing . . . And you have to weigh under nine stone, as you stand on the fuel tank while you're performing and you don't want that to break." Could a man apply? Many jockeys fulfill those physical criteria. "Er," says Rhiannon Roche, who administers the recruitment procedure and wing walks part-time, "we'd consider it." One senses that a pig would be more likely to get a job flying a Stearman. "But air shows are predominantly male, so it's nice to redress the balance— and anyway, men don't look so good in Lycra."

At this point I was unable to put off my own ascent any longer. The girls crowded around as I layered up in the shed, and we all strode onto the tarmac. Tanner led me to a biplane and showed me how to climb up: basically, you clamber onto the lower wing and over the cockpit, then swing and swivel up to the top wing. "Don't put a foot here, here, or here," she instructed helpfully, "or it will go straight through." Any sense of relief I experienced at actually accomplishing this maneuver swiftly vanished as I straightened up on the wing, looked ahead, and took in my position. You feel awfully exposed. Panic rose like milk to the boil. I began to worry that I might hyperventilate. I had malicious thoughts about the proprietors of *The Telegraph*. The photographer was already up in another plane, circling above us, waiting. "Don't worry if you don't get the shots," Norman had told him as we were leaving the shed. "She can always *go up again for a second session.*"

Tanner followed me aloft and strapped me to a harness attached to the rig—a six-foot pole sticking up in the middle of the wing, directly over the pilot. Carrington was already turning the engine over. Tanner clambered down and gave me a thumbs-up. We taxied bumpily to a distant corner of the airfield. At least the rig offered full support so that if my knees gave way or I lost consciousness—an attractive option—I would stay upright. They would have to unhook me like a crucified robber. Those photographs would play poorly in the newspaper. Carrington revved. We were about to take off. I tasted again the tuna sandwich I had eaten for lunch. Presumably, the wind would dispose of the mess, were I to be sick. But when we lifted off the ground and the trees and farm buildings shrank, I felt better. The first steep curve literally took my breath away, but apart from that—I know this is hard to believe—I felt safe. My limbs were not restricted, but my torso was tightly strapped to the harness, and I was even able to "relax back into the rig," as I had been instructed. I remember noticing that in the hollows the milky-green Cotswold fields were still rimed with a pale lattice of frost.

I stayed airborne for twelve minutes. The news that the photographer had got his shots seemed to prove the existence of God. Once I had regained the power of speech, I asked Carrington about the particular demands of flying a biplane for a wing-walking display. "A Stearman is far more difficult to fly than a 747 or a fighter," said the quietly spoken thirty-three-year-old, who, having gone solo on his seventeenth birthday, was briefly the youngest pilot in the U.K. "To start with, our planes are so light they are very affected by crosswinds. Second, you can't see straight ahead of you from our cockpits, so you need to weave as you taxi across a field. Third, when you fly for a wing walk, you have someone standing on top of you, which means a great big air brake and a load of drag. Finally, you have all the problems of an open cockpit. To me, flying a big plane would be like being a bus driver—you've lost the feel of the aircraft [one is reminded of the test pilots in *The Right Stuff* as they gradually realize, during their "astronaut" training, that monkeys could fly rockets]. We have no computers and no electronic navigation: we use a map and a compass, and we have our hands on the controls."

"Basically," Norman summed up as I handed back my goggles, "we put the buzz back into flying."

2003

Reading the Argos Catalog in Bed

With the passage of each year, the number of activities I enjoy shrinks alarmingly. These days only three things guarantee pleasure: filing, throwing things away, and reading the Argos catalog in bed. And the greatest of these is the last.

Once the telephone has ceased its clamor and the day subsides into silence, I draw up the duvet, select one section of the catalog, and assess the pros and cons of each item. I might size up the irons, say. I make notes, flick back and forward, draw up a short list. The extent of the Argos range is deeply satisfying. Twelve hundred pages bursting with things one couldn't possibly want. Fancy a nonelectric head massager with copper prongs for £14.99? (Bafflingly, the people at Argos have called it an Orgasmatron.) Nine brands of foot spa, thirty-five different kinds of headphones, hundreds of arcane kitchen appliances, zillions of "storage solutions," and a pair of furry slippers in which both feet go into the same hole. A dazzling new world unfolds in Technicolor, all in contrast to my own, real little world, which lurches on, frame by frame, in disappointing sepia tones.

Information is specific and to the point ("Makes real candy floss in minutes. Dishwasher-safe"). Neologisms are coined with sense and sensibility—"mousing," for example, which is used to mean "deploying a computer mouse rather than a keyboard." And unlike Proust's duchess, the Argos copywriter is not immune to the poetry of the incomprehensible. A fridge with "a unique twin-cooling system that keeps food fresh" (a standard requirement in a fridge, I would have thought) mysteriously also offers "a sophisticated lifestyle."

With my Argos ritual I can get the whole extended family organized in no time. My only regret is that the pet section of the catalog extends only to cats, dogs, and fish ("Radiator Cat Bed— Hangs On To Any Radiator. Fully Washable. £8.75"). If the company were to expand into rodents, I could tick off the guinea pigs as well.

Other catalogs lack the solidity of the Argos tome. Too much footling with style in place of substance, and a willful avoidance of the mundane. Argos, sensibly, embraces the mundane: And what is more poetic than everyday life? The catalog follows the rhythm of the day minute by minute, from the electric toothbrush to the electric blanket. Anthony Powell once said that he would find *Burke's Bank Clerks* more gripping than *Burke's Peerage*. I like to think that he too would have enjoyed snuggling up with Argos.

At the end of each session, I make my choice. Then I can switch off the light, dreaming of piles of razor-creased laundry swiftly dispatched with my new iron ("Self Clean, Superior Glide, Anodised Soleplate. £64.50"). I only get around to making an actual purchase about once a year. But that doesn't matter. My twenty minutes a day communing with the catalog in my fantasy life fulfills my need for order and control.

Then morning comes, and the self-doubts, like homing pigeons, return to roost.

2001

V | WHAT DO I DO NOW?

Requiem: Through Bangladesh

I pushed the swing doors of the adult education center and looked through the rain to the far end of the parking lot. It was a bleak November evening in King's Cross, the puddles reflecting the glow of streetlights and the air thrumming with traffic. I pulled my raincoat tight.

My head was leaning against a blue sign inscribed KINGSWAY COLLEGE FOR ADULT EDUCATION, LONDON BOROUGH OF CAMDEN. Rivulets trickled inside my collar, and I began reciting Bengali conjugations in my head, to take my mind off the rain. *Ami bhalo achhi, apni bhalo achhen, tumi bhalo achho.* I had enrolled for evening classes in beginners' Bengali to prepare for a trip to Bangladesh, but I loathed the boring classes and, worse, I didn't want to go to Bangladesh at all.

It was like this. Two years previously I had spent seven months in Antarctica, gathering material for a book. Ever since, sitting behind a desk at home, I had remained on the ice sheet inside my head. The project was finished, but I couldn't break free from Antarctica.

So I worked out what place might be the opposite of the South Pole.

Nobody lives in Antarctica, but Bangladesh is the most densely populated country on earth. Antarctica conjured ice-cream-cone mountains, but when I thought of Bangladesh, I saw rotting corpses floating in the sewers. And whereas Bangladesh is on the Tropic of Cancer, Antarctica was very cold indeed.

I decided to put it all behind me, secured a commission to write an essay on modern Bangladesh, and bought an air ticket to Dhaka. Now it was galling that my heart wouldn't follow my plans. My fantasy life had always been realized by travel; I had grown to rely on it. This time, it wasn't happening. The trip to Bangladesh, so thoughtfully conceived, wasn't turning out to be an expression of my inner life at all.

A car horn beeped, and I saw Peter peering through the wipers of my Ford Escort. Peter was an irascible Canadian who had been based in London for thirty years. We had spent the past six months living in each other's houses. I was still blaming everything on Antarctica, though.

Tucked neatly into the crotch of Asia, Bangladesh consists of silty lowlands squeezed between northeast India and western Burma. It is the size of England and Wales and almost entirely flat, a protean land constantly reshaped by water rushing off the Himalaya. At any one time, as much as 70 percent of the country is submerged. The overwhelming majority of its 112 million people are Sunni Muslims, making Bangladesh the third-largest Islamic nation in the world.

I arrived in Dhaka during a tropically thunderous night. The whole city smelled like a cabin lit by kerosene. The streets were pricked not with the beams of headlights but with the woozy glow of kerosene lamps swinging from the undercarriages of elaborately painted cycle rickshaws. My attempts at speech met with limited success.

The more a building had cost, the more hideous it looked. The architectural language of Dhaka said, "Nobody here cares about buildings." The only thing most people had the energy to care about was survival, and I was amazed at the resourcefulness I observed on the streets. One family had set up a production line on the pavement cleaning old nail-polish bottles. The first man was squatting in front of a mountain of empty or half-empty bottles, the cracked flagstones around him splattered like a Jackson Pollock canvas. When he had removed as much of the varnish as he could, the man passed the bottle to his brother, who soaked it in a bucket and handed it to a small boy who plunged it into another bucket, that one exuding clouds of ammonia vapor, and so it went on, until the last person, who presided over a gleaming pile of clean bottles. Once a day these were loaded into a bicycle basket, and another boy pedaled them away, clinking furiously.

In the rich residential districts of north Dhaka, I saw a slimming clinic and, in the early morning, small groups of joggers in saris and sneakers.

In Dhaka, I thought of home. I was a prisoner inside my own head instead of a free spirit in a foreign land. After all the traveling I had done, I was confused to find myself the victim of disembodied anxieties. I had so many preconceptions about what I was able to do—about my adaptability, resilience, and independence; was I losing the markers and maps of my own moods?

Perhaps, I decided after a week or two in the capital, the countryside might shake me out of this slough. One morose evening, trapped in a grim hotel room, I formed a rough plan to travel by train to the top of the country and slowly work my way down to the bottom.

At the station I arranged the first leg of the journey in less than an hour, an achievement little short of an Old Testament miracle by Indian standards. In India, I would have looked forward to a seven-hour wait in a queue followed by a tortuous conversation with the under-manager responsible for that particular branch line about why the train I wished to catch had been temporarily taken out of service on Tuesdays, Wednesdays, and Thursdays. At the end of it all, I would have discovered that the train had been replaced by another which departed at the same time and on the same days as the first one but which, because it was a temporary train, was reserved from a different station. Oh, those happy days.

Bangladesh was not a little India.

With the ticket in my pocket, I telephoned Peter.

"Hullo!" he said enthusiastically.

He said he had been in the bath; he was standing in the top hallway, dripping. I saw the light filtering through the leaves of the plane tree outside his bathroom window and falling on the tiled floor; the pools of water he would have spilled; and the hardback book open at the side of the freestanding green bath, its pages slowly sucking up water. The conversation was interleaved with the echoes and delays of antiquated technology.

After we had chatted about my trip and his news, a pause filled the line.

"Nothing's happened," I said.

"Good!" he said, even more enthusiastically than before. He seemed uncharacteristically sure of himself. Then he said, "That means we're going to have a baby, doesn't it?"

The train rattled out of Kamalpur Station and rocked past miles of huts jammed against the track, all in a state of advanced dereliction and boiling over with people. I was in first class, and an obliging steward ferried through china cups of milky tea. An hour later, the slums yielded. The emerald rice paddies were gilded with rivers and Gothic in fecundity. Women were stooping, men sitting on their heels, and children tottering under enormous wicker baskets. Drying saris garlanded the bushes. A single boat cracked the pewter surface of a stream.

My eye persistently alighted on pregnant women. They were working in the fields. I wondered if there were so many because Bangladesh is such a populous country, or whether I really was pregnant and some kind of magnetic force made them leap out at me. I found myself longing for certainty. I wished I could do a pregnancy test, but purchasing such an object was beyond the resources of my Bengali, and anyway they probably didn't exist east of Delhi. I stopped smoking anyway.

Peter's happy certainty seemed remote. I vaguely resented it: the baby—if there was one—was here, with me, not in north London, safely installed with a telephone to hand. Yet when I looked at the women toiling and bulging, I felt no sense of identification, no uplifting emotion about the universality of motherhood. I didn't feel anything at all—although something was different. I was lonely: yes, that was it. I had assumed that the onset of motherhood would be like a warm, sudsy wave, not a slow unfurling of uncertainty. It was on my mind all the time as Bangladesh uncoiled, but when I turned my attention to it, it slipped away, displaced by drongo birds, jackals, and emaciated dogs. The inner landscape was more alien than the one outside the window, and I was afraid that what lay ahead was the most foreign territory of all.

When the train stopped, blind beggars groped along to the open windows. I fell asleep in the middle of the day and was woken by a shiny elbow stump prodding at my cheek. The amputee was carrying a tin bowl in her mouth. Beyond the station, a row of men were lathering themselves on the steps of a brick tank, and behind the tank a palace was quietly decaying.

The region that became Bengal flourished as early as the ninth century B.C. It consisted of a disparate collection of states, most of which, by 450 B.C., had been permeated by the spread of Aryan culture. The states were united once or twice, and the influences of Hinduism and Buddhism seesawed until the twelfth century A.D., when Islamic invaders conquered the region and Europe groped out of the Dark Ages. The Muslim Mughals stimulated a golden age in Bengal, and in 1608 the great empire moved its capital to Dhaka.

The next invaders, the British, went on to make Bengal the heart of their Indian empire. In 1912, however, they shifted the capital to Delhi, and thirty-one years later an apocalyptic famine killed between three and five million and almost crushed the spirit right out of Bengal. At partition, East Bengal became East Pakistan, half of a brand-new Muslim country, and the majority of its Hindus fled west to India. In 1971, after civil war, East Pakistan won its independence from its western wing and became Bangladesh—land of the Bengali people.

I got off the train at Srimangal, the heart of tea country. An itinerant ear doctor was cruising for trade along the platform, a tray of weaponry suspended from his neck. I had arranged to stay in a guesthouse on a tea estate, and a man turned up to collect me in a rickshaw. It was dark, and the medieval lanes around the station were dancing with candle flame.

I walked around the terraced hills. They were quilted with tea bushes and whirring with insect wings. The roads and tracks slicing through the hills were spotted with squads of pluckers— all women—walking barefoot to work in faded saris, the baskets on their backs held by a cord tied around a cloth topknot. They carried their lunches in scarves hanging over their shoulders. Plucking is a feudal job, handed down through the generations. A few men roamed the terraces with scythes, chopping at the *jongli* bushes.

Fifty percent of the produce of the 158 northeastern Bangladeshi tea estates is exported. As these hills do not yield high-quality tea, it gets drunk mainly in Jordan, Pakistan, and Russia. While I was in the northeast, the English-language *Daily Star* ran an alarming editorial concerning "gangs of organized toll extortionists in the tea gardens." The phenomenon it went on to describe, in which local gangsters forced producers to hand over hefty payments, thereby effectively fixing the price of tea, was a typical example of the way the Bangladeshi economy functions.

Mahajons, a kind of mafia, run half the country. The government collects almost no taxes, and the state control that does exist is hugely elastic. No wonder Bangladesh remains reliant on foreign aid and that the smart districts of Dhaka bristle with the acronyms of the agencies that dish it out. Calcutta might have earned a place in the geographical imagination of the West as a cipher of disease and despair, but rich Bangladeshis go to Calcutta for medical treatment. Most depressing of all, whenever the country shows signs of struggling to its feet, another natural disaster, usually a flood or a cyclone, knocks it back down.

"Congratulations on coming to Bangladesh!" said a jolly man in a business suit, slapping me on the back. I was walking around a tea-processing plant. The leaves were being oxidized, and the air was thick with a moist and pungent aroma. On emerging from the factory part of the plant, I had collided with a pack of suited men. Despite the considerable heat, the one who congratulated me was wearing a hat like a woolly profiterole.

He explained that he and his henchmen were on a joint government-sponsored child labor commission.

Children were toiling all over the tea estates.

"Does the government want to put a stop to child labor, then?" I asked.

"Oh yes, very much," the man said with a large smile. "If they are under twelve, it is very bad."

The Lawachara evergreen and semi-evergreen tropical rain forest, folded deep within the tea plantations, had by some stroke of fate escaped the deforestation ravaging the region. The canopy swished with the beat of bird wings, screaming capped langur monkeys darted among mahogany trees, and I even saw a hoolock gibbon, a beguiling cocoa-colored ape with white eyebrows, tapering fingers, and shining eyes. It was impossible to get away from people, though, there or indeed anywhere in Bangladesh. Knots of them lurked on the loneliest path. Since white faces were a rarity, everybody was terribly interested in me. I was pleased that people tried to talk to me, and sensed I was never in danger, but I grew tired of being followed around. I felt myself turning inward, retreating into a private world of memory and imagination. Obsessed with shaking people off, I stepped smartly behind teak trees to give a curious companion the slip.

Women were more covert than men in their efforts to shadow me, their voyeurism handicapped not by solidarity but by social convention. It was surprising, at first, to learn that in Bangladesh both the prime minister and the leader of the opposition were women, but both took on almost hereditary roles, the PM as daughter of Sheikh Mujibur Rahman, "founder of the nation" (he was assassinated in 1975), and the leader of the opposition as the widow of Ziaur Rahman (President Zia, killed in 1981). For ordinary women, imprisoned within problems of their own, these figureheads are remote. Although the dowry has been banned by law, it still exists on the ground—even the continuing dowry, which must be paid regularly, like rent. Violence against women is a largely unaddressed problem in Bangladesh, and it includes the popular pursuit of throwing acid into the face of one's ex-girlfriends.

After four days on the tea estates I caught a train due south to Chittagong, second city and first port. The journey took ten hours, past bony oxen, plows, and drongo birds squatting on rotting telegraph poles. The train eventually crossed the Karnaphuli River and entered the city via a suspension bridge. According to Ptolemy, in the second century A.D. Chittagong was one of the finest ports in the East. It swapped hands many times: the Muslims and the Arakanese tossed it between them like a beach ball.

I found a hotel; it was leprous with corrosion and smelled of moldy vegetables. The next morning, on the pavement outside my window, I watched a man and a woman rolled up in blankets trying to sleep while three toddlers, who had other ideas, pulled the covering from their faces. All three children had suppurating eye infections. This image, unlike the pregnant women in the fields, made me panic. I thought about my own putative baby, shocked at the responsibility. The squalor all around enlarged my anxieties; my baby's destiny was not, of course, a childhood on the streets of Chittagong, but I could no longer apply logic to my treacherous thoughts.

I walked to the Memorial to the Martyrs of the Language Movement, a concrete lump draped with a flag and a few desiccated wreaths. On the street below, people were burning rice husks under Primus stoves. In 1948, Urdu, spoken throughout the western regions, was designated the new country's national language, even though no one in the eastern wing spoke it. In 1952, Karachi legislators went further, proposing that Bengali should be written in Arabic script. On February 21 that year Bengali-speaking students at the University of Chittagong marched in protest. Police killed five. The event, part of an orchestrated countrywide protest, was a key moment in the evolution of the independence movement, cherished still in the national psyche as proof of what Bangladeshis can achieve. The government granted Bengali official status in 1956.

At Chittagong the train line ends. I caught a bus a hundred miles south, down the narrow band of Bangladesh adjacent to the Burmese hills. Warps of water on the fields reflected the blazing sky.

I got off at Cox's Bazar, the name acquired from the town's eighteenth-century Dundonian founder. The beach there is allegedly the longest in the world. The Bangladeshi coast is entirely exposed to the Bay of Bengal, and in Cox's Bazar trucks were patrolling the main street, their loudspeakers issuing cyclone warnings. The last cyclone killed a hundred thousand people. A week after it struck, they were still hooking bodies out of trees.

Most of the people on the streets of Cox's Bazar were tribals with Tibetan features, the women carrying babies peeping out of pink woven slings. They had come down from the hills to trade at the market. The hill tribes mostly practice slash-and-burn agriculture (*jhum*), even though the government has tried to ban it to prevent further erosion of the tracts. Relations between tribals and government are strained. The day before I arrived, two activists belonging to Shanti Bahini, a loose collection of tribal peoples struggling to protect their culture and achieve some kind of political autonomy, had been arrested outside my hotel by the security forces and charged with the possession of arms.

Cyclones notwithstanding, Cox's Bazar is the main holiday resort for middle-class Bangladeshis, and they all clamored, when I appeared on the beach, to have their photograph taken with me. But I didn't mind posing for their pictures.

I went back to Chittagong by bus and on to Dhaka by train, as I had decided to travel down to the Ganges Delta on a Rocket paddle steamer, and these departed from the capital. The Ganges officially becomes the Padma when it enters Bangladesh, and the Brahmaputra is renamed the Jamuna; halfway down the country they fuse and become the Meghna. This river moves 400 million tons of earth a year and regularly rearranges the map. As for the magnificent seven remaining Rockets, built in Calcutta in the 1920s, their paddle wheels are now powered by diesel engines.

The Rockets travel four times a week between Dhaka and Khulna, a twenty-four-hour trip. I had booked a first-class cabin on the top deck. It opened onto a carpeted dining area in which a group of Bengalis were permanently hunched over pyramids of steaming rice.

I spent most of the journey sitting outside in a cane armchair as the Rocket chugged sedately down the Meghna. Hundreds of small boats puttered past, and anguished calls to prayer drifted from the banks. Great rafts of bamboo were being floated south. Schools of Gangetic dolphins leaped among mauve pontoons of water hyacinth, and riverine gypsies tethered their covered boats to coconut palms in search of customers for their herbal medicines. A steward in a crisp white jacket and dirty turban intermittently brought tea and Bengal Orange Cake biscuits, murmuring, "Good morning, sir," whenever he approached.

Once, I crept down to the lower decks. People were sprawled everywhere—hundreds of people. Right at the bottom, soldiers were lying on their backs around the engine, black boots at their sides and guns tossed against the railings.

In the morning, flotillas of small boats emerged out of the mist, the oarsmen, standing, sunk within tightly wrapped shawls.

By the time I reached Khulna, I was sure I was pregnant. I felt fine. Weary of rice and watery curried vegetables, but fine. Now I was certain about something, and that helped dislodge my anxieties. I wanted to call Peter, but no international telephones were working. "Line is failure," said a bored attendant at the STD telephone booth next to the Rocket terminal.

I found a hotel next to a derelict jute factory. For many years, yellow-flowered jute was Bangladesh's main export, and there is still a ministry for jute and a jute exchange. Jute flourishes in the humid climate of the Gangetic Plain and has been the main cash crop of wetland smallholders since about 1700. It is harvested during the floods, and to cut the plant, farmers dive down to the base six or eight feet underwater, using the stalk as a guide. Bangladeshi jute divers are said to be the most skillful swimmers in the world. The emergence of synthetics has resulted in shrinking demand and falling prices, effectively strangling the industry.

I was making my way to join a pleasure boat setting off for four days in the waterways of the Sundarbans, the dense mangrove forest along the Bay of Bengal embracing the greatest tidal delta in the world. It was only a few miles from Khulna to Mongla, the port where we were due to embark, but all travel in southern Bangladesh is circumscribed by ferries (these invariably turned out to be primitive and overladen rafts), and they are usually broken, paralyzed by *hartals* (Bangladeshi-style strikes), or simply clogged with queues. As a result, the trip took half a day and I was three hours late, though this wasn't nearly as late as everyone else.

The Sundarbans forest covers twenty-three hundred square miles, two-fifths of which are in India and three-fifths in Bangladesh. The forest, largely impenetrable on land, is crisscrossed by a network of waterways, and these we were scheduled to chug through, observing the fecund wildlife and enjoying the peace—a rare commodity in Bangladesh.

The boat, MV *Chhuti*, had ten small cabins arranged around the lower of two decks, all facing outward. Bathroom facilities consisted of two toilets in the bows, two shower cubicles, and two public washbasins. The crew bunks and galley were crammed belowdecks, and the top deck was reserved for lounging around.

The other seven passengers eventually turned up and boarded noisily. I soon learned that they did everything noisily. They were middle-class professionals from Dhaka, the ringleader a doctor in his fifties with a Mephistophelean smile. This man addressed me throughout the trip in a language tantalizingly close to English. He would begin a dialogue with enthusiastic optimism, realize that the sentiment he wished to express was beyond his capabilities, and promptly leave the sentence he had begun languishing in the syntactical desert, trunkless as Ozymandias. None of the others spoke a single word of English.

Disobliging tides meant that MV *Chhuti* was unable to leave Mongla before morning. We anchored opposite a row of thatched prostitutes' huts, the incumbents' business confined to tanker crews. When we set off in the predawn light, flocks of egrets rose from the mangrove swamps.

Mephistopheles had brought his father, wife, a son of about ten, and a teenage daughter, the last evidently inconvenienced by the presence of her parents, who seemed to annoy her a great deal. She had smeared turmeric on her face to make it brighter, a process I saw her repeating in front of the cracked mirror above one of the washbasins each morning.

The forest consisted of densely packed sundari trees, a type of mangrove yielding wood suitable for telegraph poles and paper pulp. Due to tidal shifts and the high salinity of the waterways, the Sundarbans constitute an ecological hinterland. Spotted deer, rhesus monkeys, and wild boar proliferated on land, crocodiles slunk along the riverbanks, primeval horseshoe crabs with rotating proboscises roamed the beaches, and the birds seemed almost limitless in their abundance and variety. The kingfishers had mutated into hundreds of species, tan-winged Brahminy kites followed the wake of our boat, themselves pursued by white-bellied sea eagles, and pied mynahs rose from the banks in small clouds.

The farther west in the forest you go, the more saline the waters become, with the result that the trees are shorter on the Indian side and there are fewer birds. Bangladeshis are very proud of that.

At mealtimes conversation stormed to and fro across platters of sloppy vegetable rice and fried fish. Mostly my companions ignored me, but occasionally, I suspect out of boredom, they turned their attention to the strange habits of foreigners, further subdivisions of the species apparently being considered unnecessary. The boy took a photograph of my tattoo.

The Sundarbans are the home of the man-eating royal Bengal tiger. The government claims there are 450 left in Bangladesh, but experts put the figure nearer 200. The last census on the Indian side came up with a total Indian population of 250, but this too could be optimistic. The royal Bengal, smaller and brighter in color than northern tigers, has evolved in isolation, and what makes him such a mysterious beast is his selective predilection for eating people. In particular, he likes the Bangladeshi honey collectors who arrive in the Sundarbans late in the season.

The tiger is embedded in local mythology. Bangladeshis in villages abutting the Sundarbans make offerings to the tiger god, Daksin Ray, and are careful to refer to the beast as "uncle," avoiding the Bengali word for tiger in case it provokes the spirits of the forest. Some of these small communities have lost men so frequently that they are known as *vidhaba pallis*, "tiger-widow villages."

The mythology of the tiger settled on our boat. We all dreamed about him, and I was frequently aware that the others were talking about him over meals, even though I could not understand what they were saying. I often heard a hissed call of *"Bagh!"* (tiger) from the top deck, and we would all rush up and lean over the railings, straining our eyes to see him.

But we never did. Once we spied fresh pug prints emerging from the water and a pair of red-wattled lapwings beaking around in a pile of spoor.

The best time to be on board MV *Chhuti* was otter time. For generations, in the lonely backwaters of the Sundarbans otters have been trained to chase fish. Before the monkeys wake, a gondola-shaped vessel emerges from the mist, and a pair of otters, harnessed and squeaking, dive through the milk-chocolate water while four men maneuver nets attached to six-foot bamboo poles. When they are not working, the otters live in a wicker cage strapped to the stern of the boat.

If the otters didn't come, before MV *Chhuti*'s engine began to throb, the only sound was the incantation of the old engine man reciting the Koran on the lower deck. I never heard him speak apart from his prayer sessions, but he was a hieratic presence on board our boat. His prayers helped me.

The only other people we saw in the Sundarbans were itinerant grass cutters collecting thatch and a small community of men and boys who came each summer to fish conventionally. They lived their uncertain lives in a compound of huts and slept on platforms to keep out of the way of tigers. The cracked earth of the compound was spread with coir mats on which the boys had laid out shoals of fragile silvery fish.

We landed alongside a natural jetty at dusk, and I walked in the checkered shadow of the trees, the sky flared with coral and each mangrove frond perfectly defined in the tropical light. There was no undergrowth in this forest, just hundreds of thousands of fibrous stalactites, the root system of the mangroves. I felt calm in those few days, as if I saw things more clearly. My old life seemed to be peeling away like a label from a bottle. I was able to think coherently, for the first time, about my baby. It was as if my center of gravity were altering, like a tidal shift in the great waterways of the Sundarbans.

1997

QE2 Diary

I was bloody terrified. What of "the protection of solitude" now? I sold a series to a Sunday newspaper called "Travels with My Baby." It was a panic reaction. We needed my income, and I couldn't think of any other way in which I could continue working. So when baby Wilf sprang forth, he and I spent our first year flogging around the globe. One of my first assignments was on the *QE2*, cruising from Sydney to Manila. Hardly slumming it, I admit, but it was exhausting. I saw the series through to the end, itself a reflection of the lengths to which I was prepared to go to protect my freedom. I wish in retrospect I had stayed in Starbucks with the other women from my anti-natal group, or was that antenatal? I feel I missed out on something. It was a rubbish series, too.

The *QE2* was halfway through its annual three-month around-the-world tour, and Wilf and I joined a select press trip meeting it in Sydney and disembarking in Manila ten days later. Our minder was Eric Flounders, Cunard's redoubtable PR man in London. A short, balding figure of about fifty, with abundant reserves of Yorkshire cynicism, Eric had acquired legendary status during the fiasco of the *QE2* refit some years previously. The ship made the front pages when cruisers boarded to find electrical wires coiled like snakes outside their cabins, nonfunctioning plumbing, and a wide range of other cock-ups. Eric knew where responsibility lay. But he was on the front line and after a weary week of shelling by enthusiastic reporters had taken a break in the office bathroom when a colleague banged on the cubicle door.

"Eric, it's the chairman on the phone."

"I'm on the toilet."

"He says he really has to talk to you."

"Tell him I can only deal with one shit at a time."

Eric had invited two other hacks on the Sydney-to-Manila jaunt. Brian Hitchen, former editor of both the *Sunday Express* and the *Daily Star* and currently freelancing for *The Irish Times*, was a charming old buffer with a wheeze and a twinkle in his eye. He was spherical; more accurately, he consisted of one small sphere balanced on top of a much larger sphere. Permanently attired in a panama hat and a white jacket with protruding spotted hankie, Brian was remembered by the Fleet Street diaspora for his headlines. When the emperor of Japan died, the *Star* led with EMPEROR GOES TO HELL (a tribute to its many northern readers who had slaved on the infamous railway in World War II), a statement that provoked a volley of diplomatic correspondence and a personal letter to Brian from Mrs. T. telling him that the Japanese ambassador had asked her to put a stop to the headlines. "I told him," Thatcher wrote, "that you could not be controlled."

The second hack in our small party was also called Brian, marginally less huge and similarly attired in panama and white hankie-sprouting jacket. This was Brian Vine, once managing editor of the *Daily Mail*. He was writing a piece about the cruise for that paper. It was he who, in 1974, tracked Ronnie Biggs to his Brazilian lair, and he too, the previous year, who obtained a photograph of the defense minister Lord Lambton naked in bed with a pair of tarts, smoking a joint as well. Between them the Brians had clocked up sixty years' service as foreign correspondents for the tabloids, often together. The pair of them had been shot at in Vietnam by both Americans and Vietcong, and during the Washington race riots they were teargassed, pepper-sprayed, and clubbed, all before lunch on the same day. They were great chums, a pair of likable dinosaurs who despised the six-month-old Labour government and still talked about sending messages home "by telex." They reacted to Wilf like a pair of Lady Bracknells spotting a handbag.

I reproduce here extracts from my diary.

February 16
Our party allocated a table next to the window in the Britannia Grill on the quarterdeck. The Brians complain that we aren't eating in the Princess Grill. Both have sailed on the ship more than two dozen times, and Fatter Brian has spent years greasing up the maître d'. He bitterly regrets not being able to reap the benefit. He said, "The man's built an extension to his house on what he's got off me."

The Britannia staff can't do enough for Wilf, with the exception of a waitress whom I heard announcing to a colleague this morning, "I can't stand babies." They puree anything I want and bring it to the high chair. What Wilf likes eating most is the doily on which his dish is served.

Went to the launderette at the end of deck three to do ironing, solving the problem of where to put Wilf by laying him in a laundry basket. The lower-deck wives were swinging their irons and gossiping like a Greek chorus. They seem happy here, ironing their husbands' shirts and pants.

Spotted the two Brians playing bingo. They are like a pair of old women.

February 18

The ship has been chugging up the Gold Coast, past what were once sleepy sugarcane towns and are now springboard resorts for the Great Barrier Reef. This afternoon we entered Whitsunday Passage and its archipelago, named on June 3, 1770, by Captain Cook as he surveyed the east coast of New Holland. He thought it was Whitsunday that day, but it wasn't, it was the day after. I love that: when the calendar stops mattering.

The Fat Brians have settled into a routine involving lying by the pool and complaining, their Spam-colored legs splayed on the loungers looking as if they belong to a pair of thinner men. This afternoon one Brian noted that members of the Filipino crew are now visible above decks in daylight, something that would never have gone on in Matthews's day. Victor Matthews (Baron Matthews of Southgate) is a former chairman of Cunard, and his reign is regularly invoked.

Wilf has taken his first manly steps toward independence in the QE2 nursery. Called Noah's Ark and staffed by a pair of English nannies, the nursery is located on the sundeck next to the kennels, a fact noted by the Brians as "appropriate." One of the nurses is a skinhead. Yesterday I left my boy for forty-five minutes. Today took him for two hours in the morning and two in the afternoon. Sometimes the skin-headed nanny's boyfriend is there. He is a stoker and a great supporter of Wilf's.

We were playing with an inflatable replica of the ship in the deck one lounge at about six yesterday evening when an elderly South African woman joined us. She was waiting for the casino to open. (The casino is required by law to close when the ship is in territorial waters.) The woman settled into an armchair next to ours. Since her husband died, she hasn't been able to stop gambling. "Often," she said, "I miss the bus home from the casino and have to stay there all night."

A bell rang, signaling that the casino was open. Our friend got up, then turned back toward us. "Excuse me," she said in a conspiratorial whisper. "Which of the two large men is your husband?"

February 19
Fatter Brian has a fever. He is confined to his cabin, nursed by our steward and the ship's doctor. At lunch, Less Fat Brian, lost without his henchman, wondered what the expensive doctor is going to write in the report he has to give to the patient. "You are a fat, indolent git," suggested Eric in his nasal Yorkshire twang, "and if you lost a bit of weight, you'd be less of a health hazard." In reality, we all miss Fatter Brian. He is a Falstaffian character with a softer edge than Less Fat, who refers to Wilf as "it."

Illness in our party led to a debate about death on board. There have been a number of suicides over the years, usually from deluxe cabins. "In most cases," reported Eric breezily, "a steward finds the window open in the morning." But the Reaper does his own work too: hordes of octogenarians shuffle the decks, and a couple of nonas. A rumor is going around that six passengers have expired on this world cruise so far and that they are languishing in the freezers belowdecks. A widow from Alberta is carrying on, despite losing her husband between Los Angeles and Auckland. "It's what he would have wanted," she told Eric.

Shipboard activities are advertised in a daily program slipped under the cabin door at night. There is a weight-control seminar, if one can fit it in among one's daily four meals. An event in the Grand Lounge today was billed "Your Questions Answered About God." I had plenty of unanswered questions, so I went along. A rabbi, an Episcopalian archdeacon, and a Catholic chaplain sat onstage clutching handheld mikes in front of a pot of wilting geraniums. A dozen punters were scattered throughout the red velvet seats, John Grisham hardbacks on their knees. In the gallery above them, people were drifting in and out of the boutiques. An Australian man in long purple shorts kicked off the questions. "How can you reconcile an infallible God with hurricanes?" he wondered. The trio had covered this at theological college. The chaplain began confidently with "Pain is a gift," before all three flummoxed around in original sin, coming to a standstill at free will. Soon the archdeacon and the chaplain were at it, beard to beard, over the issue of whether you were supposed to interpret the Bible literally. "Sort us out, Rabbi," drawled the archdeacon.

I wonder what they are looking for, these dogged cruisers, caught up in the frenetic round of still-life classes and trivia quizzes, barely finding time to change into their black ties and cocktail gowns for dinner. Was it what the prayer book calls "the peace which the world cannot give"? If so, I don't think Cunard can offer it either.

Mealtime conversation, which began on a modestly intellectual plane, dips a little lower with each repast. Tonight we were discussing the possibility of doing the laundry by towing it behind the ship in a large string bag. Endless speculation about fanciable candidates among our fellow passengers. What a sad lot we are: insatiable talk of shagging and none of us with a hope.

February 20

Anchored among the Whitsundays. I couldn't go on the snorkeling excursion as it was too hot for Wilf outside. But I took him on the ship's tender to Hamilton Island, a hilly tropical resort. On the tender we sat next to a woman from Barnsley on her twenty-fifth *QE2* cruise. I asked her if it was a bit different each time. "Why, no," she said. "Each time it's exactly the same. That's why I like it." Many passengers return year after year, as if cruising were a way of coping with time that lies heavy on their hands.

Most have raised kids of their own. "I wish," they say wistfully as they tickle Wilf's foot, "that mine were still that age." It seems a pity that regret should be a leitmotif of parenthood. And yet when Wilf tips his little face up to mine and smiles his gummy smile, I catch myself, already, wanting to hold back time.

Hamilton Island smelled of crushed ferns. I found a café with fans, and Wilf admired the plumed birds and the chopped-up light under the palm fronds. Bronzed young men and women padded past in bare feet, shouldering windsurf boards and grasping clumps of flippers. They were me once!

Eric so hungover at dinner he ordered consommé and ice cream. He had got drunk on the snorkeling excursion to the Reef pontoon, inadvertently snorkeling in the area roped off for fish only. The idea was that non-snorkelers could observe unmolested marine life through the glass wall of the pontoon. On this occasion they saw Eric. He gave them a wave. Back on board, he had gone to the spa to sober up before dinner, waking later in the sauna, which was by then dark and cold. His robe in the meantime had been sent to the laundry, his watch and sole pair of pebble-lensed spectacles in the pocket. Currently going through the boil cycle.

February 21

Wilf has woken at four thirty every day so far except today, when we crossed a time zone and he zinged to life at half past three. I carry him around the empty decks in a sling for three hours. His teeth are troubling him, and I'm knackered. At seven o'clock this morning he dropped off back in the cabin, and I lay down on my bed and closed my eyes. Five minutes later an announcement over the in-cabin speakers woke us both up. I burst into tears.

Fatter Brian is better. I got down to breakfast to find him and Less Fat in dispute with a waiter about their freshly squeezed orange juice.

"Squeezed this morning," thundered one. "Not two weeks

ago." They were so involved in the juice topic that they had not noticed we had arrived at Ambon in the Indonesian Moluccas. A band was stationed on the quay to welcome us, and a group of schoolchildren were singing a reedy "Waltzing Matilda." I left Wilf in the nursery and went ashore for half a day. Eric was with me, but the others took the full-day tour. The excursion was in a rackety non-air-conditioned bus. Ambon is a hole (the Allies bombed it to bits in the war), but the countryside around it is all right, mainly sago trees and mangrove swamps, and we stopped at an excellent beach where Eric and I went swimming in our knickers while the others watched a folk dance. While we were enjoying the water, a man appeared on the beach brandishing a gun in our direction. Eric manfully strode through the waves, tugging his Marks & Spencer Y-fronts as high as they would go. Much gesticulating ensued. We were, it emerged, inappropriately attired. The man departed, gun still at the ready. Eric waved me out. On the way back to the ship we watched a man coaxing eels out from under the rocks of an inlet with a hen's egg in which he had bored a hole. At a Christian village I bought a packet of clove cigarettes—I was in the Spice Islands, after all—but even unlit they stank out the cabin. There was nothing else to buy in Ambon, or so I thought. Back on board, Fatter Brian was showing off a couple of penis gourds he had picked up.

When Wilf goes to the nursery, I lie on the sundeck, reading and listening to the thwack of a golf club slicing through the air in a cage on the deck below me (the men wield irons up here while their women do the same thing five decks below). A steward, from time to time, steals soundlessly across the tawny boards, a tray at shoulder height. I like it up there. When you appear, young men spring forward to spread red foam and yellow-striped towels on a lounger. In the morning they serve beef tea, and at four Earl Grey tea and tiny sandwiches. It rained yesterday, and the stewards wrapped the few hardy punters who stayed in towels, like horses. Digestives appeared with the beef tea to help us cope with the deluge, and the tawny boards turned dark brown. Lovely. The labor ward seemed a long way off.

The Brians have persuaded Eric to let us dine in the Princess Grill, though to Fatter's chagrin the oiled-up maître d' disembarked in Sydney. Their faith in our departure from the Britannia was rewarded when the substitute maître d' asked in low tones, when caviar appeared on the order, if sirs would care for beluga rather than sevruga.

I find shipboard life sanitized. I catch myself longing for something seedy. Am influenced in part by Greene's *Journey Without Maps*, which I am reading when Wilf is asleep. The novelist acknowledged that even the smell of cooking greens off the Tottenham Court Road has something attractive about it. "It seems to satisfy, temporarily," he wrote, "the sense of nostalgia for something lost; it seems to represent a stage further back." Seediness, he went on, "is nearer the beginning than the radical and the chic." A luxury oceangoing liner is the reverse. It is a stage further on, involving doddering rich people in absurd clothes and bingo in mid-Pacific. Death stalks these ships, and the hapless cruisers stave it off with shopping and beluga. When someone dies, they must all think, "Me next?" You can see it in their faces.

February 24
Docked at Kota Kinabalu in Sabah, the Malaysian state previously known as North Borneo. Here, as at all ports, the punters rush off to use their mobile telephones. Kota Kinabalu was such a dump that I began to think fondly of Ambon. As the tour was on an air-con bus, I took Wilf. I believe he enjoyed it more than I did. Kota Kinabalu is made of stained concrete. As with Ambon, the Allies bombed it—then known as Jesselton—out of existence during the recapture of Borneo at the end of the war. There are no Malays in Sabah, only Muslim tribes and a few other ethnic groups. Our guide was a desperate individual who pretended that his grandfather was a headhunter. He pointed out, as an

attraction, "one of the largest traffic intersections in Malaysia" and explained that K.K. has twice been razed by fire. "Why don't we have a third go?" suggested one of the Brians. But Wilf was a hit among the water gypsies in the stilted villages on the fringes of the city. They ran out to touch his arm. The Brians were appalled to see that I permitted bodily contact and tutted loudly. When the children saw Fatter Brian, they patted his stomach. "They think I'm Buddha," he said amiably. I do like him.

In the Yacht Club tonight the gentlemen hosts were foxtrotting with unaccompanied women passengers. I am riveted by these characters—men employed as escorts. According to Eric, Cunard picks blokes it reckons are too old to get it up, though a few years ago a gentleman host did marry a regal American widow. He turned out to be a queen too.

February 26
Very hot all day. Booked Alison for the evening again, my regular babysitter. She is pretty, and the Brians lobbied for our nightly preprandials to be taken in my room. Alison dotes on Wilf and takes him down to the crew bar—out of bounds to us—to show him off to her colleagues.

At the twice-nightly performance in the Grand Lounge, the cruise director stands behind a velveteen drape and shouts, "It's Showtime!" his voice rising on the second syllable. Most Showtime acts are crappy cabarets featuring second-rate crooners. The Brians are convinced that Cunard recruits its dancers from an agency specializing in flat-chested women. At Kota Kinabalu, however, Petula Clark came on board, and tonight I got a front-row seat at the first of her two shows. The *QE2* Orchestra accompanied Pet, gamely doubling up on instruments, and the pianist was a hopeful American youth wearing plastic shoes under his dress trousers. He was obliged to conduct with one hand and play the piano with the other, a feat he pulled off with aplomb.

Pet was fabulous and totally unappreciated by the barbarians. During the opening bars of "Downtown," a Taiwanese couple got up and left. You could see the girl of thirty years ago as she sat at the piano herself and belted out "La vie en rose."

Had a drink with the others in the Yacht Club after. Both Brians privately offered to check on Wilf. Hope never dies; thank God!

February 27

The atmosphere among the Filipino crew growing more febrile by the hour. They are about to go home, albeit only for a day, after ten months at sea. Some of them have become fathers in that time. Sweltering heat. I joined the Brians as we approached Manila. They were sitting in the Chart Room bar complaining about the stale peanuts. Manila was steaming in the distance like an over-ripe sump. We contemplated the traffic jams and winter fogs of London. I said I had enjoyed the cruise, which was more or less true. Less Fat told me that it was pointless bringing a baby on a cruise. "As pointless as taking it to a brothel," he said. That was more or less true, too.

1998

POSTSCRIPT

Brian Vine died in September 2006. When preparing for this volume, I took the precaution of sending this piece to the other Brian: with the passage of the years, he might object. But he didn't. Instead, he sent me the following e-mail, recalling the start of the cruise.

Vine and I couldn't believe our luck when a beautiful woman in an exotic hat checked in to join Mother Flounders' Flying Circus at Heathrow. And then we spotted the basket.

"There's a bloody baby in it," Vine exclaimed. "And it's with that woman . . ."

"Never mind, Brian," I said. "We can always keep the woman and throw the baby over the side."

"Or eat it," he muttered. "I'm going to give Flounders a piece of my mind . . ."

Hitchen also pointed out that Vine was always the fatter of the two. Photographic evidence, in this case, indicates the reverse.

1998

On the *QE2*—a ship since dispatched to liner heaven—I learned that traveling was never going to be the same again. After years transforming myself in new settings, I could no longer lose my identity and become someone else. I could still stop being buttoned-up and English. I could still stop being Peter's girl-friend. I could even stop being a writer. But I could never, ever stop being Wilf's mother.

After about ten months, I began to get the hang of my new status as a double act. Improvisation was the key to keeping the show on the (almost literal) road. Once, in a town in the American heartland that might have been called Coma, I asked the motel owner if he could possibly provide a crib (cot), as I had forgotten to book one in advance. The motel didn't have such a thing, but the man kindly said he'd see what he could do. An hour later there was a knock on our door, and he wheeled in a shopping trolley. I picked magazine assignments that suited us all. In Morocco we rode camels, and the *New York Times* picture editor commissioned the man who does the Babar illustrations (the son of the author, who set the series in North Africa) to paint a picture of Daddy Babar, Mummy Babar, and Little Babar on camels for the cover of the magazine. I bought the original, and Wilf has it framed on his bedroom wall. It cost more than the fee I received for the piece.

Our second son was born in August 2002. When he was four months old, I took him to Lapland on an assignment for *The Telegraph*. Ever tried to breast-feed at minus 30? My wonderful guide and translator Lennart Pittja prepared a traditional Sámi meal in his skins-and-peat tent house. When baby Reggie and I arrived for the evening, a pair of draft reindeer were scooping snow outside with their front hooves, burying their noses into the mushy ground beneath, and whistling softly as they exhaled. Constellations of white-faced stars hung low, the abutting spruce grove a cavern of moonlight and shadows. Inside, we lounged on pelts as Pittja's herding assistant Anders rolled out flatbread and the fire hissed to life, first catching on resin in the birch bark, then crackling over pine and juniper. A small hole in the apex of the *lávvu* drew off aromatic smoke. We lay snug in our poled fortress. Pittja had cooked up a *máles*, the Sámi meal typically eaten at slaughter time, and it bubbled with ominous pungent eructations in a blackened pot. A *máles* consists of reindeer parts all boiled up together: liver, tongue, bone, and steak with a hump of canary-yellow fat. "Even the hooves are boiled!" Pittja announced, handing me a green birch skewer with which to poke marrow from the bone. I could see the flickering ion stream of the northern lights through the roof hole. Anders offered a chunk of cooked reindeer fat on a plate. "For the baby," he said. "He's not weaned yet," I said. "I know," he said. "That's what we wean them with."

From then on in, much of my working life has turned on compromise. It hasn't always involved boiled hoof. But it hasn't been a picnic, either. The history of travel writing reveals few mothers. Have a baby, and you lose your passport to the magical world of anonymity, impulse, and sleazy bars. The famous fathers of the genre usually had that most valuable travel accessory, a wife who stayed at home minding the brood. (Forget the multi-outlet electrical adapter. Get a wife!) *The Great Railway Bazaar: And the Kids Came Too*. I don't think so.

I am of course a worse mother than everyone else on the planet because I don't bake cakes or build Lego replicas of the Taj Mahal, and no doubt for other reasons too (my younger son was the first in his nursery class to yell out a rhyme for "hunt"). I said earlier that I found the sense of being a stranger in a foreign land inspiring. The school gate was different. It was more foreign than anywhere, and less inspiring. But there has never seemed a choice other than battling on. Naturally, I do less globe-trotting than I used to, and I don't mind that a bit. Who wants another tropical disease? I was always a writer before I was a traveler, and there are plenty of things I want to write about that don't involve trekking across inhospitable terrain and eating lizards, especially as I hurtle past fifty. That said, I still miss the days when I shampooed my hair in washing-up liquid, slept on the roof of moving trains, and came home when I felt like it. I hope the children have absorbed some of the rewards of travel: the power of the fleeting moment; the glimpse of another world; the whiff of a souk, recalled when the walls close in.

I have picked this short piece, out of many like it, as it is indicative of the kind of compromise that is now my stock-in-trade.

Cuba, *Sí*!

Nations rarely remain on the cusp for long, and when I heard Castro had stepped down, I decided to take my children to Cuba. Nobody knows what will happen now the wily fox is out of his lair. At least my boys will be able to say that they saw Cuba while the revolutionary flame still burned.

Before we had even checked into our hotel in Havana, Wilf (ten) and Reg (five) were squealing at the tank-sized vintage cars cruising the streets: Chevys, Plymouths, Cadillacs, Dodges—we even spotted a mauve Pontiac, with fins. My partner, a prerevolutionary North American relic himself, took to shouting out "Nineteen fifty-eight Buick!" or whatever, as every fresh model purred into view.

There were other signs of a society fossilized at a certain moment in history. The laundry list at the Hotel Nacional harked back to the heady days of Scott Fitzgerald (prices were listed for cleaning "Sport coats," "Tuxedos," and even "Drawers"). In-house entertainment featured twice-weekly water ballet in the swimming pool, all camp costumes and nose clips. The boys had never seen anything like it, and for the rest of the week Reg hurled himself off the diving board with uncontrollable vigor, toes pointed and a clothespin on his nose.

The communist experiment was everywhere evident in public buildings bristling with battalions of uniformed staff snoozing quietly through the tropical afternoon. (In the Palacio de los Capitanes Generales on Plaza de Armas, one attendant did leap up, dragging us behind an eighteenth-century armoire to ask if we would give him a pen.) Cuba enjoys zero unemployment. But salaries are painfully low, and many try their hand in the twilit world of private enterprise. We were approached by a man flogging pirated DVDs of *Saturday Night Fever*. The flourishing *agropecuarios* revealed further chinks in Cuba's armor. *Agros* are basically free-enterprise farmers' markets, and at the largest in the country, Havana's Egido, sellers touted ziggurats of mangoes, guavas, and plantains as well as sacks of garlic and sweet potatoes.

The buildings of Havana broke my heart many times over. Dilapidation is much in evidence, but the robust restoration program of the old town continues, and there are no shopping malls yet—just softly pocked marine limestone pillars and sheets billowing from first-floor balconies. People say the architecture is eclectic, but I would not agree. Cubans have made every style their own by adding baroque excrescences, whether to turn-of-the-century villas or blocky Stalinist high-rises. European fashions took a while to reach this colonial outpost, with the result that the nineteenth-century mansions have a touch of the merchant prince dwellings of Antwerp and Venice—inner courtyards, high ceilings, and marble stairs with matching handrails. But these villas are embellished with names that crowd the Miami telephone directory.

Cuban cuisine, however, called *criolla*, has a distinctly postrevolutionary tang. We ate in *paladares*, restaurants in private houses officially permitted if they seat fewer than twelve. At the Cocina de Lilliam in Miramar, a relatively affluent district characterized by small pastel villas where grandmas sit on the porches in their nineties, we dined in a courtyard among fountains and flame trees, the air heady with the perfume of butterfly jasmine. Cubans have to be inventive, given the U.S. trade embargo and general lack of funds. Wilf's grouper in coconut sauce came accompanied by a glass bowl "garnish" in which two goldfish circled. "Not for eating," said our waitress.

We partook of street food hawked from wheelbarrows or windows—from *chicharritas de plátano*, paper cones loaded with freshly fried banana chips, to my favorite, *chicharrones de empella*, fat from pork cracklings thickly spread on a wedge of bread. A heart attack in a twist of paper . . . But the highlight of Cuban guzzling has to be the Coppelia ice cream parlor, a Havana landmark of retro chic even before it featured in the 1994 awardwinning film *Strawberry and Chocolate*. Wilf and Reg quickly became experts on the merits of a *tres gracias* (three scoops) over the puny *jimagua* (two scoops). After supper, my sons played baseball on the streets of Old Havana, teaming up with local boys slogging it out with homemade bats and balls. Children effortlessly get over language barriers, and it was high fives all around when darkness drew proceedings to a close. On one occasion, observing us watching a makeshift baseball game, a set of parents invited us into a ground-floor tenement flat in a decaying mansion to view their Santería saints-day display. The voodoo-like Santería remains the most widely practiced religion in Cuba, and it reveals much about the tangled roots of the national identity, revolution or no revolution. Introduced by West African slaves and grafted onto Catholicism over centuries, the religion attracts hundreds of thousands of followers, many of whom are visible on the streets in the top-to-toe white costumes worn for a year after the rites of initiation. In the Bosque de la Habana, a wood on Río Almendares, we twice saw Santería devotees sacrificing chickens amid the Gothic fecundity of kapok trees and other hardwood monsters. It was a bit stinky, but the boys loved it.

In the 1860s, the landed gentry of Cuba revolted against Spanish rule. A decade of repression dealt with that particular revolution, but a hike in sugar prices incited another uprising, and plantation owners joined the barricades. Eventually, after thousands of deaths, the United States established a permanent naval base on the island to keep an eye on the upstarts. Its name was Guantánamo Bay. But before we left Havana, I remarked to Peter that these days the city seemed remarkably safe—more provincial backwater than crime-infested capital. "Yes," he replied, "that's one advantage of a dictatorship. Keeps the yobs off the streets."

2002

In 2005 my publishers decided it was time for a fresh edition of my travel book on Chile, published eleven years previously. Would I return, they asked, to write an introduction to the second edition? I couldn't justify a three-week trip alone for such a flimsy reason, so, as my passport out of London, I took Wilf with me, leaving little Reg with his dad, who promptly shipped him off to Slovakia with our nanny. (She is still with us, after eight years.)

Chile, *Mi Amor*

This is a young woman's book (*Chile: Travels in a Thin Country*). Rereading it now from the misty vantage point of middle age, I hardly recognize the solitary figure who shouldered a carpetbag twenty-six hundred miles from the Peruvian border to Cape Horn. Which, I wondered, had changed more in the intervening thirteen years—the thin country or the author it had so enchanted? To find out, and to prepare this new edition, I went back. Since my last visit I have absorbed myself in other places, far from Chile. But up in the Andean passes around La Junta, I found the mountains as I remembered.

On this second journey there were no vats of pisco sour, no strange men, and, disappointingly, no bad behavior of any kind. I took my eight-year-old son, Wilf, with me. I had caught my first fish in Chile, and I wanted him to do the same. It was a mother-and-son road trip.

We acclimatized in Santiago (more of that later), then flew north. There we cycled through the Atacama salt pans and swam in saline pools alongside Andean flamingos. We hiked along the rucked cliffs of the Cordillera de la Sal and under the clay chimneys and hieroglyphs that shape the valleys, and in the afternoons the desert colors shifted and elided until the moon rose over the cordillera and the sun set over the flats. High up, in the puna land above thirteen thousand feet, we saw vicuña grazing on cropped grassy slopes and viscachas—tailless rabbits—feeding in the swamps. We made our base in San Pedro, the oasis village where I had spent Christmas on my last trip. Everyone told me San Pedro had changed. More agencies were offering trips to Bolivia, many suspiciously cheap, and suspiciously close to the cocaine route, but Club Med still seemed a long way off.

Wilf was at the age of perpetual questioning and maniacal classification, the latter involving the categorization of everything into Best Ten and Worst Ten—fruits, cars, people we had met that day. Oh, for an hour to escape the questions! The morning would kick off at 6:30 (if I was lucky) with "Mum, does the Labour Party like the queen?" and end, at whatever hour we returned to our lodging, with "Mum, what's your top-ten Premiership goalkeepers?" But he made many friends. While I struggled to breathe life into my moribund Spanish, football provided Wilf with an international language. He had many "conversations" debating the virtues of Frank Lampard over Thierry Henry, and he watched countless reenactments of the way in which Uruguay had recently been knocked out of the World Cup qualifiers by—and this was the detail Chilean boys loved most—*Australia!*

Later, in the south, we rode horses through Valdivian rain forest from Cochamó to La Junta, a three-day trek following an eighteenth-century trading route over the Andes (fish went over from the Chilean coast and cattle came back from the Argentinean pampa). The path was alarmingly narrow in places and so stony that horses must be reshod every three weeks. But the Chilean saddle, at least, is more forgiving than its ridged English counterpart. We were in ranching country, and Wilf was desperate to see a genuine *huaso* cowboy. It didn't take long. The first we spotted was still wearing the traditional heavy wooden stirrup clogs (I had taken one of these ornate stirrups home last time, and it remained stabled on the mantelpiece, a source of wonder to Wilf and his brother, who regularly tried it on). But the other end of our cowboy was plugged into an iPod.

We celebrated Christmas on a dairy farm in San Antonio on the island of Chiloé. Every surface in the small wooden-tiled farmhouse was crowded with blocks of waxy cheese. When we woke up on Christmas Day, we telephoned the other half of our family back in England and exchanged two gifts I had stowed in the luggage before leaving London—a micro flashlight for Wilf and a lipstick for me. Our hosts, Hardy and Marie-Luisa, spit roasted a sheep (on Christmas Eve the lanes of Chiloé were colonized by small boys each leading a sheep home on a rope). And it was on the San Antonio River, in Hardy's rowing boat, that Wilf caught his fish.

Even on Chiloé, still in many respects a backwater literally and metaphorically isolated from the mainland, a gleaming supermarket had recently opened in the center of Ancud, instantly dispossessing the jumble of tiny shops circling it. It was called Full Fresh—a typically ill-conceived mangling of English—and its plastic bags were already cartwheeling through the streets. But on the remote Pacific coast of the island, men were still harvesting hairy brown *pelillo* seaweed, diving with primitive hoses clamped in their mouths.

Everywhere we went, I found that Chile was flourishing. It has lately been enjoying one of the most impressive growth rates in the world, let alone in South America. You can even get decent coffee in a few places now: when I was last there, the entire country was in thrall to Nescafé, gourmet restaurants even offering the granules in silver pots with hot water on the side. Roads have advanced: the Carretera Austral had crept toward Tortel, Chiloé's west coast was finally punctured, and the throbbing new network around Puerto Montt was a veritable spaghetti junction. The infamous Santiago buses had been regulated, and fleets of smart yellow-and-white vehicles were hurtling up and down the

Alameda in place of the disparate flotilla of boneshakers I used to know. A multiplicity of measures had been introduced to reduce the smog of the Santiago bowl, and new environmentally friendly green buses were about to be phased in. People were fatter, mobile phone sirens had entered the aural mix, and the premium network, called Movistar, was touted everywhere. As we waited for our luggage in Calama airport, a billboard above the carousel informed me that I could be checking e-mails on my BlackBerry. Last time it took me three days to locate a functioning landline in Calama. I found the most dramatic changes of all in the south, around Puerto Montt. The town itself had doubled in size, largely as a result of the burgeoning farmed-salmon business. Chile has overtaken Norway as global leader in the industry, and highways radiate from the coast opposite Chiloé, where most of the fish are harvested, to the airport outside Puerto Montt, the roadsides clotted with warehouses, "ice markets," and the golden arches of three McDonald's.

Many things had not changed. Economic success had not towed in its wake the Argentinean swagger, and anyway the strong dollar was hurting exporters—the old story of Chilean history. At the *marisquerías* in Santiago's central market the café patrons were still hustling for their lives, and their customers were still spooning shellfish juice into glasses of cloudy white wine. Wilf gobbled up his first empanada at a sawdust-floored stand-up joint next door to the market, jostled alongside elderly Santiagans lunching on the hoof. Whenever we squashed onto one of the new buses and headed for the Plaza Italia, our driver and all the other drivers spent the whole journey honking, just as they had in the deregulated epoch. The Andean foothills of the Santiago bowl were still wreathed in cadmium smog, as I remembered them, and people told me that the previous August, the worst month for pollution, the government advised people to avoid sport, and numbers of the young and the old were hospitalized. And despite abundant evidence of what economic pundits called "the Chilean tiger," 95 percent of wealth remained in the hands of the old central valley elite. I was regaled with volumes of horror stories, from the shocking state of public health care in rural areas to the endemic lawlessness and deprivation of the La Legua district of Santiago.

After a few weeks' worth of conversations back on Chilean soil, it became clear that Argentina was no longer the enemy it had been during my last visit: its spectacular economic collapse had rendered old rivalries futile. Bolivia had taken up the baton. Still fighting for access to the sea, Bolivia seemed to be getting nowhere in any department, its recent gas reserves failing to yield the promised foreign bonanza and, as Chileans loved to trumpet, its left-wing president, Evo Morales, a member of the *cocaleros* (coca growers) party. Since my last visit almost the whole continent had drifted left (Colombia apart), presumably as a reaction against an increasingly aggressive and interventionist United States. Morales was even shouting about kicking all U.S. interests out of Bolivia. But many Chileans felt that a succession of their own governments had sold out to the United States as part of the country's rise to prosperity. Down in the south we traveled for a week with a guide studying for a doctorate in botany. One day Wilf asked him when Chile became independent of Spain. After a short lecture on national history, Juan concluded ruefully, "We belong to the United States now."

The word "eco" was now much in evidence, in newsprint, on product details, and in conversation. Always deployed with sound and fury, it invariably signified nothing. The chopping down of the Chilean forests was continuing apace, and I learned of many other cases in which the corporate interests of multinationals were favored over environmental concerns or the well-being of local people. I was appalled in the Norte Chico, or "Little North," the band of country between the central valley and the Atacama Desert, to see the destruction already perpetrated on the Huasco valley. The Canadian mining titan Barrick Gold had detected what might be the world's biggest gold deposit under three glaciers straddling the border at the head of the valley. Corporation bosses immediately launched the Pascua-Lama project, and in 1997 Presidents Eduardo Frei of Chile and Carlos Menem of Argentina signed a treaty granting both glaciers and land to Barrick and agreeing that the territory should not be subject to the laws of either country. (All land above ninety-eight hundred feet in Chile belongs to the government and can't be sold, except, apparently, in this case.) Barrick actually planned to move the glaciers. Whether it shifts them or not, as much as 40 percent of the ice has already degraded as a result of Pascua-Lama construction operations. The disastrous consequences for the ecosystem are yet to be realized.

I saw Wilf learning to love Chile, as I had done. It was deeply gratifying, and I wondered if pleasure becomes a vicarious commodity when you turn into a parent. I was one step away from Chile this time. You don't have the same sense of the open road when you travel with a child. Responsibility is like a barricade. Comfort, safety, and decent hotels don't provide the same rush as traveling hard, either. The hit of hot water after days without it; the dusty journeys standing up in the back of a truck, jolted to pieces and cooked alive; the total exhaustion of a ten-hour hike— these were part only of my past. I regretted the safety of the life that is now mine and longed for the freedom I once had—the liberating sense of being alone without responsibilities and without the disillusion the years tow in their wake, and with a whole world to discover. I was forty-four when I went back to Chile. I would have hoped that the tension between domesticity and discovery might have slackened off by that advanced age. It was what Karen Blixen called the choice between the lion hunt and bathing the baby.

I picked up a few novels while I was back. A new generation

of Chilean writers was trying to get the past in order—though at least magic realism had more or less died a natural death, thank God. In the dictatorship, wrote Roberto Bolaño in *By Night in Chile* (Bolaño was born in Santiago in 1953 and was imprisoned under Pinochet), "Chile itself, the whole country, had become the Judas Tree, a leafless, dead-looking tree, but still deeply rooted in the black earth, our rich black earth with its famous 40-centimetre earthworms."* On the whole it seemed to me that politics in Chile had converged on the center ground, as it had in other parts of the world. Our visit coincided with a presidential election. When I read the manifestos of the candidates, there appeared little to choose between them—except for the communist man, and he ended up polling just 5 percent. We happened to be in Santiago when the results came in. I was pleased to be present on the day Chileans returned their first woman president. Our hotel was being used as the base camp of one of the losing candidates (four stood), and at one o'clock in the morning I was woken by a crowd of his supporters. The candidate duly arrived amid a defiant maelstrom of Latin flag-waving as hordes of aides rushed around with press passes swinging round their necks. At one point the television cameras panned up to me, watching from a third-floor window in my pajamas.

We ended our trip at Hacienda Los Lingues, the estate near San Fernando in the central valley that was my sanctuary last time around. Los Lingues has been in the hands of the same family since the king of Spain dished out the best land to the first conquistadores in the sixteenth century. The current owner's son, my old friend Germán, had visited me in London since my first trip, and we had stayed in touch. He was still running the haci-

---

*Bolaño won international fame in 2008 with his door-stopping novel *2666*. But he was not able to enjoy his success. After decades of vagabonding and dishwashing, he died in 2003, aged fifty.

enda as a hotel, now commuting from Santiago on a 1,200cc motorbike wearing a riding hat instead of a helmet. He had given up drinking but was otherwise the same brash and lovable figure, erupting with volcanic energy and soft as a marshmallow in the middle.

For three days Wilf and I rode the Los Lingues Aculeo thoroughbreds, swam in the new pool, and heard the strangulated pleas of the peacocks as we dined on the circular terrace next to the fountain with Germán and his parents. On the fourth day I left Wilf with a gang of children from various familial branches and climbed onto the back of the motorbike. Germán had cooked up an ambitious scheme to bottle wine under the hacienda label in a joint venture with Los Vascos, one of the most prestigious wineries in Chile. He had invited me to join him for a meeting at the Los Vascos vineyards fifty miles to the south.

The ribbon development south of Santiago melts away as one leaves San Fernando. The southern heartlands take on softer edges here, beyond the detritus of the copper mines and the intense-cultivation U.S.-owned fruit farms strung out between the capital and Rancagua. As we hurtled down the Pan-American, deciduous beech forests climbed higher up the slopes of the Andes, the glaciers in between feeding a succession of broad, gravelly rivers. At Santa Cruz, Germán wheeled off the highway, and slowing down by about half a mile an hour, we roared into the seventy-five-mile-long Colchagua Valley. A subtribe of the Mapuche known as Chiquillanes first settled the land ("Colchagua" means "Valley of Small Lagoons" in their language). The industrious Inca who conquered them built the first pre-Hispanic irrigation works on Chiquillán soil and introduced agriculture. In the middle of the sixteenth century the Jesuits pitched up and, needing Communion wine, planted Chile's first vines on the fertile plains next to the Tinguiririca River.

We screamed into the brick courtyard of the smart Los Vascos headquarters and made unsuccessful efforts to clean up the dust and sweat from the journey. After presenting ourselves at reception, we were greeted warmly by Claudio Naranjo, the genial boss of Los Vascos Chile. The winery is 60 percent owned by the Rothschilds, and Claudio exuded the understated grandeur of the French establishment within which he had trained. We were joined, on a tour of both cellars and vineyards, by Marco Puyo, chief winemaker at Los Vascos, and a corpulent magazine magnate from Santiago wearing a toupee of such magnificent absurdity that it was difficult to focus on anything else in his presence. After a stately procession among stainless steel tanks, pneumatic presses, and pungent rows of new oak barrels, we piled into Claudio's jeep and headed to the highest point of the ninety-acre estate. Wedged between the Andes, dominated here by the 14,038-foot Tinguiririca volcano, and the Pacific Ocean just twenty miles to the west, the Colchagua region was regarded by European investors as viticultural Shangri-la. An abundance of irrigating meltwater, low humidity, zero frost, maritime breezes that temper the effects of the summer sun, deep semiarid sedimentary soil containing a mixture of fine-textured loam clay and loam silt, an exceptionally long growing season—these factors create a near-perfect *terroir*.

Over lunch in an elegant guesthouse set back from the company offices on a trimmed lawn, we sipped the flagship 2001 Le Dix, an intense purplish-ruby wine with an aroma redolent of vinous Ribena. The magazine magnate could hardly contain his enthusiasm. "It's gorgeous," he breathed, the toupee going up and down like a pedal bin. That morning, Claudio had heard that Le Dix had won a top wine award *in France*. "Delightful!" gurgled the magnate. "New World wins on Old World turf." The others winced politely. Nobody uses the terms "Old World" and "New World" much anymore, either in wine or in any other business. It was not just a condescending label. It was wrong. Since my first visit to Chile, archaeologists in Peru have uncovered evidence of Andean civilizations as old as any in the world.

As we walked back to the motorbike, I asked Germán how he felt, as a nondrinker, about becoming professionally involved in wine, and whether it wasn't unusual to offer Hacienda Los Lingues vintages when the estate only produced table grapes. "Well," he said, donning the riding hat while swinging a long leg over the fender, still hot from the outbound journey. "I consider it a badge of honor. I am the world's first teetotal winemaker without any vineyards."

When it was all over and we were sitting in a plane high over the Andes, I realized the most conspicuous sign that Chile had moved on had been the absence of Pinochet. Not the physical absence—the old monster was still crouching in his lair, adored by pocket demagogues still ranting about the general who was "the savior" west of the Andes. I mean the metaphorical absence. Back in the early 1990s, I sensed him everywhere, stalking the national imagination and permeating life itself. The memories were still fresh then. In the intervening years the world had witnessed the bizarre sequence of events surrounding Pinochet's detention in London and Surrey from the winter of 1998 to the early spring of 2000, after the eighty-two-year-old had landed in Britain to be treated for a spinal hernia (he had wanted to go to a Paris hospital, but French authorities refused him a visa). He was arrested just before midnight on October 16, 1998, on the initiative of a Spanish magistrate operating under the auspices of the Progressive Union of Public Prosecutors. The action triggered an unprecedented episode of international litigation, and I had gone down to Devonshire Street as it played itself out to stand with the protesting Chilean refugees holding candles up to the milky net curtains of the London Clinic. On March 2, 2000, Pinochet was spirited home in a military jet. Back on a Chilean tarmac, he rose from his wheelchair, Lazarus-style.

It would have been preferable, for the record of humanity, if Pinochet had been fairly tried for his alleged crimes. I did not blame the foreign secretary, Jack Straw, for not allowing his extradition to Spain: he was trying to follow the due process of a murky area of international law. But what about those who spoke up in defense of Pinochet? The former ambassadors and ministers and "distinguished columnists" who queued up to testify that he was a good man and that thousands of murders and thousands of acts of medieval torture should be forgotten? As Salvador Allende said in his last speech, delivered after Pinochet's Hawker Hunters had taken off to bomb the Moneda Palace with the country's democratically elected president still inside, "History will judge them."

2005–2006

POSTSCRIPT

Will I take off again, once the children are grown? I mean really go, without the return half of an air ticket in the inside pocket of my bag? I don't know. But I might.

APPENDIX

0 Miles   1   2

0 Kilometers   2

Toward the end of 2002, the BBC commissioned me to write a short story on the theme poste restante for the Radio 4 afternoon slot. But I was strictly a nonfiction writer, I informed the producer politely. She had got mixed up: I didn't do fiction. No, she explained, there was not a mistake. She knew what I did. How different could it be?

Poste Restante

McDonnell sat with his chin on his forearm, leaning on the lip of the glassless train window and squinting at the green guinea fowl skittering across the savanna. An up-train from Mombasa, he had read in yesterday's *Standard*, had on Saturday struck a rhinoceros on the bend of the track between Wangala and Buchuma, a few hundred yards from where they were now idling. The animal had lurched into an acacia thicket, and the driver of McDonnell's train had pulled up for a precautionary scout, mindful that two tons of temper might be looking for a target. The air burned with the smell of sage.

McDonnell sat back inside the carriage. Across a curve in the track he watched the driver lower his field glasses and pull himself nimbly back up onto the footplate. At the western edge of the plain, a rim of rock trembled in the heat. As the train sprang forward, McDonnell saw the engine tunnel through the acacias, cetacean steam puffs leaping free from the branches and dissolving in the blue. In the distance he thought he spotted the squat outlines of the Kilifi Sisal Plantation, and he wondered with much lively interest whether the workers there were yet cutting.

McDonnell had sailed out to East Africa in 1919, full of cautious hope. He had been granted a small acreage near Voi in the Soldier Settlement Scheme that the Colonial Office had devised to attract settlers to the Kenya Protectorate. He had planted sisal, a crop that grew tolerably well on the waterless coastal plains, and one in perennial demand in the foreign markets as its fiber made the toughest ropes. McDonnell's plantation lay in a pocket of dry hills in the depths of elephant country, close to the border with Tanganyika Territory.

He was thirty-one. Tall and supple, with brown eyes and hair straight and coarse as straw, McDonnell was the kind of man in whom acute self-awareness was not matched by an ability to translate knowledge into action. When the war interrupted his university career, he had taken a naval commission and commanded a division of armored cars in Belgium. In 1917 he was invalided out with an intestinal disorder. Since the armistice he had zigzagged from this to that but fallen victim, in the end, to the seditious effects of his father's success. He knew this.

His father had been a prominent Conservative MP for two decades, and briefly a member of Salisbury's last cabinet. He was a genial, revered figure with a shock of white hair that shot up like an Olympic flame. Besides excelling as a statesman and wit, he was a serious claret drinker and a committed adulterer, sins to which his diffident son could only aspire. McDonnell saw him in his mind's eye as the train screamed toward the coast, and it seemed to him that the old man dwelled in an age when figures larger than the junior McDonnell roamed the earth.

The lyre-shaped horns of a herd of hartebeests snagged his attention. The colors of these plains were burnt, McDonnell noted, like pottery colors, and the trees had a delicate foliage that grew in horizontal layers, not in bows or cupolas as they did in Europe. Out here, he reflected, it was above all a question of scale. He found it difficult, when writing his letters, to convey to his family the vastness of the East African plains. There was no break and no order, and the air vibrated with the bark of a hundred thousands zebras. The sounds and fears that were traumatizing twentieth-century England were neither heard nor felt in Africa. When he stood among the live green shadows of the forest on the edge of his plantation, he heard nothing but the stillness of the eternal beginning.

Sisal was a laborious crop. Five years after planting out his first bulbils, McDonnell was only now contemplating harvest. Every morning he had dressed to the hiss of a pressure lamp and slipped into his fields as hoops of mist lay in the valley and the bulk of the Mwakingale Mountains flushed flamingo. He had watched the tough little plants bristling up, their shardy leaves and woody stems resembling oversized pineapples. He had recently entered into a joint arrangement with a neighboring settler to purchase a decorticator, the machine that stripped sisal poles down into fiber. After a lot of hard work he was at last poised to enjoy a successful harvest. This time he would repay his father's capital and show him that this project had succeeded where the others had faltered.

Toward three o'clock, the palmy outlines of Mombasa appeared ahead, crenellated against a mackerel sky. McDonnell took his felt terai hat from the rack. He made this journey every Tuesday and knew that in nine minutes the train would squeal into the equatorial torpor of Mombasa station. From there, McDonnell would walk to Tyrwhitt's store and thence to the post office, which by that hour would be flying the white pennant with two blue crosses in the center, indicating that the weekly mail from England was ready for collection.

The platform was thick with hawkers, porters, and general

strappers. McDonnell pushed through to the arched entrance, then took a few steps up the slope leading to the street. A ship's horn rose above the clamor. McDonnell pulled down the brim of his terai and turned in to an alley. He was fingering an envelope in his pocket containing his weekly letter to his father, written the previous night after the digestive African darkness had swallowed his sisal. McDonnell was a man who found writing easier than speaking. His next letter, he noted to himself with satisfaction, would almost certainly be the one to report total success. He had waited five years to write it. The first fibrous crop would obliterate the years of unspoken paternal disappointment and silent reproach.

McDonnell's shoe crunched a red palm nut into the hard mud floor. Above his head, a line of washing drooped across the limestone arabesques. The air was close and infused with a smell of cloves and dung. On a step to the right, an elderly man in a turban was reading a book. When McDonnell reached the end of the alley, he turned left and made his way to Tyrwhitt's store, where he climbed the semicircle of steps and pushed open the double door.

When he had finished with his order at Tyrwhitt's, he walked in the direction of the post office. The rickshaw boys pounded past, their backs gleaming and their carts teetering with sacks of coffee beans and graying boards of dried kingfish. McDonnell loosened his collar. The hard red mud was steaming.

"McDonnell!"

He turned around and saw the gently perspiring but still impressive figure of Matthew Head advancing toward him.

"I have some news that might meet with your approval," Head shouted above the clatter of carts and the Kiswahili banter of rickshaw boys and Zanzibari traders. The Englishmen shook hands. Head was able to speak normally. "Felicity is returning next month," he said.

"For good." The ghost of a conspiratorial glance glimmered behind the flawless manners. Felicity was Head's sister. She had come out for a visit the previous year, on a trial run, and was shortly to return to live with Head at the house he had built out of coral blocks at the northern entrance to the deepwater creek of Takaungu. McDonnell had been much taken with her.

The pair walked together in the direction of the post office, momentarily flattening themselves against a burning corrugated-iron wall to allow a Model T Ford to nose past. The driver nodded an acknowledgment to Head. McDonnell had often noted that his friend cut a dignified figure. Head was a hardy type who adapted well to extreme environments: he was the human equivalent of a sisal plant. The year after graduating from Balliol, he had taken his chances in East Africa. He was in Nairobi in August 1914 and like many settlers signed up with the King's African Rifles and served until the armistice, pushing the Schutz-truppe right the way down through German East Africa and out the other side. He subsequently established himself as a white hunter, which is to say, he was hired out to lead safaris. His clients were American millionaires (one had made his fortune manufacturing slot machines). For a single client, Head employed a hundred porters in addition to trackers, skinners, and personal staff—and he had to shoot meat for all of them. McDonnell admired his fearlessness. It was famous throughout the colony.

Like many settlers going about their business in the blazing Mombasa streets, both Head and McDonnell had sought a better world in Africa. They were not hoping for a feudal haven on the plains or trying to turn their backs, as it might have appeared, on the chaotic change of the twentieth century. They were born Victorians, but in choosing Africa, they were looking for fresh images of humanity. Head was a natural traveler who craved the freedom of wide open spaces. McDonnell was hesitant and more of a plodder. But he felt so sure that once he had shown his father he was a decent and capable fellow like Head, he would be able to proceed with his life—on a firmer footing, as it were.

"Leave a note for me at the club," said Head as they reached the junction east of the post office. "Let me know when you'll be coming up for a few days. I know Felicity will be looking forward to seeing you."

McDonnell walked in the checkered shadow of the palms. He hummed a few bars of a popular song that had been buzzing around his head since he bicycled the five miles to the station that morning. The farm was going to work. It was as if he had been hitting a tuning fork for five years and finally got it right. It was a good feeling. He drew level with the low monolithic magnificence of the post office and trotted up the twelve steps. It was cool inside. McDonnell turned to the left and walked to the last counter. A white sign was hanging over it painted with black letters. They read, POSTE RESTANTE.

McDonnell smiled at the Indian behind the counter. The man got up from his seat and vanished through an inner door. McDonnell took off his terai and smoothed down his hair. He felt fine. He determined to take a walk over the Nyali Bridge before returning to the station. The Indian came back holding some envelopes.

"Here you are, Mr. McDonnell," said the man.

"Thank you," said McDonnell. He walked back across the cool hall and out onto the steps. He had three letters. One, he saw from the handwriting, was from his sister. Another was stamped with the name of his bank. He lifted it up and looked at the third envelope, which lay underneath. It had a black border. McDonnell tasted again the oranges he had eaten on the train. The heat lay on his shoulders like a leaden cape. He opened the envelope.

"Regret to inform you," said the stiff card inside, "your father passed away this morning."

2002

POSTSCRIPT

After this story was broadcast, listeners wrote in to ask anxiously whether it was all made up. The buggers had been accusing me for years of inventing stuff in the nonfiction, now they were worried in case I hadn't made up every line of the short story. Which of course I had not. How could I? I borrowed a location from a photograph, hair from an uncle, and a theme from my heart.

About the Author

A couple of years ago my friend Jeremy Lewis and I conceived the idea of a book of obituaries with entries written by the subjects themselves. We drew up, over lunch, a list of famous people to whom we would write, soliciting self-penned obituaries that were to be frank, wide-ranging, and, as far as possible, score settling. The volume was to be called *Reports of My Death*. To accompany the letters, Jeremy and I wrote our own obituaries, to give prospective contributors something to go on.

SARA WHEELER
B. 1961

Sara Wheeler was a nonfiction author who wrote mainly about foreign lands, but she always said that the only thing she really wanted to explore was what it is to be human. Her most well-known book remains the worldwide bestseller *Terra Incognita: Travels in Antarctica*. Wheeler said that the hundreds of letters she received from readers telling her how that book had changed their lives propelled her out of bed in the morning.

Wheeler was born in Bristol in 1961 to a long line of builders and decorators. Investigation of the family tree was abandoned when it emerged that in four hundred years no Wheeler had ventured beyond the city walls of Bristol. The young Sara benefited from a state-funded education, and the direct-grant system operational in the West Country in the 1970s provided her with a ticket out into the world beyond, just as grammar schools facilitated escape for so many northern boys. To the bafflement of the builders and decorators, she took an exhibition scholarship in classics to Brasenose College, Oxford.

She became a writer by the standard route: a job in publishing after college and the slow, painful acquisition of a freelance portfolio. She got her first book commission in 1990—and she was off. Readers warmed to her idiosyncratic blend of scholarship and poor behavior. Her account of a six-month journey down Chile (the working title was "Keep the Mountains on the Left") was reprinted more than a dozen times in both Britain and America, and her biography of Captain Scott's man Apsley Cherry-Garrard, author of the polar masterpiece *The Worst Journey in the World*, won major acclaim and was subsequently made into a television film. Wheeler was constantly astonished at how kind reviewers were to her, feeling that she deserved much less. In 1999 the Royal Society of Literature awarded her a fellowship.

In many ways she was happiest on her frequent travels, making a small home in a tent or an igloo or a compartment on a Bangladeshi train. The American government once appointed her writer in residence at the South Pole, a role she cherished, comparing the total absence of topography at 90 south to biological haiku. Wheeler once told an interviewer that she never felt foreign on the road. If there was a hell in her imagination, it was the curtain department of John Lewis.

Like many writers, she had an intimate relationship with the bottle. She regretted having to give up, but she did, and was teetotal for many years. There were also far too many unsuitable boyfriends. Wheeler finally settled down with Peter Graham, a clever and amiable Quebecer, and together they raised two sons, Wilfred and Reginald, the lights of both their lives. The family home was a Victorian butcher's shop on the edge of Hampstead Heath

(Wheeler ran on the heath most days and was never happier than at the Ladies' Pond). Wheeler and Graham never married, and their relationship was not straightforward, but she stayed with him till the end—or, more to the point, he stayed with her.

She had a small band of intimates that changed little in composition as the decades took their course. They included the reprobate writer Jeremy Lewis, whom Wheeler met after stealing some of his phrases for her book on Chile (he retaliated by picking out the thieved phrases in a review, citing them as examples of Wheeler's fine powers of description). For many years the pair represented the *Literary Review*, of which Wheeler was a contributing editor, at the annual PEN quiz at the Café Royal. They were eventually expelled from the team for drinking throughout the questions and failing to answer a single one, a debacle that reached a conclusion when Lewis fell facedown into the crème brûlée.

Wheeler joined the Labour Party at eighteen (another revolt against the blue-collar Tory family) and never abandoned it, despite everything. She also found a deep faith that sustained her through dark times and for three decades worshipped at St. Mark's, Regent's Park, a temple of high Anglicanism. Her books, especially the last one, *The Magnetic North: Notes from the Arctic Circle*, included regular ruminations on the marginalization of spirituality in contemporary culture. Wheeler valued ritual in her private religious life, and she used to say that if she had her time again, she would be a Catholic (usually adding that she would also be a lesbian).

Like so many writers before her and surely after, she loved the London Library. The author A. N. Wilson enjoyed recounting the story of finding Wheeler gluing on false eyelashes in the topography stacks. Wheeler served a term as a trustee; she also served on the Council of the Royal Society of Literature and on the boards of various charities.

Wheeler's life in many ways was directed by her only sibling,

310 | About the Author

Mathew, fifteen months her junior. She was close to him. Mathew was profoundly brain damaged at birth, and had severe behavioral problems, including, as an adult, extreme violent episodes. He dominated her childhood from a practical point of view, and in an emotional sense he dominated her adulthood too, as she always felt she had to run fast enough for two. Her sorrow at Mathew's inability to find happiness never diminished, and perhaps contributed to the awareness of the sad absurdity of life that underpins all her work.

Acknowledgments

I would like to thank the admissions committee of the Hawthornden International Retreat for Writers for granting me a residential fellowship. It gave me the time and space to put this collection together. I am immensely grateful for this opportunity.

"Malawi: Dead in the Long Run," "Colorado: Bringing Lynx Home," "Kerala: Killing Elephants, and How to Avoid It," "Jan Morris," "Chen Yifei: An Artist in China," "Wing Walking: Oh, the Terror," "Writing Ronald Reagan," "Gertrude Bell," "Fiction Never Lies: V. S. Naipaul," "Worst Dressed," "Captain Scott: Evolution of a Hero," "Chewing Cement: Martha Gellhorn," and "Wilfred Thesiger" were first published in *The Daily Telegraph*. "Albania" was commissioned by *The New York Times* but never appeared because of a deterioration in relations between Albania and the United States.

BBC Radio 4 commissioned and broadcast "Frozen Ten Years" and "Poste Restante." "No, No, Nanook" was first published in *Vanity Fair*, and I wrote "Solovki: Russia in Miniature" for *Condé Nast Traveller*. "Sybille Bedford" was delivered as a lecture at the French Institute.

"The End of the Bolster: Romance in Poland," "Tierra del Fuego," and "And So the Years Passed" were originally essays in anthologies, respectively *Brief Encounters*, *Extreme Earth*, and *Lives for Sale*. "Mary Kingsley" introduced a Folio Society edition of *Travels in West Africa*, while "Shackleton" and "Apsley Cherry-Garrard: Bad Trips" introduced Pimlico editions of, respectively, *Shackleton's Boat Journey* and *The Worst Journey in the World*. "Captain Scott: Lights in the Darkness" appeared as an essay in a limited edition of platinum Herbert Ponting prints. "Requiem: Through Bangladesh" appeared in *The Penguin Book of Women's New Travel Writing*. "Chile, *Mi Amor*" was the introduction to a second edition of my own book *Travels in a Thin Country*.

"The South Pole," "Freya Stark," "Henry Stanley," and "Reading the Argos Catalog in Bed" were first published in *The Times* of London. The *Literary Review* commissioned "Norman Lewis," and *Slightly Foxed* commissioned "Tété-Michel Kpomassie." "Domestic Manners of the Americans" and "Fucking the Tea Cozy: Bruce Chatwin" appeared in *The Independent*. "Almost Castrated: Robert Byron" was first published in the *New Statesman*, "Fridtjof Nansen" in *The Guardian*, and "Shackleton's Ross Sea Party" in *The New York Times*. *The Oldie* commissioned "Learning to Belly Dance" and "Learning to Striptease." The *Mail on Sunday* commissioned "Cuba, *Sí!*"

Grateful thanks to the editors concerned. I have, where necessary, made deletions to avoid repetition, added material in the interest of clarity, and corrected solecisms to save face.

Sincere thanks to my wonderful editor at Farrar, Straus and Giroux, Courtney Hodell, and her more than helpful assistant, Mark Krotov. Also to my agent in New York, Kathy Robbins, and her assistant, Micah Hauser. Similarly to their counterparts in London, respectively Dan Franklin, Steven Messner (and his predecessor, Tom Avery), Gillon Aitken, and Imogen Pelham. Finally, thanks to Harry Parker, Lucinda Riches, and Peter Graham.

OKANAGAN REGIONAL LIBRARY
3 3132 03697 3412